# Biblical Studies
# In
# Final Things

By

William E. Cox

**PRESBYTERIAN AND REFORMED PUBLISHING CO.**
Phillipsburg, New Jersey
1980

ISBN: 0-87552-152-5

Library of Congress Catalogue Card Number 67-11794

Printed in the United States of America

TO

MY WIFE

OSA

# CONTENTS

# INTRODUCTION

What is next on God's program? How will the end of time come? Will anyone be saved after the trumpet of the Lord sounds? These and many similar questions are on the lips of Christian people everywhere. In our generation there is an increased interest in eschatology (final things). Laymen are becoming more and more concerned and interested in these important theological questions. Bible conferences are being held in many parts of the world. The chief interest at these conferences would seem to be in God's program for the future and fufillment of prophecy.

We are witnessing a return to the Bible, and the theology of our day is coming to be known as a biblical theology. In view of this fact there is need for a fresh look at the teaching of the Bible concerning eschatology. Some things are unknown to us; these things God has reserved for his own knowledge. Man must be content at many points to say, "I do not know." For example, Jesus said that no man could know the time of the end of the world. And in Matthew 24 Jesus dealt with two great subjects at the same time — in the same sentences he spoke sometimes of the coming destruction of Jerusalem in A.D. 70, and sometimes of the end of the world at his second coming — and no person can say with final authority which sentence refers to which subject in every case.

We have said that God has kept some things from man's understanding, and this seems self-evident. However, eschatology is more of a labyrinth than it need be! Much of our confusion stems from a hyperliteral treatment of apocalyptic sections of the Bible, such as the book of Revelation and parts of Daniel and Ezekiel. Whereas John states he wrote in order to *unveil* (Rev. 1:1), many have interpreted as though John meant to *conceal* God's plan. The book of Revelation, as well as the books of Daniel and Ezekiel, was written in symbolic language, not to confuse, but to enlighten God's people. John's apocalyptic language had a perfect meaning to the Christians of his day. Our task is to get back to the historical setting and to decipher the numerology and symbolism of the book. While this is not an easy thing to do, it is made easier when one becomes a seeker after meaning rather than a connoisseur of terms.

This book has two paramount purposes: (1) to present from the Scriptures themselves, as accurately as possible, a clear arrangement of God's plans and program for the future; and (2) to help eradicate from our minds some things — held by many sincere people — which the Bible *does not teach*. For in this, as in most great doctrinal areas, there have sprung up man-made beliefs and "traditions of men." It is just as important to unlearn false beliefs about God's Word as it is to gain new insight into areas of truth.

It is hoped that many readers will be "Berean Christians" and will "examine the scriptures to see whether these things be so" (Acts 17:11 paraphrased). This group will say with Paul, ". . . let God be found true, but every man a liar. . ." (Rom. 3:4).

It is also hoped that all who read this book will do so with Bible in hand, and that each Scripture reference will be turned to, in order that the Holy Spirit may speak through the Word.

The futurist view of eschatology (final things) all too often is equated with orthodoxy. For this reason it seems well to point out that the writer of this book believes explicitly in the infallibility of the Scriptures, taking the entire Bible, Old and New Testaments, as the Christian's inerrant guide. This is to say that the writer of this book accepts *all* clear teachings of the Bible, such as miracles, the virgin birth, the deity of Christ, his blood atonement, the bodily resurrection, the literal, visible second coming, and other such teachings. He chooses, however, to carry his orthodoxy back to the Bible, and not to take it from John Nelson Darby, the Plymouth Brethren who advanced this theory about 1830.

When we say that Darby advanced the futurist theory, this is not meant to say that Darby was the first to teach futuristic beliefs about unfulfilled prophecies. There have been Bible scholars from apostolic times who held that many prophecies, from the Old Testament as well as from the New, are yet to be fulfilled. In fact, it would be hard to find a conservative student of the Word today who does not hold many eschatological beliefs. Certainly the writer of this book holds many such beliefs.

It was John Darby, however, who crystallized the futurist school of thought dealt with in this book. The Plymouth Brethren, with Darby as their chief apostle, broke with all previous Bible students and invented their own ultra-dispensational system of eschatology, with the Jew as the main piece on the chessboard. Alexander Reese has well said: "The fact that so many eminent men, after independent study of the Scriptures, reached similar conclusions regarding the subject of Christ's coming and Kingdom, creates a strong presumption — on premillennial presupposition — that such views are scriptural, and that nothing plainly taught in Scripture and essential to the Church's hope, was overlooked. About 1830, however, a new school arose *within the fold of pre-millennialism* that sought to overthrow what, since the Apostolic Age, have been considered by all pre-millennialists as established results, and to institute in their place a series of doctrines that had never been heard of before. The school I refer to is that of 'The Brethren,' or 'Plymouth Brethren,' founded by J. N. Darby" (Alexander Reese, *The Approaching Advent of Christ*, p. 19).

Some might inquire as to the necessity for this book, since it deals with a subject for which no person has the final answer. A fresh approach to eschatology is needed for at least two reasons. First of all, the misunderstandings on this subject have tended to hold conservative Christians apart and to hinder them from having a united witness for Christ. And secondly, all of us have an insatiable curiosity as to what lies over the mountain. This curiosity has a right to be satisfied in so far as the Bible allows.

In no other phase of Bible study will there be found the differences of opinion that exist concerning prophecy and eschatology. The two subjects are closely related. One can find every extreme represented in this field. Someone has aptly remarked that eschatology often has been the plaything of undisciplined minds. Certainly many do let their minds run rampant in dealing with this subject. It would almost seem as though some try to outdo each other in weird, fantastic interpretations of prophecies concerning future events. Just about every event in history as well as every uncouth person has been proclaimed as absolute fulfillment of scriptures relating to antichrists, demons, dragons, the number of the beast (666), and so forth and so on. And when men and events proved not to be the fulfillment, folk were not overly disheartened, but merely went in search of another person or event. Germany, Italy, Russia, Hitler, Mussolini, Stalin — all have been paraded as specific characters depicted in apocalyptic books of the Bible.

moment, some of these theories are in the public fancy, and have gathered to their support the names and sponsorship of a few prominent pastors, evangelists, writers, or radio preachers does not disturb Conservatives in the least" (*Christ's Kingdom and Coming*, p. 17).

As we attempt to steer this straight course through the Scriptures, we shall seek out the spirit of each passage rather than the letter. We shall keep in mind Paul's warning that the letter kills while the spirit gives life. This is to say that ours will not be a hyperliteral approach.

The more the writer has reflected upon, and studied about, New Testament eschatology, the more he has been impressed by the massiveness of the subject. No one knows better than he that even now the task is imperfectly accomplished. Many avenues have not been investigated, and many points in the book will need to be scrutinized and elucidated by men of greater ability whose imaginations have been stimulated by their reading. It can only be hoped that this work will serve as a road map to guide into the far reaches of this great subject, which in fact will never be completed so long as we mortals "see through a glass dimly." Many things the Lord has reserved unto himself until we "know as we are known." We have attempted to keep plagiarism at a minimum, giving credit where we knew it to be due. Most, if not all, of the ideas contained in this book have been garnered from persons who blazed the trail ahead of us, after they, themselves, had gained their markers from someone who went before them. It is hoped, however, that the logical arrangement of the fragments of truth contained in the book may be somewhat new and helpful.

The present writer was raised up under the influence of the *Scofield Bible*, and for a few years preached it religiously. He knows something of the struggle required to let loose of this fascinating theory of interpretation. His change of mind came from a close study of the Bible, and not from books. Since discovering scriptural proof that Scofield and Darby were inconsistent, he has done extensive research for several years and has read widely on both sides of the subject.

It is the sincere desire of the writer that God may so use this book that many evangelical Christians will be drawn closer together, and that much of the animosity created by Darby's theories will be

Although all the theories of interpretation with reference to eschatology cannot be mentioned, we shall try to deal with those that have made the greatest impressions upon theological thought. Our desire is to seek the scriptural view, however, and not to follow any one theory. We accept the entire Bible, without apology, as divinely inspired and therefore infallible in its original manuscripts. And knowing that those original manuscripts are no longer available to us, we further believe without apology that God has so protected the extant copies that we still have an infallible Bible when it is correctly translated.

This does not mean that we look on the Bible as a fetish or as a "paper pope." These cliches, originated by liberals who wish to discredit the Bible and its followers, too long have made conservative men afraid to "stand alone on the Word of God." We believe that even as God inspired men to write the Scriptures, he also gave us minds with which to seek out their thoughts. For certainly each writer was permitted to use his own terminology and style of writing. Even a cursory reading of the Bible makes this fact evident. We believe, too, that the Bible contains much figurative and poetic language; and that while most of the Scriptures are to be taken literally, some must surely be interpreted in a spiritual sense.

Perhaps our approach to the Scriptures has been described best by Jesse Wilson Hodges, who said: "PRACTICAL CONSERVA-TISM. This term represents still another approach to Bible interpretation. It applies to that school of thought which seeks to steer a straight course through the Scriptures, swinging neither to the left towards rationalism nor to the right towards extreme emotionalism and literalism. Conservative scholars and teachers neither sympathize with the Modernists in their so-called 'higher criticism,' nor with those extremists who pretend to believe that we have in the King James Version, for example, a perfect translation both of the Hebrew Old Testament and the Greek New Testament. Language scholars know, of course, that such is not the case; for if this were the case, we should never need to revise the King James Version.

"Conservative teachers refuse to enter the field of speculative theorizing, whether on the side of Rationalists or on the side of Literalists. Neither do they lend themselves to speculative and novel theories concerning 'things to come,' especially when these theories rest upon figurative and symbolic language. The fact that, for the erased as we work more diligently to advance the kingdom of our blessed Redeemer. It is sent forth, not as an instrument of argument, but rather in a spirit of love for the real teachings of God's Holy Word.

Unless otherwise noted, all quotations from the Bible are from the American Standard Version, published in 1901 by Thomas Nelson & Sons. Portions of the Scriptures have been italicized to call attention to the particular point being proved by their use.

WILLIAM E. COX

# I

## DEFINITION OF TERMS

Voltaire is quoted as having said, "If any man will reason with me, first let us define our terms." This would seem to be in order at the very beginning of the book. Although the subject dealt with herein is of special interest to every minister, the interest by no means stops there. One of the healthiest signs of our generation is the increased interest among laymen concerning theology. The sincere desire of the author is that this book will be read by Christians from all walks of life, laymen and ministers alike. The terminology of the present work will be familiar to the average minister; but many laymen may not be conversant with it. Thus these definitions.

It would be next to impossible to write a book of this nature — since the subject matter is specifically theological — without using some theological terms. Although such terms have been kept to a bare minimum, it seemed well to define them at the outset in order that all may read with ease and understanding.

DISPENSATIONALIST: One who believes God has divided time into seven distinct periods. The dispensationalist believes that God has a different means of testing man in each of the so-called dispensations, or periods of time. He further believes that man's salvation is dependent upon his obedience to these testings.

ESCHATOLOGY: A study of final things. Something that is "eschatological" is something that will happen in the end of time.

EXEGESIS: The art of examining a word within a passage of Scripture to learn its literal meaning. To "exegete" a passage is to seek out the exact meaning of each word within that passage.

FUTURIST: One who centers his theological beliefs around national Israel, and believes that most prophecies concerning Israel are to have a literal fulfillment *in the future*, after the Christian church has been taken out of the world.

HERMENEUTICS: The art of interpreting the Scriptures. To exegete is to bring out the literal meaning of a passage, while hermeneutics is the *interpreting* of the passage.

MODERNISM: While a significant distinction may be made between "modernism" and "liberalism," in this book the term "modernism" is used in contradistinction to the conservative orthodox position of historical, or biblical, Christianity. In general, by "modernists" we refer to those who reinterpret the basic doctrines of Christianity in such a way as to de-supernaturalize them. Modernists and liberals differ widely in the extent to which they consistently follow their naturalistic premises.

PRETERIST: One who believes that the prophecies concerning national Israel have been historically fulfilled, for the most part. He also believes that the church has superseded national Israel and is known as the "Israel of God." The preterist believes that any unfulfilled prophecies concerning Israel will have a spiritual fulfillment *in the church.*

The word "preterist" is used for lack of a better word to serve as an antonym for "futurist." It is important to emphasize the fact that the word is used throughout the book *only* with reference to national Israel. The author believes explicitly in predictive prophecy and still looks to many events that are yet future.

RAPTURE: This is a term applied to the church being caught up in the air to meet Jesus at his second coming.

The above definitions are thumbnail sketches for the lay person, and are not meant as technical dictionary definitions. They are deliberately oversimplified.

Many words used in this book are not meant in any way to be used in the same sense as they are often used by modernists. By "progressive revelation," for example, we do not mean to subscribe to Fosdick's evolutionary approach to the Scriptures. We mean rather that there is clear evidence to the fact that God's program has become plainer with passing generations, and that the New Testament, for instance, gives the reader a much clearer apprehension of God's marvelous works than does the Old Testament.

By "historical approach" the author does not mean anything like that which Albert Schweitzer meant when he spoke of the "historical Christ." We simply mean by this that the Bible can be more fully understood when one becomes acquainted with the historical background of a particular prophecy, and when he does not ignore historical events which can be seen to fulfill, clearly, certain passages. When we speak of "figurative language," certainly we do not mean to subscribe to the pure allegorism of the Roman Catholic theologian. We concur with Ramm when he makes the literal have control over the spiritual, and when he says that we should interpret prophecy literally unless the evidence is such that a spiritual interpretation is mandatory. We further concur, however, when he says that the literalistic approach does not blindly rule out figures of speech, symbols, allegories, and types; but that, if the nature of the passage so demands, it readily yields to the second sense.

By "accommodation" we do not mean that God used already existing superstitions in order to teach people. We simply mean that an infinite God spoke in a manner to be understood by finite man. In order to be understood, he sometimes used symbols and figures of speech they would understand.

It is hoped that these definitions will make for a better understanding of this all-important subject.

## II

### GOD'S ETERNAL COVENANT

Someone has said that if one could look into the heart of God, one would see there a cross; and certainly it is true that God foreordained salvation which was to be received through Calvary. This is, and has been, the *only* plan in God's program for the salvation of all men who would accept his promises.

It would seem that when the Bible speaks of "old" covenant and "new" covenant, it is a matter of accommodation. That is to say that God is accommodating his language to the understanding of finite man. For, to be sure, God is all-knowing, and in his mind there has always been but one plan for the salvation of man. This is evident from such scriptures as the following:

". . . We have found him, of whom Moses in the law, and the prophets, wrote, Jesus of Nazareth, the son of Joseph" (John 1:45). "But now apart from the law a righteousness of God hath been manifested, *being witnessed by the law and the prophets*; even the righteousness of God through faith in Jesus Christ *unto all them that believe.* . ." (Rom. 3:21,22). "Knowing that ye were redeemed, not with corruptible things, with silver or gold, from your vain manner of life handed down from your fathers; but with precious blood, as of a lamb without blemish and without spot, even the blood of Christ: *who was foreknown indeed before the foundation of the world, but was manifested at the end of the times for your sake*" (I Peter 1:18-20).

Every inspired writer who spoke in the Scriptures of *old* and *new* covenants could well have added the words of Paul, "I speak after the manner of men. . ." (Rom. 6:19). For in God's sight there has always been but one eternal plan, which he has unfolded through a progressive revelation to man.

This one plan was hinted at even as Adam and Eve were driven from the Garden of Eden (Gen. 3:15), and when God covered them with the skins of animals, requiring the shedding of blood to make an adequate coverage (Gen. 3:21), thereby giving a type of Calvary where the blood of Christ was poured. out in order to institute the new covenant and make adequate coverage for our sins. However, from man's perspective, that plan has been unfolded in sections as he was able to grasp it, and these integral parts of God's eternal whole have been referred to (by accommodation) as *the covenant of Abraham, the Mosaic Covenant, the New Covenant* (Jer. 31:31), and so forth. Examples of the progressive revelation can be seen from such scriptures as the following: "God, having of old time spoken unto the fathers in the prophets by divers portions and in divers manners, hath at the end of these days spoken unto us in his Son, whom he appointed heir of all things, through whom also he made the worlds" (Heb. 1:1,2). "And I heard, *but I understood not*: then said I, O my Lord, what shall be the issue of these things? And he said, Go thy way, Daniel; for the words are shut up and sealed till the time of the end" (Dan. 12:8,9). "But blessed are your eyes, for they see; and your ears, for they hear. For verily I say unto you, *that many prophets and righteous men desired to see the things which ye see, and saw them not; and to hear the things which ye hear, and heard them not*" (Matt. 13:16,17). "I have yet many things to say unto you, but ye cannot bear them now. Howbeit when he, the Spirit of truth, is come, he shall guide you into all the truth" (John 16:12,13). ". . . whereby, when ye read, ye can perceive my understanding in the mystery of Christ; *which in other generations was not made known unto the sons of men*, as it hath now been revealed unto his holy apostles and prophets in the Spirit; to wit, that the Gentiles are fellow-heirs, and fellow-members of the body, and fellow-partakers of the promise in Christ Jesus through the gospel" (Eph. 3:4-6).

In these verses to the Ephesians Paul was saying that although what he was revealing was not new in the plan of God, it had nevertheless been kept hidden from other generations,[1] and was revealed

---

[1] Paul was not saying that this mystery—the fact that Gentiles were scheduled to be made fellow-members of the body of God — concerning the church was not prohesied in the Old Testament. Nor is he saying that Old Testament saints did not know it was coming. For Paul to make such a statement would contradict his teaching that Hosea and others had prohesied the bringing of the Gentiles into the covenant promises. The key to Paul's statement, in Ephesians 3:4-6, is found in his words "as it hath now been revealed unto his holy prophets in the Spirit.
This word "as" indicates a comparison. Paul would say that the church was prophesied in the Old Testament. He would say further, however, that

only after the birth of Jesus into the world. It also explains that this covenant (though hidden till then) had always included the coming of Gentiles into the covenant: ". . . *that the Gentiles should be fellow-heirs, fellow-members of the* [*same*] *body.*" Let us now look separately at these facets of God's eternal covenant.

### God's Covenant with Abraham

Someone has said that the best way to exegete Scripture is to read it and just see what it says! Good advice, and yet all too often neglected while we get our interpretations from traditions of men. At this point we need to mark the words of Jesus where he said, ". . . *in vain do they worship me*, teaching as their doctrines the precepts of men" (Mark 7:7). Certainly the futurists have read many things into the covenant with Abraham which were never a part of that covenant. So let us read it and see what it actually says.

First of all, the covenant with Abraham was not given to a Jew, nor was it given exclusively *for* Jews. This may come as a shock to many who have been reared on cliches and "Jewish theology." Abraham had been called out of Ur of the Chaldees and had received the covenant long before Israel as a nation came into existence. Let us bear in mind that Israel as we know it today originated with Jacob, who lived two generations after Abraham: "And he said unto him, What is thy name? And he said, Jacob. And he said, Thy name shall be called no more Jacob, but Israel: for thou hast striven with God and with men, and hast prevailed" (Gen. 32:27,28).

Now, having established the fact that Abraham was not an Israelite or Jew when he received the covenant, let us proceed to look at the covenant God made with him. Another fact which appears is that the covenant was not coupled with the law, or with circumcision. "Now this I say: A covenant confirmed beforehand by God, the law, *which came four hundred and thirty years after*, doth not disannul, so as to make the promise of none effect. For if the inheritance is of the law, it is no more of promise: but God hath granted it to Abraham by promise" (Gal. 3:17,18). "How then was

---

God's progressive revelation gave the New Testament apostles more light concerning the details than was granted those in the Old Testament.

it reckoned? . . . *Not in circumcision, but in uncircumcision"* (Rom. 4:10).

Whom did this covenant include? Was it for Jews only? This is an important point, because more has been read into the old covenant than is there. At no time has it been limited one hundred percent to Hebrews (although futurists leave this impression). From the very beginning it has included slaves, strangers, and the like, many of these being Gentiles (compare II Chron. 6:32,33; Num. 15:15). Ruth, the grandmother of King David, was a Gentile! Jesus' lineage is traced through her: ". . . and in thee shall *all the families of the earth be blessed"* (Gen. 12:3). "As for me, behold, my covenant is with thee, *and thou shalt be the father of a multitude of nations"* (Gen. 17:4). Compare also Romans 4:16,17 and Galatians 3:8,26-29.

What the *spirit* of the Old Testament teaches is that the old covenant people was made up *primarily* (but not entirely) of Israelites. God arbitrarily chose that nation to be an example to the world. He gave them special training and insight in order that they might be a "peculiar people" and evangelize the entire world. But this we need to learn (the futurists ignore it), *Israel failed God!* (see Rom. 9:31,32; 10:21). Since the covenant was conditional, the contract is broken, and God is not bound to *Israel as a nation.* His covenant now is with the faithful remnant, and with the Gentile believers; these two groups constitute the Christian church, which today is the Israel of God (Gal. 6:16). We shall deal later with the conditional aspects of the covenant.

### The New Covenant

The incarnation set the process of eschatology in motion. Since the second "when the time was fully come . . ." the people of God have been living in the last days and enjoying the benefits of the new covenant promised for that golden age. A whole host of New Testament scriptures show conclusively that the new covenant prophesied by Jeremiah (31:31-34) was established with the church made up of both Jews and Gentiles without distinction. When our Lord instituted the Lord's Supper, he told his disciples: "For this is my blood of the [new] covenant, which is poured out for many unto remission of sins" (Matt. 26:28). The book of Hebrews makes clear the fact that the new covenant was instituted at the first advent of Christ. Let the interested reader read the book of Hebrews, and especially chapters 7 through 12, for verification of this fact.

The writer of Hebrews points out that the new covenant has replaced the old one (Heb. 7:18; 8:6-13; 10:9). The new and better covenant was made necessary by the fact that the old had weaknesses and also because of disobedience (compare Heb. 8:9b with Ps. 89:39 and Jer. 31:32). This new covenant includes both Jew and Gentile believers (Rom. 2:28,29; Gal. 3:6-9,28,29; 6:16; Phil. 3:3; James 1:1; I Peter 1:1; 2:9; Eph. 2:11-19). Although the covenant was made with Judah and Israel of the Old Testament, it was fulfilled in the spiritual Israel of the New Testament, that is, the church. Even this, however, was prophesied in scriptures such as Zechariah 2:11. Compare also Romans 15:8-12.

Because a correct appreciation of the new covenant is so important to a correct understanding of eschatology, and because the establishment of that covenant was one of the most important accomplishments of the first advent, let us deal in detail with Hebrews 8:6-13 as it relates to Jeremiah 31:31-34.

"But now hath he obtained a ministry the more excellent, by so much as he is also the mediator of a better covenant, which hath been enacted upon better promises. For if that first covenant had been faultless, then would no place have been sought for a second. For finding fault with them, he saith, Behold, the days come, saith the Lord, That I will make a new covenant with the house of Israel and with the house of Judah; Not according to the covenant that I made with their fathers in the day that I took them by the hand to lead them forth out of the land of Egypt; For they continued not in my covenant, and I regarded them not, saith the Lord. For this is the covenant that I will make with the house of Israel After those days, saith the Lord; I will put my laws into their mind, and on their heart also will I write them: And I will be to them a God, And they shall be to me a people: And they shall not teach every man his fellow citizen, and every man his brother, saying, Know the Lord: For all shall know me, From the least to the greatest of them. For I will be merciful to their iniquities, And their sins will I remember no more.

In that he saith, A new covenant, he hath made the first old. But that which is becoming old and waxeth aged is nigh unto vanishing away" (Heb. 8:6-13).

We make the following observations with reference to this passage of inspired Scripture: (a) The new covenant is already a reality as evidenced by the use of the present tense and past tense in verse 6, "*But now hath he obtained . . . he is also the mediator of a better covenant, which hath been enacted. . .*"; (b) even at the time Jeremiah made his prophecy in Jeremiah 31:31, God had already termed the then existing covenant *old*, thus preparing the way for a new one (vs. 13); (c) the quotation in Hebrews 8:8-13 is from Jeremiah 31:31-34, thus making it clear as to which covenant the writer of Hebrews said Jesus had already enacted.

In Hebrews 10:14-20, the writer of Hebrews is still dealing with this new covenant. There he makes it clear that any person who has come under the shed blood of the cross is a member of the new-covenant people (10:14). He again identifies Jeremiah's predicted covenant as being the one he has in mind (10:15-17). In verses 18 and 19 he credits the cross as being the means of enactment, then refers again (vs. 20) to the new covenant as a present reality ". . . the way he dedicated for us, *a new and living way.*"

We need to bear in mind that this is a *new* covenant only from man's point of reference. It is not an innovation which came as an afterthought in God's mind. On the contrary, it is merely an un-veiling of that for which the *old* covenant was the forerunner. Paul taught that the old was a schoolmaster to bring us to the new.

Augustine taught that the old covenant had hidden within it the new covenant, which it typified in "secret fashion." In the book of his *Institutes*, Calvin insisted that there was but one covenant with two distinct dispensations, and that the only difference beween the two was one of administration.

The new developed from the old, even as the present kingdom will some day culminate in the perfected kingdom at the return of Christ. The church has the same affinity to the nation of Israel as has the New Testament to the Old Testament, or as grace has to the law.

Many students of eschatology fail to recognize the phenomenal changes wrought by Jesus' sacrifice on Calvary's cross! This was a dividing line in the plan of God's program for his people. The following are among the many changes brought about by Calvary:

1. The Old Testament was superseded by the New Testament.
2. Law was superseded by grace.
3. Animal sacrifice was superseded by the blood of the Lamb.
4. The sabbath was superseded by the Lord's Day.
5. The old covenant was superseded by the new covenant.
6. Israel (as a nation) was superseded by the church (spiritual Israel).

To say that the old way will some day be revived is to say that the atonement of Christ on the cross is not sufficient or complete. George Ladd remarks, "Scripture says nothing about the end of the church age and a restoration of the Jewish age" (*The Blessed Hope*, p. 136).

### When Fulfilled?

#### 1. Futurist Belief

The futurist believes in a new covenant. However, he does not expect that covenant to be enacted until after the church has been raptured. In other words, he feels that God will finish his work with the church during the present "church age"; and that God then will remove the church from the world, start the "prophetic clock" again — which is now standing still — make a separate appearance to Israel — this after a seven-year tribulation period (some would say half way through this seven-year period) — will establish the new covenant *with national Israel*. This is to take place during Scofield's seventh "dispensation," which is to be set up after the church is removed, at the *second* coming of Christ. According to this theory of interpretation, the new covenant does not include the church at all.

The futurist realizes that Christ established a covenant with his church at his first coming, but the futurist makes this a separate and different covenant than that promised to Israel.

#### 2. Preterist Belief

The new covenant was established at the *first* coming of Christ, and it was established *with the church* — which is the *fullness* — of which Israel was only a type (compare Eph. 1:23). Thus the new covenant includes every believer in Jesus Christ, or the "Israel of God," mentioned in Galatians 6:16. What saith the scripture?

When Jesus instituted the Lord's Supper, he told his followers, "For this is my blood of the new testament, which is shed for many for the remission of sins" (Matt. 26:28, KJV). In the second chapter of Acts, Peter quotes Joel's prophecy concerning the last days, and says that the new covenant has been ushered in. Joel had prophesied that God would "pour out my Spirit upon *all* flesh," and that "*whosoever*" should call upon the name of the Lord should be saved. These are the key words in Peter's sermon, and they are the key characteristics of the promised new covenant. The writer of Hebrews, in chapter 8, verse 11, quotes Jeremiah 31:34, where the prophet was prophesying the characteristics of the new covenant, and points out that this is the covenant Christ had established with his church. The characteristic referred to was the fact that it would no longer be necessary for Israelites to act as teachers of the laws of God, since these laws would be known to all people alike.

The late G. Campbell Morgan had this to say concerning the Christian church and the new covenant: "The prophet put the new covenant into definite contrast with the old covenant. Most distinctly did he affirm that the new covenant should not be according to the covenant made with the fathers in the day that they were delivered from the bondage in Egypt; but that it should be a new covenant, something in advance of the old, and different from it. . . .

"This is an exact description of the covenant under which Christian people live. This is the communion of the Holy Ghost. Yet how we still hanker after laws and rules and regulations. How we of the Christian church and Christian dispensation still perpetually put ourselves back under the Hebrew economy, the imperfection of which was revealed by the spiritual interpretations of Christ, and declared in the holy apostolic writings, which affirm that the law made nothing perfect, nor could do so, and that it was therefore abolished. . . . The spiritual covenant in which we live, is far ahead of the covenant made with Noah, Abraham, or Ezra.

"It is this very covenant that the prophet [Jeremiah] saw the glory of, while he was yet imprisoned, and expressed in the language of this triumphant song. . . ." (*Studies in the Prophecy of Jeremiah*, pp. 177-80).

Dr. George Ladd, of Fuller Seminary, made the following statement: "The same double fulfillment is to be recognized in the prophecy of the new covenant which God will write in the hearts of His people. As the prophecy was given in Jeremiah 31:31-34, it had to do only 'with the house of Israel, and with the house of Judah.' The Church does not appear in the prophecy at all. However, the Spirit of God Himself in Hebrews 8:7-13 applies this prophecy to the new covenant made by our Lord with the Church. Scofield recognized that this prophecy, given exclusively to Israel, has its fulfillment in the Church, when he says of Hebrews 8:8, 'The New Covenant rests upon the sacrifice of Christ, and secures the eternal blessedness, under the Abrahamic Covenant, of *all who believe*' (italics ours). *The new covenant, promised in Jeremiah 31, was made by our Lord with the Church and is now in effect.*

". . . we have the principle clearly established that prophecies which in the Old Testament have to do with God's future purpose for Israel have their fulfillment both in the Church and Israel, . . . We are on church ground, not Jewish ground in Acts 2 and Hebrews 8 even though the Old Testament predictions appear to be exclusively on Jewish ground. . ." (*The Blessed Hope*, p. 133).

## Characteristics of the New Covenant

### 1. Prophesied in the Old Testament

Isaiah 61:8; Jeremiah 31:31; Malachi 3:1; Galatians 3:16.

### 2. Mediated by Christ

Hebrews 8:6; 9:15; 12:24. Someone has remarked that Jesus is the Omega of the old covenant and the Alpha of the new. Romans 10:4 tells us that he is the "end of the law to all who believe," and in Hebrews 8:6 we read that he mediated a new and better covenant. In this respect Jesus could be said to be an anti-type of Samuel of the Old Testament. Samuel was in a transitional period and had the privilege of being the last of the judges and the first of the prophets. Jesus likewise fulfilled one covenant and instituted the other.

### 3. Better Than the Old Covenant

The key word in Hebrews would seem to be "better." The author points out that Jesus brought in a *better* priesthood, *better* law, *better* sacrifice, *better* offering, *better* covenant, and so forth. He also asserts that all this was foreshadowed in the Old Testament, and that Jesus had ushered in the new and better covenant at his first coming, by his death on the cross. Compare especially Hebrews 7:22; 8:7; compare also Galatians 4:24-31, where the two covenants are compared and contrasted.

### 4. Replaces the Old Covenant

Hebrews 7:18,22; 8:6,13; 10:9. The new and better covenant was made necessary by the fact that the old one had weaknesses and also because of Israel's disobedience. Compare Psalms 89:39; Jeremiah 31:32; Hebrews 8:9b.

### 5. Includes Both Jew and Gentile Believers

Romans 2:28,29; Galatians 3:6-9,28,29; Philippians 3:3; James 1:1; I Peter 1:1; 2:9; Ephesians 2:11-19. Although the covenant was made with Judah and Israel of the Old Testament, it was fulfilled in the spiritual Israel of the New Testament, that is, the church. Even this, however, was prophesied in scriptures such as Zechariah 2:11. Compare also Romans 15:8-12.

The apostle Paul unveiled a mystery to the effect that God had planned from the beginning to include Gentiles in his covenant people. Paul did not teach, as the futurists do, that the church itself was in a mystery form, but he revealed a mystery *concerning* the church. He also taught that Gentiles were grafted into the same olive tree as Israel.

Throughout the New Testament, the church — or Christians — is referred to in Old Testament terminology, which up to that time was used only with reference to national Israel. Although both James and Peter begin their epistles with Jewish terminology, there can be no doubt that both were writing to members of the Christian church. These inspired men addressed first century Christians — Jew and Gentile — as Israelites. In the church they recognized the "faithful remnant," that is, the "Israel of God." A close study of the

New Testament will reveal that Christians are recipients of a better covenant — instituted by Christ — and that this covenant has superseded the old covenant, which looked forward to Christ's first advent.

A quotation from *The Topical Bible Concordance* (D. M. Miller, p. 19) would seem to be a fitting conclusion for this chapter on the covenant:

## COVENANT, THE

Christ, the substance of:  Isa. 42:6; 49:8.
Christ, the mediator of:  Heb. 8:6; 9:15; 12:24.
Christ, the messenger of:  Mal. 3:1.

Made with:
   *Abraham*  Gen. 15:7-18; 17:2-14; Lu. 1:72-75;
                 Acts 3:25; Gal. 3:16.
   *Isaac*  Gen. 17:19,21; 26:3,4.
   *Jacob*  Gen. 28:13,14; I Chron. 16:16,17.
   *Israel*  Ex. 6:4; Acts 3:25.
   *David*  II Sam. 23:5; Ps. 89:3,4.

Renewed under the Gospel:  Jer. 31:31-33; Rom. 11:27;
                                   Heb. 8:8-10,13.
Fulfilled in Christ:  Luke 1:68-79.
Confirmed in Christ:  Gal. 3:17.
Ratified by the Blood of Christ:  Heb. 9:11-14,16-23.

## III

## REALIZED ESCHATOLOGY

The world has never realized a greater event than that which Christians know as the incarnation, or first advent, of our Lord. If we might paraphrase a statement of Tennyson, more things were accomplished by our Lord's earthly sojourn than this world ever dreamed. And yet, no event in history has been so misunderstood, or so lacking in appreciation. Much of this misunderstanding has grown out of the tendency to minimize the first advent in order to relegate everything of any importance to the end of time. This grows out of the failure to realize that the *last days* have already begun. In their tendency to "stand gazing up into the sky," that is, in their being overly concerned with the second coming, some have tended to minimize the importance of Jesus' first advent. These are not in reality two separate events, but rather two steps in one plan. The two comings complement each other, and one could not be complete without the other. If it were necessary to emphasize the importance of one event over the other, the first would tip the scale to its side. Nor is this meant to minimize the importance of the second coming, as will be evidenced in later chapters. Our aim here is to focus attention on the importance of the first advent.

This importance is evidenced by the fact that on at least three occasions the curtains of heaven were drawn aside, and God the Father expressed his pleasure in the work of God the Son. In his great intercessory prayer, recorded in John 17, our Lord laid claim to a perfect earthly ministry.

"I glorified thee on the earth, having accomplished the work which thou hast given me to do" (John 17:4).

The apostle Paul summarized the importance of the first advent vividly in the following words: ". . . He who was manifested in the flesh, Justified in the spirit, Seen of angels, Preached among the nations, Believed on in the world, Received up in glory" (I Tim. 3:16).

It is because of the success of the first coming of our Lord that Christians have such great confidence as they look forward to his glorious appearing. Had our Lord failed in any way to accomplish his mission during his earthly ministry, then there would be no assurance that he would not fail in his second appearance also. Because of his finished work on Calvary, every Christian can look with confidence for his appearing in glory. No event will ever surpass the death, burial, and resurrection of Jesus Christ. The second coming of our Lord ought to be looked for with expectancy — and it will be an astounding event in the timetable of God's program — but it should never be cause for minimizing the perfect accomplishments of the incarnation.

It is impossible to chart a course of travel on a road map without first knowing one's present location on the map. By the same token — in order to follow the eschatological events of the Bible — we find it necessary first of all to determine our own location in God's calendar. This is another way of saying that we must determine what ground has already been covered before we can possibly know what part of the eschatological road map remains to be traversed. Much confusion has grown out of past happenings being proposed as things which lie out in the future. A surveyor is in a hopeless quandry unless and until he can locate a known marker. Unless he is sure of his starting position, all his conclusions will be completely in error. So let us first find our line stakes; then we shall more accurately mark off our boundaries and see what yet lies ahead.

C. H. Dodd in his book, *The Parables of the Kingdom*, maintains the point of view that the first advent of Jesus fulfilled all eschatology. On the basis of this thesis, Dodd contends that all prophecy has already been fulfilled, and that, consequently, no teaching of the Bible is concerned with anything beyond the apostolic age. He coined the phrase, "realized eschatology," and said, "The eschaton has moved from the future to the present, from the sphere of expectation into that of realized experience" (p. 50).

We do not agree with Dodd's all-or-none theory on this matter of eschatology, and feel that he has done violence to many eschatological teachings of Scripture. In order to arrive at his "realized eschatology," Dodd found it necessary to get around many Scripture passages which spoke of things that were future to the age of the apostles. This he did by discrediting the passages, by referring to some of them as fraudulent passages. Others he simply explained away. He even went so far as to state that Jesus had been mistaken in some of his prophecies! Thus we would differ from Dodd on both his Christology and his attitude towards the Bible.

Having made the above statements, however, there is no gainsaying the fact that Dodd has a kernel of truth in what he said concerning much that is wrongly called eschatology. While we feel that he has carried a good element of truth too far, and even though we do not agree with his ultimate conclusions, it must nonetheless be admitted that his thesis concerning realized eschatology contains within it a great germinal truth. That is to say, much which has been relegated to the future is in reality a matter of actual history. The following are fulfilled prophecies which many mistakenly place in the future.

### Daniel's Seventieth Week

Daniel the prophet was inspired to predict events that were to take place over a period of seventy weeks. Most students of the Bible are agreed that these "weeks" were Hebrew heptads, or weeks of years. This would make each of these prophetic weeks equal to seven years. On this there is general agreement. There is disagreement, however, as to when the heptads were to be fulfilled. Some teach that the fulfillment will not take place until after the rapture of the church, and that it will precede an earthly kingdom which is to last for one thousand years. If this "gap theory" be correct, then the gap has already lasted longer than the entire period that was prophesied. This is incompatible with all the known rules of prophecy.

It makes a great deal of difference whether only sixty-nine of these weeks have been fulfilled, or whether all seventy of them have already come to pass. One who realizes that the entire seventy weeks are a matter of fulfilled prophecy will have an altogether different approach to the New Testament, and to eschatology in general, than will the person who looks for the seventieth week to be fulfilled out in the future. If the seventieth week lies behind rather than ahead of our generation, then it is ludicrous to say that the book of Daniel is a "key" to the interpretation of the book of Revelation. If all of Daniel's prophecy was fulfilled by the first advent of our Lord, then another key would need to be found when one studies the Revelation. These two books would then need to be treated as two separate volumes, each dealing with a different period of history. We believe this to be the case.

Neither the book of Daniel nor any subsequent part of the Bible mentions or even hints at a gap between the fulfillment of the sixty-ninth and seventieth weeks of Daniel's prophecy. Daniel was told that these seventy weeks would be divided into three periods: a seven-weeks period (7x7 = 49 years), followed by a sixty-two weeks period (62x7 = 434 years), followed by one week (1x7 = 7 years). All are agreed that the first two of these three periods occurred consecutively, and that they included happenings up to the time Jesus began his public ministry. Since period two followed period one without any intervening gap, and since there is nothing to indicate that there would be such a gap between periods two and three, it is logical to conclude that period two extended to the beginning of the ministry of our Lord, and that period three began with the beginning of that ministry and consequently was fulfilled long ago.

A statement by the late Dr. H. A. Ironside seems appropriate at this point. In a book entitled *Lectures on Daniel the Prophet* (p. 163), Ironside made the following statement with reference to the prophecy of Daniel 9: "But in answer to his prayer God makes known to him that in seventy weeks, or sevens of years, *all prophecy in connection with his people Israel will be fulfilled*" (italics added). This is a true statement, the only difference being that Dr. Ironside relegated the seventieth week to the period following the rapture of the church instead of acknowledging that it was fulfilled during the first century.

In order to show that the seventieth week of Daniel is history rather than eschatology, let us examine the passage in question (Dan. 9:24-27).

## The Setting

Daniel was with his people in their exile in Babylon during the sixth century B.C. It was during this exile that he had the vision concerning the seventy weeks. Daniel had studied the prophecies of Jeremiah, which predicted that the exile would last seventy years

(Dan. 9:2). Realizing that his people were being punished for their sins against God, Daniel admitted sin on the part of his people and also on his own part, and asked for forgiveness. Daniel's prayer was heard (Dan. 9:20-23), and it was at that time that he was given the vision of 490 years — at the end of which a blessing was to come upon Israel in the person of the Messiah.

### Purpose of the Seventy Weeks

"Seventy weeks are decreed upon thy people and upon thy holy city, to finish transgression, and to make an end of sins, and to make reconciliation for iniquity, and to bring in everlasting righteousness, and to seal up vision and prophecy, and to anoint the most holy" (Dan. 9:24). In this verse the purpose is given as having six objectives in mind: (1) to finish the transgression, (2) to make an end of sins, (3) to make reconciliation for iniquity, (4) to bring in everlasting righteousness, (5) to seal up the vision and prophecy, and (6) to anoint the most holy. All of these objectives were included in Jesus' words from the cross: "It is finished."

"Know therefore and discern, that from the going forth of the commandment to restore and to build Jerusalem unto the anointed one the prince, shall be seven weeks, and threescore and two weeks: it shall be built again with street and moat, even in troublous times" (Dan. 9:25). According to this verse Daniel is told that Messiah will come at the end of sixty-nine weeks, that is, 483 years. These years are to be made up of two successive periods, seven weeks plus sixty-two weeks. Daniel is told the starting point and also the culmination of the first sixty-nine weeks. The building of the temple was to take place during the first seven weeks; this happened under Zerubbabel's reign. The end of the sixty-nine weeks was to be marked by the coming of Israel's Messiah.

### The Seventieth Week

"And after the threescore and two weeks shall the anointed one be cut off, and shall have nothing: and the people of the prince that shall come shall destroy the city and the sanctuary; and the end thereof shall be with a flood, and even unto the end shall be war; desolations are determined. And he shall make a firm covenant with many for one week: and in the midst of the week he shall cause the sacrifice and the oblation to cease; and upon the wing of abominations shall come one that maketh desolate; and even unto the full end, and that determined, shall wrath be poured out upon the desolate" (Dan. 9:26,27). There is general agreement among evangelicals as to the interpretation of the ninth chapter of Daniel up to verse 26. There the harmony ends. Many different interpretations have been placed upon verses 26 and 27. It is around these two verses in fact that all the controversy rages concerning the seventieth week and also concerning the abomination of desolation spoken of by Daniel. Perhaps the quickest way to deal fully with these two verses and at the same time to conserve space would be to give a resume of the two schools of thought.

### 1. Historic Christian View

Immediately after these sixty-nine weeks — that is, during the seventieth week — Messiah will be cut off from among the living; this will not be because he has sinned, but rather for the sins of others. As a result of this cutting off, the Roman soldiers will come under their leader, Titus (the prince referred to by Daniel), and both Jerusalem and the temple will be destroyed by them. The end will come at the hands of a "flood" of soldiers, and it is already determined (because of the punishments called forth by the sins of Israel) that the entire siege will be a time of desolation. During this one week (the seventieth week of Daniel's vision) Messiah will confirm a covenant with "as many as receive him" (compare John 1:12 and also the words of our Lord at the institution of the Lord's Supper: "This is my blood of the *new covenant* which is shed for many. . ."). In the middle of that seventieth week (here note that the Lord's ministry lasted approximately three and one-half years, at which time he was *cut off* from among the living) he will cause the sacrifice and oblation to cease, and, as punishment for this dreadful sin against Messiah, the temple will be abominated and made desolate to the extent that all the wrath God has stored up for Israel will be heaped upon her at that time.

## 2. Dispensationalist View

At the end of sixty-nine of the seventy weeks Messiah will be cut off from among the living; this will not be because he has sinned, but for the sins of others. And the people of the prince (antichrist) will destroy the city and sanctuary, and the end thereof will be with a flood. This is taken to refer to the end of time, after the church has been raptured, when antichrist will appear to bring tribulation upon the Jewish nation. This group believes there is a gap between the sixty-ninth and seventieth weeks, which Daniel was not told about and therefore could not predict.) And he (the antichrist) will confirm a covenant with many for one week; and in the middle of the week he will cause the sacrifice and oblation to cease. (This prediction is taken to mean that, after the rapture of the church, there will be a period of seven years [one week] during which the antichrist will make a covenant with national Israel; the covenant will be broken half way through this week and the sign of this break will be the fact that antichrist forces the cessation of the temple sacrifice — the temple having been rebuilt and the sacrifices resumed after the church was raptured.) And for the overspreading of abomination he will make it desolate even until the consummation, and that determined will be poured upon the desolate (note that those who hold this theory also believe God is reserving punishment for Israel, but they do not believe Israel will receive such punishment until after the church has been raptured). After antichrist breaks the covenant, according to this interpretation of Daniel, Israel will see her mistake in following him and will turn to Jehovah worship. In retaliation for this, antichrist will bring on the abomination of desolation and the "great tribulation," which will last three and one-half years — the second half of the seventieth week.

In the above two summaries, we have used parentheses to separate our own explanations from the actual rendering given the passage by the two schools. We believe that an impartial study of the two interpretations will reveal that the first is smooth and logical, while the second requires a number of assumptions which lack scriptural bases.

Perhaps the greatest point of difference between the two schools of thought concerning chapter 9 of Daniel is the pronoun "he" in verse 27. The historic view of the church always has been that this word refers back to the anointed one (the Messiah) of verse 26. The dispensationalist insists that verse 27 takes up a completely new subject by beginning to predict the antichrist, who is to appear just before the second coming of Christ.

There is absolutely no scriptural justification for saying that Daniel speaks in one breath of the first coming and crucifixion of Christ, then in the next breath jumps to the subject of the second coming. Nor is any scriptural proof offered for this interpretation; it is simply assumed to be so. Daniel clearly is prophesying the first coming, crucifixion, and results thereof.

In both verses 26 and 27 Daniel foretells the crucifixion — this took place in the middle of the seventieth week, after the ministry of our Lord had lasted three and one-half years — and the resultant wrath of God which followed the crucifixion. The avenging prince was not the antichrist, but Titus, who headed the Roman troops as they destroyed Jerusalem and desecrated the temple in A.D. 70. The sacrifice and oblation ceased in the sight of God when Jesus died on the cross during the middle of the seventieth week. Here was the perfect fulfillment of which the Old Testament sacrifices and oblations were mere shadows. Although the unbelieving part of Israel refused to acknowledge Jesus as the end of oblations, in A.D. 70 God made it utterly impossible for them to offer their sacrifices. This was done by having the temple completely demolished.

In order to acquaint the reader with the seriousness of the sufferings of the Jews at the destruction of their city, this would seem an appropriate point to insert some passages from *Wars of the Jews*, by the Jewish historian Flavius Josephus. Josephus was an eyewitness to the city's destruction, and estimates that some 97,000 Jews were taken captive during the siege, while more than a million were slain, in addition to more than 1,300,000 killed during the seven years of war preceding the siege and destruction.

These vast numbers were not all inhabitants of Jerusalem, but had collected at Jerusalem from all parts of Palestine for the Passover and were bottled up by the Romans. Josephus also points out that whereas the city had been taken by enemy action six times during its previous history, this was the first time God had elected to send a conqueror against it at the time of one of its solemn festivals.

Those slain in the siege were not all, by any means, direct victims of the Romans, but were victims of famine and of fighting between insidious factions which opposed each other before and during the siege. These factions, while fighting each other, destroyed most of the grain stores in the city, thus bringing about famine. If these grain stores had been preserved, Josephus believed, the city could have withstood a siege of several years.

These following passages are quoted from *The Works of Josephus*, as translated by William Whiston:

". . . so they first were whipped, and then tormented with all sorts of tortures, before they died, and were then crucified before the wall of the city. This miserable procedure made Titus greatly to pity them, while they caught every day five hundred Jews: nay some days they caught more. . . . So the soldiers, out of the wrath and hatred they bore the Jews, nailed those they caught, one after one way, another after another, to the crosses, by way of jest, when their multitude was so great, that room was wanting for the crosses, and crosses wanting for the bodies" (p. 800).

"However, when Titus, in going his rounds along those valleys, saw them full of dead bodies, and the thick putrefaction running about them, he gave a groan; and, spreading out his hands to heaven, called God to witness that this was not his doing; and such was the sad case of the city itself" (p. 804). (It should be noted here that, during the siege, Titus was continually pleading with the people to surrender the city and thus save themselves and it, but they were prevented from doing so by the zealots and seditious leaders.)

"Yet did another plague seize upon those that were thus preserved [deserting to the Romans]; for there was found among the Syrian deserters a certain person who was caught gathering pieces of gold out of the excreme of the Jews' bellies; for the deserters used to swallow such pieces of gold [to prevent being robbed], . . . But when this contrivance was discovered in one instance, the fame of it filled their several camps, that the deserters came to them full of gold. So the multitude of the Arabians, with the Syrians, cut up those that came as supplicants, and searched their bellies. Nor does it seem to me that any misery befell the Jews that was more terrible than this, since in one night's time about two thousand of these deserters were thus dissected" (pp. 805-06). (Titus, it should be noted, was not to be blamed for all the cruelties, since things some-times got out of hand for him. In this instance, he threatened death to any Roman soldier found guilty of killing a Jew for the sake of dissecting his body and searching it for gold.)

Toward the latter part of the siege, one woman was found to have slain her infant son and to have roasted his body for food. To robbers who came to her door searching for food she said: "This is mine own son, and what hath been done was mine own doing! Come, eat of this food; for I have eaten of it myself; do not pretend to be either more tender than a woman, or more compassionate than a mother; but if you be so scrupulous, and do abominate this my sacrifice, as I have eaten the one half, let the rest be reserved for me also" (pp. 818-19). Josephus' translator observes in a footnote at this point that there is no known parallel to this in history, either be-fore or after. Some recorded cases, such as victims of shipwreck, have the added element of there being no alternative for survival. But in this case, and others intimated to have happened at this time, the "Romans were not only willing, but desirous, to grant those Jews in Jerusalem both their lives and their liberty, and to save both their city and their temple. But the zealots, the robbers, and the seditious would hearken to no terms of submission. They voluntarily chose to reduce the citizens to that of extremity, as to force mothers to this unnatural barbarity. . . ."

"And now the seditious rushed into the royal palace . . . [and] slew all the people that had crowded into it, who were in number about eight thousand four hundred, and plundered them of what they had" (p. 828). (This took place after the temple had fallen, but before the "mopping up" operations in the city were completed.)

". . . nor was there any place in the city that had no dead bodies in it, but what was entirely covered with those that were killed either by the famine or the rebellion; and all was full of dead bodies of such as had perished, either by that sedition or by that famine" (p. 829).

It is our belief that Daniel 9, compared with other inspired scriptures, makes plain the conclusion that Daniel prophesied con-cerning events that took place in connection with the first advent of our Lord, and therefore are matters of history. The futurists admit that all prophecy was to be fulfilled *during the seventy weeks* prophesied by Daniel. Since all seventy of those weeks were fulfilled by our Lord, then all prophecy concerning Israel *as a nation* has been fulfilled.

### The Abomination of Desolation

Because of the special emphasis put on this phrase by many, it seems well to devote a separate section to it. Literally, it means "the abomination that makes desolate." As mentioned in the preceding section, the futurist, or dispensationalist, takes this phrase by Daniel to refer to an event which is yet future. We shall show from the Scriptures that this refers to a matter which is now history. This prediction, as a part of the seventieth week, was fulfilled in A.D. 70, when the Roman armies under the direction of Titus literally destroyed the temple. This was predicted by our Lord as punishment upon Israel for the crucifixion of their Messiah.

The seventy weeks of Daniel 9 were predicted as being made up of three successive stages: (1) a period of seven weeks during which the temple would be rebuilt, (2) a second period of sixty-two weeks, culminating in the first advent of the Messiah, and (3) a third period of one week, which would constitute the earthly ministry of the Messiah, half way through which the crucifixion would take place.

We need to keep in mind that the abomination of desolation was not the main theme of Daniel's prophecy, but rather a mere by-product. The vision of the seventy weeks was given in answer to a penitent prayer for deliverance, and was meant to bring comfort to the faithful. Only the unbelievers would suffer during the abomination. The "elect remnant" would be protected, and to them it was to be a time of deliverance, as everlasting righteousness was to be brought in by means of the crucifixion. As one examines the entire section dealing with the seventy weeks (Dan. 9:24-27), one gains the following sequence: (1) although the Israelites would return to Palestine at the end of seventy years as predicted in Jeremiah 25:12, their real spiritual deliverance must await a period of seventy heptads, which is seventy times seven years; (2) during the early part of these seventy heptads Israel would be blessed by the rebuilding of her temple; and at the conclusion of the seventieth heptad the sixfold purposes enumerated in verse 24 would have been accomplished (all these blessings were to be brought about by the Messiah, who should appear at the beginning of the seventieth heptad); and (3) during the seventieth week (heptad) the Messiah would be crucified. This would have a twofold result — it would bring in everlasting righteousness for the faithful, while it would bring upon the unfaithful the abomination that makes desolate!

In Matthew 23, our Lord used a phrase almost identical to the language of Daniel's ninth chapter (Matt. 23:32), and said that all the stored-up wrath of God was to come on *that* generation (vs. 36). Then he proceeded in Matthew 24 to predict the abomination of desolation which he said would be the greatest tribulation ever suffered by Israel. It is interesting at this point to recall the footnote by Josephus' translator to the effect that the Jews had never suffered such tribulation in all their history as a nation. In order to gain the full significance of this statement and prophecy, we must look back to Daniel's prophecies, then compare them with our Lord's words in Matthew 23 and 24.

In Daniel 9:24 we are told that the seventy weeks would, among other things, "finish transgression," and "make an end of sins. . . ." Most expositors take this phrase "finish transgression" to mean that by the end of the seventy heptads predicted by Daniel, Israel's sins and transgressions would have reached their very lowest depths, that the cup of their transgressions would be filled to overflowing; so much so that God could no longer tolerate their sinfulness (the crucifixion would be the breaking point of God's patience), therefore his wrath would pour out in the form of the abomination of desolation, that is, the destruction of Jerusalem and the temple, bringing the Jewish state to an end.

B. H. Carroll, the late president of Southwestern Baptist Theological Seminary, certainly needs no introduction as an Old Testament exegete of outstanding ability and devotion. His interpretation of this statement is representative of the great theologians: "The finishing of the transgression: This refers to the transgression of the Jews as a people, and by 'finishing' is meant the filling up of the measure of their sins, just as the Canaanites, their predecessors in the Holy Land, retained it until the measure of their sins was full; so, according to Moses, it would be with the Jews, that when the measure of their iniquities is full, they shall be cut off, lose their title to the land, and be scattered over the whole earth" ("Daniel and the Inter-Biblical Period," *An Interpretation of the English Bible*, p. 118).

Our Lord himself took up this prophecy concerning "the finishing of transgression," some six hundred years after Daniel's vision, and said it would be fulfilled in *that* generation, which of necessity would make it during the first century. The actual fulfillment came in A.D. 70, by means of the Roman armies under Titus. But first, our Lord's prophecy on the matter: "Woe unto you scribes and Pharisees, hypocrites! for ye build the sepulchres of the prophets, and garnish the tombs of the righteous, and say, If we had been in the days of our fathers, we should not have been partakers with them in the blood of the prophets. Wherefore ye witness to yourselves, that ye are sons of them that slew the prophets. Fill ye up then the measure of your fathers. Ye serpents, ye offspring of vipers, how shall ye escape the judgment of hell? Therefore, behold, I send unto you prophets, and wise men, and scribes: some of them shall ye kill and crucify; and some of them shall ye scourge in your synagogues, and persecute from city to city: that upon you may come all the righteous blood shed on the earth, from the blood of Abel the righteous unto the blood of Zachariah son of Barachiah, whom ye slew between the sanctuary and the altar. Verily I say unto you, All these things shall come upon this generation. O Jerusalem, Jerusalem, that killeth the prophets, and stoneth them that are sent unto her! how often would I have gathered thy children together, even as a hen gathereth her chickens under her wings, and ye would not! Behold, your house is left unto you desolate. For I say unto you, Ye shall not see me henceforth, till ye shall say, Blessed is he that cometh in the name of the Lord" (Matt. 23:29-39).

We make the following observations concerning this passage from the Word of God: (1) our Lord addressed himself to the Jewish leaders of his day; (2) in verse 32 he uses a phrase almost identical to that of Daniel 9:24, "Fill up ye then the measure of your fathers"; (3) as Daniel said that this "filling up" of sin would be followed by the wrath of God in the form of the abomination that makes desolate, our Lord prophesied that those whom he addressed would bring sin to its lowest ebb (this they did by crucifying him) for a purpose, that is, "That upon *you* may come all the righteous blood . . . ," so that God's stored-up wrath can be released upon *your* generation; (4) in verse 36 our Lord prophesied that all he spoke about there would come upon that present generation; and (5) in verse 28 our Lord pronounced desolation upon the temple. After their rejection of Messiah the temple would no longer be God's house, but would simply be "*your house.*" And so it was until it was completely destroyed in A.D. 70. Our Lord "caused their sacrifices to cease," in fulfillment of Daniel's prophecy, and God took no more pleasure in their oblations. Verse 39 is often held out as a promise to restore the temple worship, but this must be *read into* our Lord's statement.

When was this prophecy fulfilled which first was made by Daniel, then reiterated by our Savior? It came to pass in A.D. 70, with the destruction of Jerusalem and the abolition of the Jewish state. When he had said that this generation would fill up the measure of the sins of Israel, and that the act would be followed by punishment and desolation, our Lord went on to predict and describe the destruction of Jerusalem. This prediction apparently is a part of the same discourse dealt with in Matthew 23, and it is recorded in Matthew 24 as well as parallel passages in Mark 13:14 and Luke 21:20. A comparison of these three passages makes it evident that "the abomination of desolation, which was spoken of through Daniel . . ." (Matt. 24:15), and "Jerusalem compassed with armies. . ." (Luke 21:20) are used by our Lord as synonymous terms. Thus we see that the abomination spoken of by Daniel and the destruction of Jerusalem in A.D. 70 were one and the same thing.

This same event is referred to by the apostle Paul: ". . . the Jews; who both killed the Lord Jesus and the prophets, and drove out us, and please not God, and are contrary to all men; forbidding us to speak to the Gentiles that they may be saved; *to fill up their sins always: but the wrath is come upon them to the uttermost*" (I Thess. 2:14-16).

Paul spoke after the ministry of our Lord but before the fall of Jerusalem. His statement was quoted because of its similarity to the phrase in Daniel and also that used by Messiah. While there was a brief transition period between the predictions of Jesus and Paul and their actual fulfillment in A.D. 70, it is only too obvious that both had Daniel's prediction in mind and that both saw its fulfillment as at hand in their generation.

In comparing scripture with scripture it is important to keep in mind the time element and to observe historical events which follow. Note that our Lord—in Matthew, Mark, and Luke—and Paul spoke previous to A.D. 70, while the apostle John wrote after that date. Our Lord took up the prophecy of Daniel concerning the abomination that makes desolate; all three of the synoptic gospels recorded it; Paul referred to it in reference to his generation. In the Gospel of John there is no mention of the teaching at all. Now this is more than coincidence. John would not have been inspired to ignore such a great prophecy made by our Lord and recorded by all the others. The reason for the omission is obvious. Since John wrote *after* the historical fulfillment of the prophecy, there was nothing for him to predict. By the time John was inspired to do his writing, the fulfillment of that prophecy had become history.

We conclude, then, that the abomination that makes desolate was predicted by Daniel to follow the seventieth week, that during that seventieth week our Lord reiterated the prediction, that Paul saw it approaching, that eye-witnesses such as the Jewish historian Josephus recorded the actual event as it happened in A.D. 70. "And now the Romans, upon the flight of the seditious into the city, and upon the burning of the holy house itself, and of all the buildings round about it, brought their ensigns to the temple, and set them over against its eastern gate; *and there did they offer sacrifices to them,** and there did they make Titus imprecator, with the greatest acclamations of joy.

"*Take Havercamp's note here: 'This (says he) is a remarkable place'; and Tertullian truly says in his Apologetic, ch. xvl, p. 162, that the entire religion of the Roman camp almost consisted in worshipping the ensigns before all the (other) gods" (text and footnote quoted from *The Works of Josephus*, as translated by William Whiston, p. 826, italics added).

The abomination of desolation is a matter of history, therefore, rather than a matter of eschatological speculation.

### The Great Tribulation

"For then shall be great tribulation, such as hath not been from the beginning of the world until now, no, nor ever shall be" (Matt. 24:21). For a number of years this writer was led to believe that this great tribulation spoken of by our Lord was to take place during the latter half of a seven-year period which was thought to follow the rapture of the church. Upon closer study of the Scriptures, however, he has learned that this was another prophecy dealing with the destruction of Jerusalem in A.D. 70. The words of our Lord reveal that the great tribulation was one facet of the punishment resulting from the "finishing of transgression," spoken of by the prophet Daniel.

While predicting the abomination of desolation and giving instructions as to what Christians should do when it came (Matt. 24:15-21), Jesus says by way of description, ". . . then shall be great tribulation. . . ." We take this word "then" to mean "at that time."

Here we have spoken of the great tribulation of Israel. This had its fulfillment — as was stated earlier — in A.D. 70. However, there also is to be a great tribulation of the church in the end of time; this will be dealt with in a later chapter.

### The Time of Jacob's Trouble

"Alas! for that day is great, so that none is like it: it is even the time of Jacob's trouble; but he shall be saved out of it" (Jer. 30:7).

"The time of Jacob's trouble," like the great tribulation of Matthew 24, has been put forth by the dispensationalists as predicting a time following the rapture of the church. In fact, the two events are looked upon as being identical.

Nothing about the context from which this verse is taken would seem to warrant such an interpretation as the one the dispensationalist puts on it. Jeremiah was predicting the return of Israel (often referred to in the Old Testament as "Jacob") from their Babylonian captivity. He referred to this captivity as "the time of Jacob's trouble." Adam Clarke is representative of the historic Christian interpretation of this passage: "Alas! for that day is great. When the Medes and Persians, with all their forces shall come on the Chaldeans, it will be the day of Jacob's trouble — trial, dismay, and uncertainty; but he shall be delivered out of it — the Chaldean empire shall fall, but the Jews shall be delivered by Cyrus. Jerusalem shall be destroyed by the Romans, but the 'Israel of God' shall be delivered from its ruin. Not one that had embraced Christianity perished in the sackage of the city" (*Clarke's Commentary*, Vol. IV, p. 330).

Here, then, is another item of recorded history which has been wrongly relegated to the sphere of future eschatology.

## Ezekiel's Valley of Dry Bones

The entire thirty-seventh chapter of Ezekiel is sometimes interpreted as being a portrayal of a future restoration of the nation Israel to Palestine and of a golden rule there. By "future" we mean that it is said to be future from our twentieth century. Most of the outstanding commentaries representing the historic view of the church have taken this chapter to be a prediction of the restoration of Israel from her Babylonian captivity; this restoration took place in 536 B.C.

Ezekiel used descriptive poetic language, which is a common characteristic of most of the Old Testament prophets. He pictured the nation in captivity as a lifeless person. It is not difficult to gain such a picture of Israel as she is said to have "hung her harps on the willow trees and refused to sing," because of her depressed spirit. Being inspired to predict that God would deliver Israel from this captivity, Ezekiel spoke poetically of the lifeless body being imbued with life. Verse 11 makes it evident that Ezekiel represented Israel as the dry bones, while verses 14 and 21 interpret the "resurrection" as signifying the restoration to the land.

It is difficult to see how anyone could read eschatology into such a passage as Ezekiel 37, when the chapter itself explains Ezekiel's meaning. Clarke gives the historical setting and outline for chapter 37: "Under the emblem of the open valley being thickly strewed with very dry bones is represented the hopeless state of the Jews when dispersed throughout the provinces of the Chaldean empire. But God, contrary to every human probability, restores these bones to life, thereby prefiguring the restoration of that people from the Babylonish captivity and their resettlenment in the land of their forefathers, 1-14. The prophet then makes an easy and elegant transition to the blessedness of the people of God under the Gospel dispensation, in the plentitude of its manifestation; when the genuine converts to Christianity, the spiritual Israel, shall be no longer under the domination of heathen and anti-christian rulers, but shall be collected together into one visible kingdom, and constitute but one flock under one Shepherd, 15-28. The vision of the dry bones reviving is considered by some as having a remote view to the general resurrection" (*Clarke's Commentary*, Vol. IV, p. 523).

Before leaving this chapter of Ezekiel, we ought to mention the reference to the two sticks, beginning with verse 16. This too is looked on by some as being unfulfilled prophecy. Again Ezekiel gives his meaning: ". . . and one king shall be king over them all; and they shall be no more two nations, neither shall they be divided into two kingdoms any more at all." Those who look on this as a reference to the end of the world contend that the northern and southern kingdoms have never been united since the prediction was made.

However, a study of Isaiah or Romans will reveal to the interested reader that God's plan has never depended upon the entire nation of Israel, but only upon the faithful remnant. Among this faithful remnant were such men as the apostle Paul, who by his own testimony was a member of one of the *northern* tribes (Rom. 11:1). The myth of the so-called "lost ten tribes" has been exploded many times over. When the faithful remnant of Israel — numbering some fifty thousand — returned from exile after Ezekiel's prophecy, there were among them members of both the northern and southern kingdoms. Clarke interprets this verse simply: "I will make them one nation. There was no distinction after the return from Babylon."

While Ezekiel's prophecy in chapter 37 had future spiritual ramifications, these were fulfilled at the first advent of our Lord as he became the Greater David of verse 24, and the one great Shepherd over the entire house of Israel, uniting all believers into one flock. Jesus also became the true Tabernacle of verse 27. John says that God took on human flesh and *tabernacled* among his people. This type of exegesis is branded by the dispensationalists as "spiritualizing," while they claim to give all prophecy a "literal" meaning. It is safe, however, to say that there are no absolute literalists with reference to this chapter. For example, the dispensationalists say that Ezekiel predicted a future return to the land by national Israel. Now this would require that Israel be *living* at the time she returned to the land; however, verses 12 and 13 of Ezekiel 37 say that they would be brought back from the grave, then returned to the land! So that the dispensationalists, too, "spiritualize." And, while David was long dead, verse 24 says that "David" would again be king over the restored people. The dispensationalist here, again, does not hesitate to spiritualize this verse and make it apply — as we also apply it — to our Lord.

We do not agree with Dodd that the entire eschaton is already a matter of history. Eschatology will not be complete until the visible second coming of our Lord to earth. However, we do feel that many events — which some view as yet future — already have been historically fulfilled, or at least set in motion. Included in these are the kingdom (millennium), Daniel's seventieth week, Ezekiel's valley of dry bones, all promises to *national* Israel, the new covenant of Jeremiah 31:31-34, Israel's great tribulation, and the time of Jacob's trouble.

## IV

## THE KINGDOM OF GOD

In these last days, also called "the fulness of time," God has a present kingdom. That kingdom is both new and at the same time old. It is new in that it took on a completely new and clearer manifestation at the first advent of our Lord; and yet it is old in that it existed long before our Lord ever came to earth in bodily form. This is an eternal kingdom (Ps. 145:13). In the Old Testament, as well as in the New, the eternal kingdom of God (or of heaven) was a spiritual kingdom and was made up only of those who were genuine followers of God, those who had been born from above (John 3:3-6). This eternal kingdom must never be confused with the earthly material kingdom of national Israel, which came to an end in A.D. 70 with the destruction of Jerusalem by Titus. The people of the old covenant entered the kingdom by looking forward through faith to the Lamb of God, while we of the new covenant exercise faith in the finished work of the cross.

The word "kingdom," like any other word in the Bible, must be examined in its context. This word would seem to be used in at least four distinct ways in the Bible: (1) the kingdom of national Israel, which had its beginning when Saul was made king over Israel (up to that time Israel had been a theocracy); (2) the kingdoms of this world; (3) the kingdom of Satan; and (4) the kingdom of God.

The last named of the above-mentioned kingdoms is altogether different from the other three. Whereas they are temporal, it is eternal; and whereas they are material, it is spiritual. One of the three has already come to its end, and the other two have only a limited duration. The kingdom of national Israel came to a definite end in A.D. 70. This event was predicted by our Lord himself in chapters 23 and 24 of Matthew, and is a matter of historical record. The Scriptures teach that the kingdom of Satan is diametrically opposed to the kingdom of God, and that the brightness of our Lord's second coming will put down Satan and bring his kingdom to an end. We also read in the Revelation that in the end of time the kingdom of this world will become the kingdom of our Lord. Thus the only one of the kingdoms of Scripture to be eternal is the kingdom of God.

Daniel, who wrote nearly six hundred years before Christ, predicted an eternal kingdom to be set up by the Messiah (Dan. 2: 44). Nor is this the only place in the Old Testament where this kingdom was prophesied. The Old Testament seers and prophets were given a vision of Messiah's coming and reign. He was to be a king, and his kingdom was to appear as soon as he appeared. The Bible nowhere pictures the king without his kingdom. Nor is there a verse of Scripture anywhere in the Bible speaking of a postponement of the messianic kingdom. The Messiah was to be a Greater David and would sit upon a throne just as soon as he appeared in the world.

That these prophecies were applied to the first advent of our Lord is evident in many passages in the New Testament. For example: (1) the angelic announcements of the birth of Christ were couched in vivid language from those prophecies in the Old Testament (to say that these *birth* announcements referred to the *second* advent borders on the ridiculous); (2) those Jews who believed in Jesus attempted to crown him their king (the fact that they made the mistake of literalizing the prophecies does not change the fact that they looked for their Messiah to be a king); (3) the believing Jews were constantly addressing Jesus in language which the Old Testament applied to the millennial kingdom, whereas all unbelieving Jews rejected these praises being given him since they *did not* accept him as Messiah. A clear example of this is found in the account of Palm Sunday, where Jesus is addressed in language reserved for the messianic kingdom alone. Nor did Jesus disclaim these titles. On the contrary, he said that the very stones would have so addressed him had the people not done so.

In the second chapter of Daniel, the prophet was interpreting the dream vision of Nebuchadnezzar. In the seventh chapter Daniel himself saw a vision of these same events and there gave some details not covered in chapter 2. Among other things Daniel saw that the ruler of the coming spiritual kingdom was to be called "son of man." This is the very title our Lord applied to himself *at his first advent.*

Daniel's account of the spiritual messianic kingdom follows after an account of four physical kingdoms which were to precede it

(Dan. 2:31-45). During the time Daniel was an exile in Babylon the king of Babylon had a dream which none of his soothsayers could name or interpret. Daniel told the king what his dream had been and then interpreted it for him. The dream (vision) concerned five kingdoms. Through a comparison of chapters 2 and 7 of Daniel with actual historical events, little doubt is left as to the identity of the first four kingdoms of Nebuchadnezzar's vision. They were Babylon (Chaldea), Medo-Persia, Greece, and the Roman Empire.

The fifth kingdom is also described in these chapters of Daniel as well as in the New Testament. It is in direct contrast to the other four kingdoms. The following characteristics of this kingdom are spelled out for us in Daniel 2 and 7: (1) Whereas the other four kingdoms were set up by men, this one was to be set up by God himself. (2) It was to be a visible kingdom, i.e., it was to have live subjects; these were to reign in the kingdom by authority given them by a "son of man." (3) It was to be a progressive kingdom, filling the whole earth. (One is reminded here of Jesus' description of the kingdom as a grain of mustard seed which grew into a large tree, or a small piece of leaven — yeast — which permeated the entire lump of dough.) (4) This kingdom was to be eternal as contrasted to the four kingdoms which were temporal. (This is the only kind of a kingdom ever mentioned in the prophecies which looked forward to the coming of Messiah; it is unscriptural indeed to limit it to one thousand years duration.) (5) This fifth kingdom was to be set up "in the days of those kings," i.e., while the fourth kingdom was still in existence (2:44).

Before fixing the time of the messianic kingdom, Daniel gave a vivid description of the four successive world empires: Babylon, Medo-Persia, Greece, and Rome. Then follows his description of the fifth kingdom: "And in the days of those kings shall the God of heaven set up a kingdom which shall never be destroyed, nor shall the sovereignty thereof be left to another people; but it shall break in pieces and consume all these kingdoms, and it shall stand forever" (Dan. 2:44).

This passage fixes the time clearly for this kingdom. While verses 28 and 45 state that it is to come "hereafter" in the "latter days," it is well to keep in mind that this was future from Daniel's day rather than future from the twentieth century. The New Testament makes clear the fact that the first advent of Christ ushered in the latter days (see Heb. 1:1,2).

A most important factor is the statement by the prophet that this fifth kingdom would be set up in the days of those four kingdoms. Now parts of all four kingdoms would have been present in the Roman Empire since each world power took over the previous empire, assimilating their people, customs, etc., into the succeeding kingdom. Thus, in order for Daniel's prophecy to have been accurate, the promised messianic kingdom would need to have been established during the days of the fourth empire (Roman). History clearly records the fact that the Roman Empire (the fourth kingdom of this prophecy) became extinct in A.D. 476. So that Daniel's fifth prophetic kingdom was of necessity established some time prior to that date.

It does not satisfy the mind of a thinking person to contend that the long-extinct Roman Empire will some day be revived in order that a millennial kingdom may be established during that reign! This is a mere speculative argument from silence, for which there is not one verse of Scripture offered.

The *method* of fulfillment prophesied by Daniel also fixes the *time* of the fifth kingdom. Daniel predicted that the Roman Empire would be destroyed by a stone cut out without hands, i.e., from heaven (vss. 34,35). Daniel said (poetically) that this stone would fall upon the feet of the image and thereby cause the entire image to collapse. A cursory glance at the New Testament will show that this stone was Christ, and that these predictions came to pass during his first advent (Matt. 21:42,43; Luke 20:17; Acts 4:11; Eph. 2:20; I Peter 2:6,7; etc.).

Commenting on Daniel's interpretation of Nebuchadnezzar's vision, B. H. Carroll said: "So when a man asks when was the kingdom of heaven set up, . . . then, as a Baptist, I answer: Jesus set up the kingdom in his lifetime, as the Gospels abundantly show" ("Daniel and the Inter-Biblical Period," *An Interpretation of the English Bible*, pp. 68,69).

Before one can correctly understand the teachings of Scripture concerning God's kingdom, the fact must be established that God has but *one* such kingdom. While this kingdom is referred to by different terms in the Bible (kingdom of God, kingdom of heaven, kingdom of our Lord, kingdom of Christ), all such terms are used interchangeably, and all are synonymous, describing one and the same kingdom. Dr. Harold J. Ockenga, pastor of the famed Park Street Church in Boston, writing an introduction to *The Uneasy Conscience of Modern Fundamentalism*, by Carl F. H. Henry, says: "It has always been easiest for me to think of the Kingdom as one, but with several forms — theocratic, church, millennial — but *all* the Kingdom of God" (pp. 13,14).

The most acceptable definition of the kingdom of God among evangelicals is "God reigning in the hearts of his people." This reign transcends time and space. Some would limit the kingdom to a period of one thousand years, place it in the future altogether, and give it a prescribed location. This is foreign to the teachings of those scriptures which plainly teach that God's kingdom is eternal (Psalm 145:13), and that it is not involved with geography at all (Luke 17:20,21). Even a cursory glance at such scriptures as Colossians 1:13; Matthew 10:4; 11:12; 21:13; Mark 1:14,15; 4:26-29; Luke 17:20,21; and Revelation 1:6 will show that although the kingdom is to be perfected at the second coming of our Lord, *he very definitely established a present kingdom on earth.*

Dr. Wilbur M. Smith once wrote: ". . . one must not talk about any Kingdom of God as existing in our generation, for this was a theme that only liberals were preaching, and any statement pointing to the Kingdom must be placed at the end of this age. . . . Since then I have learned to think differently, in fact, must even confess that I am compelled to disagree with many of my friends today who think that 'the Kingdom' must not be mentioned except in relation to some distant event. . . .

"Furthermore when our Lord said at the beginning of His ministry that unless a man was born again he could not enter the Kingdom of God, I believe He meant that everyone who is born again has entered the Kingdom of God, and the new birth brings him into that Kingdom. . ." (quoted from the preface of Dr. George Ladd's book, *Crucial Questions About the Kingdom of God*, pp. 9,10).

Concerning the kingdom in reference to geography, Dr. Ladd said in that same book: "The primary meaning of the New Testament word for kingdom, *basileia*, is 'reign' rather than 'realm' or 'people.' A great deal of attention in recent years has been devoted by critical scholars to this subject, and there is practically unanimous agreement that 'regal power, authority' is more basic to *basileia* than 'realm' or 'people.' The essential meaning is not realm, but authority" (*ibid.*, p. 78).

Dispensationalists build much of their argument upon the assumption that the kingdom of God and the kingdom of heaven are two separate kingdoms. However, the following scriptures show conclusively that these two terms are used interchangeably. "And from the days of John the Baptist until now *the kingdom of heaven* suffereth violence, and men of violence take it by force" (Matt. 11:12). "The law and the prophets were until John: From that time the *gospel of the kingdom of God* is preached, and every man entereth violently into it" (Luke 16:16). "From that time began Jesus to preach, and to say, Repent ye; for the *kingdom of heaven* is at hand" (Matt. 4:17). "Now after John was delivered up, Jesus came into Galilee, preaching the gospel of God, and saying, the time is fulfilled, and *the kingdom of God* is at hand: repent ye and believe in the gospel" (Mark 1:14,15). "Blessed are the poor in spirit; for theirs is the kingdom of heaven" (Matt. 5:3). ". . . Blessed are ye poor: for yours is the kingdom of God" (Luke 6:20). "And as ye go, preach, saying the kingdom of heaven is at hand" (Matt. 10:7). "And he sent them forth to preach the kingdom of God. . ." (Luke 9:2). ". . . The kingdom of heaven is like unto a grain of mustard seed. . ." (Matt. 13:31). ". . . How shall we liken the kingdom of God? . . . It is like a grain of mustard seed. . ." (Mark 4:30,31). ". . . Suffer the little children, and forbid them not, to come unto me: for to such belongeth the kingdom of heaven" (Matt. 19:14). ". . . Suffer the little children to come unto me; forbid them not: for to such belongeth the kingdom of God" (Mark 10:14). ". . . It is hard for a rich man to enter into the kingdom of heaven" (Matt. 19:23). ". . . How hardly shall they that have riches enter into the kingdom of God" (Luke 18:24).

In the above Scripture passages two inspired writers spoke of the same event; yet one used the term "kingdom of God," while the other used the term "kingdom of heaven." Matthew 4:12 fixes the ministry of Jesus referred to in that context as being immediately after the imprisonment of John. Mark 1:14 fixes his account as being the same event. The only explanation is that the two terms were synonymous.

The fact needs to be clearly established that God's eternal kingdom is spiritual in nature, and can be entered into only by means of the new birth. It is a grave error to say, as many do, that the present kingdom is a mixture of good and evil. This may be true to a technical extent in that the saints who make up the kingdom are still possessed of a sinful nature which they will not be rid of until redemption is completed with the glorification of the body (Rom. 8:23). It is unscriptural, however, to teach that there are both saved and unsaved in the kingdom of God. Tares are in the kingdom only to the extent that they mingle among the kingdom members. They are in but not of the kingdom — even as kingdom members are in the world but not of the world (Matt. 7:21). Mere professors have never entered the kingdom of God. The *field is the world;* but the *kingdom is not the world!* That the kingdom is entered only through regeneration is shown by the following scriptures:

"Even as Abraham believed God, and it was reckoned unto him for righteousness. Know therefore that they that are of faith, the same are sons of Abraham. And the scripture, foreseeing that God would justify the Gentiles by faith, preached the gospel beforehand unto Abraham, saying, In thee shall all the nations be blessed. So then, they that are of faith are blessed with the faithful Abraham" (Gal. 3:6-9).

"For I say unto you, that except your righteousness shall exceed the righteousness of the scribes and Pharisees, ye shall in no wise enter into the kingdom of heaven" (Matt. 5:20).

Jacob wrestled with God and gained a new name along with a new nature. Read Genesis 32:24-28.

"Not every one that saith unto me, Lord, Lord, shall enter into the kingdom of heaven; but he that doeth the will of my Father who is in heaven" (Matt. 7:21).

The Lord made it unequivocally clear that the new birth was necessary for entrance into the kingdom. And here we need to keep in mind that there is but one kingdom for God's people; so that it does not change the picture to say our Lord spoke of *another* kingdom. When speaking of the spiritual kingdom our Lord knew of but one, because there has always been but one.

In the parable of Matthew 13:24ff, Jesus said that the Son of man sowed only *good* seed in the field, and that the enemy (Satan) had sowed the weeds. In explaining the parable to his disciples, our Lord said (vss. 33f) that the field was the world, and the good seed means the sons of the kingdom, while the weeds referred to the sons of the evil one. Now, if the weeds are members of the same kingdom as are the good seed, then the words "sons of the kingdom" are non-sensical, since they serve no purpose of description at all. When Jesus speaks in verse 41 of sending forth his angels to gather the weeds out of the kingdom, he can be referring only to the kingdom of this world. Otherwise, there is a contradiction within this very short statement of our Lord. Those of us who look on the Scriptures as being infallible cannot subscribe to this, but must interpret scripture by scripture.

"Jesus answered and said unto him [Nicodemus], Verily, verily, I say unto thee, except one be born anew, he cannot see the kingdom of God . . . except one be born of water and the Spirit, he cannot enter into the kingdom of God. That which is born of the flesh is flesh; and that which is born of the Spirit is spirit" (John 3:3-6). This verse is very enlightening at this point. Having stated the necessity of the new birth for entrance into the kingdom — indeed before one can even "see" (comprehend) the kingdom — Jesus went on to elucidate this necessity by saying that before the new birth a person was merely "fleshly" (carnal), whereas upon receiving the new birth he became "spiritual" (heavenly). The only thought to be gained from this statement of our Lord is that it is utterly inconceivable that a merely carnal person could be a member of the kingdom.

Although the kingdom of God is eternal, and although — as has been pointed out — there is but one such kingdom, it is not unusual for the three separate phases of this kingdom (past, present, future) to be spoken of in the Scriptures as though they were separate entities. For example, Jesus said that he who was least in the king-dom (as it would be after his death) would be greater than John the Baptist (Matt. 11:11). This statement came after he had referred to John as being among the greatest of all prophets of the kingdom as it existed during the previous era, that is, the Old Testament era. We need to remember that John was technically an Old Testament prophet. This statement — that some would be greater than John — could not possibly refer to the kingdom in its future consummated form, since John surely will be there with the other believers and certainly will not have a position inferior to theirs at that time. On the other hand, Jesus referred to the future aspect of the kingdom as if it were a separate entity in the many places where he spoke of coming in his Father's kingdom, referring to the second advent at the end of this age. These are for the sake of emphasis and are not to be construed as constituting three different kingdoms, any more than the three members of the Trinity — which often are spoken of in their separate roles — are to be looked on as three separate Gods! Salvation is also spoken of in a threefold sense—past, present, and future. We *were* saved at conversion, we *are being* saved from this present age, and we *shall be* saved from the wrath to come.

As the kingdom of the Old Testament was a mere shadow of what we enjoy in this new age (through the finished work of Calvary), so the kingdom of our day will be dwarfed by the majesty of the fuller realization at the appearance of our Lord in all his glory.

In this respect, this eternal kingdom did indeed become new at the incarnation; and the Old Testament saints could look *forward* to a *new* kingdom, even as we today look forward to a new kingdom to be ushered in at the second coming. This is quite different from saying that because there is a future aspect, the kingdom does not exist today, or that it did not exist in the Old Testament era. It is also erroneous to conclude, on this basis, that the coming kingdom will be a completely separate kingdom from the one now existing. We concur with John Bright on this point.

"It is at once apparent that the idea is broader than the term, and we must look for the idea where the term is not present. Indeed, it may come as a surprise to learn that outside the Gospels the expression 'kingdom of God' is not very common in the New Testament, while in the Old Testament it does not occur at all. But the concept is by no means confined to the New Testament. While it underwent . . . a radical mutation on the lips of Jesus, it had a long history and is, in one form or another, ubiquitous in both Old Testament and New. It involves the whole notion of the rule of God over his people, and particularly the vindication of that rule and people in glory at the end of history. That was the Kingdom which the Jews awaited" (*The Kingdom of God*, p. 18).

The key to the kingdom of God, according to Matthew 16:19, is the gospel, that is, the good news that God was in Christ reconciling the world unto himself. Only this key will unlock the kingdom and permit entrance through faith in Jesus Christ, who is the door to the kingdom (John 10:9).

As there is but one kingdom of God, even so God recognized but one gospel. That is the gospel preached by our Lord during his earthly ministry. This is the same gospel preached by John the Baptist, all the apostles, and all the inspired writers of the New Testament. Paul also preached this same gospel, and even pronounced a curse upon any who would dare preach "another gospel." Nor was this gospel foreign to the old covenant, for Paul stated in Galatians 3:8 that this same gospel had been presented to Abraham, who was saved by believing it, and who thereby became the father of all the righteous.

John Bright speaks of this gospel, this proclamation (kerygma), as the primary element in the New Testament, and points out in his excellent treatment that the existence of this gospel is itself proof of the fact that the promised kingdom has come. This fact is corroborated by such passages as Luke 10:23,24; Mark 1:15; and Romans 1:1-3. Bright says this gospel announced that the new age proclaimed by the prophets had begun; that the long-awaited Messiah had come, who is none other than this Jesus who did mighty works, died and rose again according to the Scriptures; that this Jesus has been exalted to the highest heaven to sit at the right hand of God, from whence he will shortly come again "to judge the quick and the dead."

Upon hearing and believing this gospel, one is immediately translated into the present kingdom of God's dear Son (Col. 1:13), and ceases to be a member of the kingdom of Satan. He becomes a recipient of the blessings as well as the corrections of that kingdom and will never come into condemnation as will the members of Satan's kingdom. God's kingdom exists today as an incomplete realization awaiting its perfection at the appearing of the King of Glory. Incomplete as it is, however, *the kingdom is a present reality.* Kingdom and life are synonymous in the New Testament. To enter into life is to become a member of the kingdom of God.

How wealthy is he who accepts the wonderful invitation of that great Shepherd of the sheep, "I am the door; by me if any man enter in, he shall be saved, and shall go in and go out, and shall find pasture" (John 10:9).

### The Present Position of the Saints

Far from being defeated and doomed to failure, the saints during these last days are the body of Christ. They are members of the

church, which is the very fullness of God (Eph. 1:23). As members
of the messianic kingdom, the saints are reigning with Christ. To be
sure, this is not a perfect reign — nor *can* it be, so long as we remain
in the flesh (Rom. 8:23) — and there is a better future in store
for the saints of God.

Every genuine believer in Christ — those who have experienced
the birth from above through repentance and faith in Christ — is
reigning with him in his kingdom. Before being born again we were
members of the kingdom of Satan. At conversion, however, our
citizenship was transferred, old things passed away, and all things
became new. There would be more dynamic Christian living and
less apologetic Christianity if Christians could get a clear biblical
view of their present standing in Christ. Christians are *already* heirs
of God, joint-heirs with Jesus Christ. They are members of a
kingdom that started out as a mustard seed and has grown to the
size of a sturdy tree.

"For all things are yours; whether Paul, Apollos, or Cephas,
or the world, or life, or death, or things present, or things to come;
all are yours; and ye are Christ's; and Christ is God's" (I Cor. 3:
21b-23).

"Giving thanks unto the Father, who made us meet to be partakers of the inheritance of the saints in light; who delivered us out
of the power of darkness, and translated us into the kingdom of the
Son of his love; in whom we have our redemption, the forgiveness
of our sins" (Col. 1:12-14).

We concur with John Bright again at this point: "Thus the
New Testament faith in the victory! And in that victory, it declares,
the Christian may participate here and now. In fact the new age has
already dawned, and the Church is living in that age. The miracle
of Pentecost is proof that the end-time has begun for the outpouring of the spirit spoken by Joel has taken place (Acts 2:16-21; cf.
Joel 2:28-32; II Cor. 1:22; Eph. 1:13,14). The Christian has been
delivered out of the present evil age (Gal. 1:4), has 'tasted . . .
the powers of the age to come' (Heb. 6:5), has transferred his
citizenship to that age (Phil. 3:20). He has been freed from the
demonic power of evil (Col. 1:13) into the Kingdom of the Son"
(*ibid.*, p. 232).

Certainly this is not a picture of defeat. This picture of hope
is not meant to be taken as concurring with the postmillennialists,

who teach that the world will get better and better until Christianity almost completely permeates society. It is simply to say that the saints of God are on the victory side in spite of the fact of their being in the "narrow way" which is found by only a minority of the population of the world. By losing their lives, the saints have gained them! Theirs is the abundant life.

## V

## ISRAEL AND THE CHURCH

We come now to a study of the biblical relationship between national Israel and the Christian church. A correct understanding of this relationship is absolutely essential to a correct understanding of the Bible. While opinions vary on many individual points, there would seem to be two *main* schools of thought on this subject. The first of these may be called the historical Christian view, being that view held by the great majority of the church fathers, Protestant reformers, and Bible commentaries. The second view originated with John Nelson Darby around A.D. 1830, and is best known today as dispensationalism. I feel that the historical Christian view is biblical and sound, while the more recent view (which view I once held) is artificial and forced. Let us look at these two interpretations.

The historical Christian teaching always has been that national Israel was a type of the church, and that the church replaced Israel on the Day of Pentecost. This view holds that God made two sets of promises to Israel — natural promises and spiritual promises. All earthly promises to Israel have been either fulfilled or invalidated because of disobedience. All spiritual promises are being fulfilled through the church, which is made up of Jews and Gentiles alike.

Main Points of Historical Christian Teaching

1. God has always had but one spiritual people, represented by the remnant in every generation.

2. God's promises to Israel were conditional.

3. All earthly promises to Israel have been either fulfilled or invalidated through disobedience and unbelief.

4. Israel was a type of the church and was superseded by the church.

5. The church was prophesied in the Old Testament, *in Old Testament language.*

6. Christ was, and is, the only Hope of Israel. And Israelites (Jews) will be saved only if they accept him during *this* age.

7. The first advent of Christ completed Israel's redemption, and manifested the Israel of God (the church) referred to in Galatians 6:16.

8. Christ instituted a Jewish-Gentile church.

9. All unfulfilled spiritual promises to Israel are being fulfilled through the Christian church.

10. This does not represent a change in God's plan, but evidences progressive revelation.

Dispensationalists teach that God has two separate peoples — Israel and the church — and two separate plans for them. Israel, they say, is "an earthly people," while the church is "a heavenly people." Not only does God have two separate plans for these peoples, but two distinct destinations. They teach that Israel will spend her eternity on the earth, following an earthly millennium of one thousand years, while the church will spend eternity in heaven after the millennium. They say that Israel was indeed a type of the church, but then go on to teach that this is the one and only type in the entire Bible which was never meant to have an antitype (fulfillment)! Dispensationalists teach that Jesus, at his first advent, offered to Israel an earthly millennium; that Israel rejected this offer; that God then postponed his plans for Israel; and that the church was instituted as a temporary (parenthetic) plan until after the second advent.

Main Points of Dispensationalist Teaching

1. God has two bodies (peoples) — Israel, and the church.

2. God's promises to Israel were unconditional, and therefore are still binding.

3. God's promises concerning the return to the land, rebuilding the temple, etc., were never fulfilled. They are therefore still future.

4. Although Israel was a type of the church, they will always remain separate.

5. Christ instituted the church as a "parenthesis."

6. Christ came the first time to establish an earthly millennial kingdom with Israel.

7. Israel rejected him, then God postponed this plan until the second advent.

8. Christ instituted a Gentile church.

9. Israel is God's earthly people; the church is God's heavenly people.

10. Israel's destiny is to remain on earth forever; the destiny of the church is to spend eternity in heaven.

Many people confuse the real issue between dispensationalists and the majority of Christian Bible exegetes. The real issue is well stated by Dr. George E. Ladd: "We must first clarify the nature of dispensational theology. The heart of the system is not seven dispensations nor a pretribulation rapture of the Church. It is the notion that God has two people, Israel and the Church, and two programs — a theocratic program for Israel and a redemptive program for the Church. Israel is a national people with material blessings and an earthly destiny; the Church is a universal people with spiritual blessings and a heavenly destiny" (*Christianity Today,* October 12, 1959).

Dr. Ladd's statement is substantiated by this statement from the pen of the late Dr. L. W. Chafer, who was a leader in the dispensational movement in this country. "The dispensationalist believes that throughout the ages God is pursuing two distinct purposes: one related to the earth with earthly people and earthly objectives involved, which is Judaism; while the other is related to heaven with heavenly people and heavenly objectives involved, which is Christianity" (*Dispensationalism,* p. 107).

Here, then, is the crux of the argument concerning Israel and the church. The paramount aim of the dispensationalist is to keep these alleged two groups separate. This accounts for their alleged postponements, gaps, and parentheses in God's program. This is why they will turn heaven and earth upside down in order to win one convert to their school of thought. And why they make this one belief a test of Christian fellowship. This is why dispensationalists are accused of taking glory which ought to go to Christ, and giving that glory to the non-believing nation of Israel. This writer believes they are guilty of this charge.

Jesus taught, in John 10:16, that there was one fold and one shepherd. Paul, the great theologian, certainly knew nothing of God's having two bodies. Let Paul speak: "For he is our peace, who made both one, and brake down the middle wall of partition, having abolished in his flesh the enmity, even the law of commandments contained in ordinances; that he might create in himself of the two one new man, so making peace; and might reconcile them both in one body unto God through the cross, having slain the enmity thereby" (Eph. 2:14-16).

Paul says here that God took two men (peoples) and created one man (people) from these two. Nor does the apostle teach that God had two peoples even before this. Rather, he teaches that God took Israel (who were his people) and added the Gentiles to them — grafted the Gentiles, who up to that time had not been God's people — into the same olive tree. The prophet Hosea had predicted that those who were not God's people should be called his people. This prophecy was fulfilled when the Gentiles were grafted as a wild shoot into the original olive tree of God (Israel).

Just what difference does it make whether one believes God has two peoples rather than one? Many have asked if this is not a minute theological point. The importance of this premise grows in magnitude as one studies the dispensational ramifications growing out of it. The New Testament teaches us that the church is the very apex in Christ's redemptive work and that Calvary was its purchase price. An example of this teaching is Ephesians 1:22,23: "And he put all things in subjection under his feet, and gave him to be head over all things to the church, which is his body, the fullness of him that filleth all in all." Whereas the Bible calls the church the very *body of Christ* and the very *fullness of God*, the dispensationalist teaches that the church is doomed to failure, that it is a temporary instrument, and that national Israel will have a far greater ministry, following the removal of the Holy Spirit, than the church will have under the guidance of the Holy Spirit. Is this a minor point?

Whereas our Lord himself taught that he carried out the complete will of God the Father, during his earthly ministry, the dispensationalist theology has it that Jesus fully expected to establish the counterpart of David's earthly kingdom (the millennium); that he thought he was going to establish just such a millennium; but that the non-believing part of national Israel frustrated his plans by refusing to accept his offer of himself as an earthly king along with an earthly kingdom. They teach that if the Jews had accepted Christ, the cross would not have been necessary. Is this point important in the light of such scriptures as the following?

"Jesus therefore perceiving that they were about to come and take him by force, to make him king, withdrew again into the mountain alone" (John 6:15).

"Now is my soul troubled: and what shall I say? Father, save me from this hour. But for this cause came I unto this hour" (John 12:27).

". . . Christ: who was foreknown [foreordained] indeed before the foundation of the world, but was manifested at the end of the times for your sake" (I Peter 1:19,20).

"But *when the fulness of the time came*, God sent forth his Son. . ." (Gal. 4:4).

Many more passages of Scripture could be brought to bear on this subject. These, however, should suffice to show that the events of the first advent were not accidents of chance. They show too that the cross was no afterthought in God's plan of redemption.

This teaching about Israel and the church leads much deeper into theology. However, it is not within the scope of this book to deal in further detail with this point. The reader will find much helpful information in *An Examination of Dispensationalism*.[1]

Oswald T. Allis (*Prophecy and the Church*, p. vi of the Preface) has given a concise distinction between dispensational teaching concerning the church, as opposed to the views of the great majority of Christians: "According to one view, the Church is the fulfillment of prophecy; according to the other, it interrupts that fulfillment. According to one view the Church age is the 'day of salvation'; according to the other view the Church age is only an episode, even if a very important one, in that day of salvation; and the salvation of Israel and of 'the enormous majority of mankind' will follow the removal of the Church."

### Conditional Promises

One premise held by futurists and dispensationalists is that all promises to national Israel were unconditional, and that they are binding upon God regardless of the actions of the nation Israel. Here especially the student of the Bible needs to search out the *spirit* of the Old Testament and not to become enmeshed in the *letter*. Many

1. Cox, William E., *An Examination of Dispensationalism*. Philadelphia: Presbyterian and Reformed Publishing Company, 1963.

Jews of Jesus' day had made this mistake, and the result was their total blindness to Jesus' teachings.

Certainly John the Baptist recognized conditions to be binding upon Israel. The fact is recorded in Matthew 3:7-12 that John recognized one such condition to be *fruit-bearing*. John refused even to baptize the leaders of Israel unless they showed evidence of meeting this condition — "Bring forth therefore fruit worthy of repentance" (vs. 8).

Knowing that they believed themselves to be living under unconditional promises which would accrue to all the descendants of Abraham, John blasted their false hopes by saying: "And think not to say within yourselves, We have Abraham to our father: . . . And even now the axe lieth at the root of the trees [including national Israel]: every tree therefore that bringeth not forth good fruit is hewn down, and cast into the fire" (Matt. 3:9,10). According to these scriptures, John did not accept the Jewish tradition that to be a natural descendant of Abraham placed one under unconditional promises. John believed and preached that the promise was only to those who "brought forth good fruit." This, then, was a condition.

The paramount condition of the law was the acceptance of that to which the law itself pointed — the Messiah. Romans 10:4 tells us that Christ is the *end* of the law. We take this to mean that he was that to which the entire law pointed. Then any person who rejected Christ — as did many of the Jews, then and now — is "guilty of the whole law." They have broken the main condition and therefore God is not obligated to force them to be saved.

Jesus recognized that the reception of him was a condition of the covenant with Israel. We have recorded for us in John's Gospel (8:31-47) an account of a conversation between a group of Jews — who believed in an unconditional covenant — and Jesus. Jesus brusquely shattered their false hopes. He distinguished between *national Israelites* and *spiritual descendants* of Abraham.

When told by Jesus that they should continue in his word, the Jews immediately fell back upon their ancestry and claimed self-sufficiency because of their being descendants of Abraham. Jesus acknowledged that they were natural descendants of Abraham (vs. 37); but then went on to say that if they were genuine *spiritual* descendants they would have done the works of Abraham. These "works of Abraham" would have been the acceptance of Christ (compare Gen. 15:6 with John 8:39,40,42,47). Jesus concluded that these men, who were definitely natural descendants of Abraham, were the children of Satan and not true Israelites. His proof of this was the fact that they failed to meet the condition of the covenant with Abraham, that is, they failed to believe in the Messiah of God.

It is important at this point to interpret scripture *with* scripture. The prooftext method of interpreting the Bible — this is the method of taking isolated verses out of context — always leads to confusion. A denomination (Disciples of Christ) was founded by Alexander Campbell, who read such passages as Acts 2:38 to the exclusion of all other passages on baptism. The futurist has made this same mistake in reading the Old Testament passages concerning Israel. He reads such passages as II Samuel 7 as blanket unconditional promises, while ignoring other passages such as I Kings 9:4-9, where the conditions are spelled out. In almost every Old Testament passage used by the futurist to prove unconditional promises to Israel, there are parallel passages dealing with the same account, which lay down definite conditions binding upon the recipient of the promise.

So we see that to take isolated passages from the Bible and build a doctrine on them is a dangerous thing. Whereas Acts 2:38 would appear — if taken by itself — to teach baptismal regeneration, there are many other passages which leave no doubt that the candidate must first become a believer in Christ if his baptism is to be valid.

Perhaps we should also remind ourselves of John's statement that the whole world would not hold the teachings of Christ. By this we mean to say that many of God's teachings are taken for granted and are not mentioned every time he deals with a particular subject. In the Old Testament God taught people both blessings and cursings (Josh. 8:34), but did not spell them out in every statement he made. That is to say, the *condition* was not mentioned every time the *promise* was given. However, it is impossible to read *all* the Old Testament without seeing both. When the conditions are not spelled out, they are always understood.

Jonah's prophecy to Nineveh was conditional. Although it is never mentioned in the prophecy of Jonah, the condition was repentance. Proof of this is the fact that *Nineveh was not destroyed in forty days*. This in spite of the fact that God had instructed Jonah to prophesy: "Yet forty days, and Nineveh shall be overthrown." No provision was mentioned. From all appearances the prophecy was unconditional. However, we know that there was a condition in the mind of God, because he did not destroy Nineveh in forty days. They had met the condition (understood) by repenting, and thus God had withheld the destruction at that time.

If one were intellectually honest in seeking out the spirit of the Old Testament, he would see just as many definite promises to *destroy* Israel as to *redeem* her. Here the futurist, like everyone else, takes these threats to be provisional. He realizes that God meant to destroy Israel *unless* they repented. In view of the following scriptures, by what authority does one place a provision or condition upon the promises to destroy, while saying there are no conditions attached to the promises to redeem?

"And it shall come to pass, *if thou shalt hearken diligently unto the voice of Jehovah thy God*, to observe to do all his commandments which I command thee this day, that Jehovah thy God will set thee on high above all the nations of the earth. . . . But it shall come to pass, *if thou wilt not hearken unto the voice of Jehovah thy God, to observe to do all his commandments and his statutes which I command thee this day*, that all these curses shall come upon thee, and overtake thee" (Deut. 28: 1-15).

"If ye forsake Jehovah, and serve foreign gods, then he will turn and do you evil, and consume you, after that he hath done you good" (Josh. 24:20).

Compare also Genesis 17:9-14; Exodus 19-5; Deuteronomy 30:15-19; Joshua 8:34; I Kings 2:3,4; 9:2-9; 11:11; II Kings 21: 8b; I Chronicles 28:7b; II Chronicles 7:19-22.

While it is not spelled out each time, it is obvious that the conditions were laid down when God made his covenant promises to Abraham. Before he received the blessing, Abraham was given a command: "Now Jehovah said unto Abram, Get thee out of thy country, . . . unto the land that I will show thee: and [then] I will make of thee a great nation. . ." (Gen. 12:1,2).

In Genesis 15:6 we read that Abraham "believed God" and that it (Abraham's belief) was counted unto him for righteousness. Belief here was a condition (understood).

In Genesis 17:9 God very definitely lays down a condition before blessing: "And God said unto Abraham, And as for thee, thou shalt keep my covenant, thou, and thy seed after thee throughout their generations."

A very definite condition was circumcision (Gen. 17:30), with God spelling out the fact that for anyone to disobey this condition would cut him off from the covenant (vs. 14). In 17:23 we read that Abraham immediately was obedient. In Genesis 22:1-12 we have the account of God's testing Abraham's obedience by challenging him to sacrifice his only son on the altar. In verse 12 God is recorded as having said to Abraham, ". . . now I know that thou fearest God, seeing thou hast not withheld thy son, thine only son, from me." In the verses which follow the account, God specifically says he blessed Abraham *"because thou has obeyed my voice."*

According to Genesis 26:5, God renewed the covenant with Isaac *"because Abraham obeyed my voice and kept my charge. . . ."* Compare this verse with Hebrews 11:8.

Many of the foundation stones of the Darbyite beliefs are ruled out completely when one discovers that the Old Testament promises to Israel were conditional and that Israel failed to observe these conditions. Thus it was necessary for God to institute a *better* covenant (compare Jer. 31:31,32; Heb. 8:6,7,13).

A simple chart will show that there were two parties to the contract between God and national Israel:

| PROMISES | CONDITIONS |
|---|---|
| Gen. 12:2 | Gen. 12:1 |
| 15:5 | 15:6 |
| 17:4 | 17:9 |
| 14:2-8 | 17:9 |
| 17:10,11 | 17:14 |
| | Ex. 13:4,5 |
| Deut. 28:1-14 | Deut. 28:15 |
| 30:15,16 | 30:17-19 |
| | Josh. 8:34 |
| | 24:20 |
| II Sam. 7 | I Kings 2:3,4 |
| | 9:4-9 |
| | 11:11 |
| | 21:8 |
| | I Chron. 28:7 |
| II Chron. 7:16-18 | II Chron. 7:19-23 |

These are but a few of the conditional passages. The interested reader will find many such passages throughout the Old Testament, where the promises have *parallel passages*, showing that conditions were attached. At least five conditions stand out clearly as we read the Old Testament covenant promises to national Israel: (1) faith, (2) obedience, (3) circumcision, (4) faithfulness, and (5) acceptance of Christ at his *first appearance*.

### Fulfilled Prophecy Concerning Israel

The disputed promises were made to Abraham and were essentially four in number:

1. Promise of the Messiah (first advent). Compare Genesis 22:18 with Galatians 3:16.

2. To make the descendants of Abraham into a great nation (Gen. 12:2).

3. The inheritance of the land of Canaan by Abraham's descendants (Gen. 22:7; 13:14,15; 15:18f; 17:2-8).

4. A great posterity (Gen. 13:16; 15:5,6; 17:2-8).

All four of these promises having to do with national Israel have been fulfilled literally. Some of them had ramifications now being fulfilled through the church, *which includes the believing remnant of national Israel.* These latter ramifications include "all the nations of the earth," and were not restricted to national Israel (compare Gen. 22:18 with Rom. 4:16,17).

Paul assures us that this fulfillment will not include the entire nation of Israel, but only the believing remnant: "And Isaiah crieth concerning Israel, If the number of the children of Israel be as the sand of the sea, *it is the remnant that shall be saved. . . .* And, as Isaiah hath said before, *Except the Lord of Sabaoth had left us a seed*, we had become as Sodom, and had been made like unto Gomorrah" (Rom. 9:27-29).

Paul prided himself on being an integral part of that remnant. However, Paul found his joy in the church — the body of Christ — rather than resting his faith in his nationality.

It would be well to begin our examination of the fulfilled promises with the books of the Law, which include the Abrahamic covenant. Let us be reminded again that this covenant consists of four main promises to Abraham: (1) Messiah, (2) Land of Canaan, (3) Father of great nation, and (4) A great posterity. It is readily agreed by all students of Bible history that Moses was God's instrument for fulfilling the prophecy to Abraham of the return from captivity in Egypt. Compare the book of Exodus with Genesis 15:12-16. Let us, therefore, move on to the covenant proper.

Paul gives us unmistakable proof for the fulfillment of the messianic promise of the Abrahamic covenant. In Genesis 22:18 God had promised Abraham: ". . . and in thy seed shall all the nations of the earth be blessed because thou hast obeyed my voice."

It is only as we read the New Testament and look back through that new light that we learn this passage was messianic. In dealing with the messianic part of the Abrahamic covenant, Paul says to the Christians at Galatia: "Now to Abraham were the promises spoken, and to his seed. He saith not, And to seeds, as of many; but as of one, And to thy seed, *which is Christ*" (Gal. 3:16).

Paul seems to be alluding here to the fact that Abraham had two seeds, that is, his natural descendants, and his spiritual descendants. Paul then makes it clear that one who is a mere natural descendant of Abraham has no part in the covenant, but only those who, like Abraham, believe in Christ (compare with John 8:56). These believing descendants include Gentile as well as Jew.

In Galatians 4:22-31 Paul elaborates upon this subject and teaches that the natural Jew (unless a believer) is like the children who were born to Abraham through Hagar the bondslave, whereas the believer, whether Jew or Gentile, is like the descendants of Isaac (children of the promise). He sums up his argument by these words, "Howbeit what saith the scripture? Cast out the handmaid and her son: for the son of the handmaid shall not inherit with the son of the freewoman. Wherefore, brethren, *we are not children of a handmaid, but of the freewoman*" (vss. 30,31).

Will anyone deny that the apostle Paul was speaking to members of the Christian church? Or will any dare to say he was speaking about future generations? Will the futurist say this is a "Jewish passage," and does not include the Christian?

What about the promise to Abraham of becoming a great nation? Will anyone deny that this was exemplified and fulfilled under Moses and Joshua when the descendants of Abraham were brought out of bondage in Egypt and made into a great national power under the leadership of Moses? Or when they were marshalled under the military leadership of Joshua and marched across the land of Canaan? If any doubt the historicity of this promise, let them read any or all parts of the books of Exodus and Joshua. Surely Herod and the heathen kings of Canaan thought Israel was a great nation!

Looking now at the third promise involving the giving of the land of Canaan, let the Scriptures speak for themselves: "Behold, I have set the land before you: go in and possess the land which Jehovah sware unto your fathers, to Abraham, to Isaac, and to Jacob, to give unto them and their seed after them" (Deut. 1:8). "and he brought us out from thence, that he might bring us in, to give us the land which he sware unto our fathers" (Deut. 6:23). "Be strong and of good courage; for thou shalt cause this people to inherit the land which I sware unto their fathers to give them" (Josh. 1:6).

Note that God promised Joshua that he (Joshua) would have the privilege of giving the land to the Israelites. Note also that it was the land which God *had promised to their fathers.* These fathers would be Abraham, Isaac, and Jacob. Did God keep the promise to Joshua? The futurist cannot allow it. Let us pursue the Scriptures further.

"So Joshua took the whole land, according to all that Jehovah spake unto Moses; and Joshua gave it for an inheritance unto Israel according to their divisions by their tribes. And the land had rest from war" (Josh. 11:23). "So Jehovah gave unto Israel all the land which he sware to give unto their fathers; and they possessed it, and dwelt therein" (Josh. 21:43).

We could summarize these promises concerning the land of Canaan being inherited by Israel, as follows: The land was promised through Abraham; the promise was renewed to Isaac, Jacob, and Moses. It was fulfilled literally through Joshua. Some Bible scholars find the actual fulfillment in Solomon's day. Compare I Kings 4:21 and 5:4 with Genesis 15:18. How sad it is then that some theologians are still arguing that they are yet future! Much of the futurist belief rests on the assumption that God has never given Israel all the land promised through Abraham.

Concerning ourselves now with the promise to Abraham that he would have many descendants, let us again read the Scriptures and see just what they have to say on this subject. In Deuteronomy 1:10 we read: "Jehovah your God hath [note the past tense] multiplied you, and behold, ye are this day as the stars of heaven for multitude."

"Their children also multipliedst thou as the stars of heaven, and broughtest them into the land concerning which thou didst say to their fathers, that they should go in to possess it" (Neh. 9:23). Compare this with Genesis 15:5, and with I Kings 4:20, II Chronicles 1:9, and Hebrews 11:12.

This is not to argue that there are not future implications to these prophecies. Many prophecies have a dual meaning. Many of these we have mentioned definitely have eschatological fulfillments yet to come. These, however, are secondary meanings and will be fulfilled through all believers, including the church. Therefore, there will not be one kingdom for Israel and another for the church! The earthly promises to national Israel have been fulfilled. God took away the first that he might establish the second. See Hebrews 10:9.

The thesis of this chapter is that every Christian is a spiritual Israelite, and that Christians are therefore subject to all unfulfilled promises. If this be true, then nothing eschatological will happen apart from the church. Futurists agree that the "church age" ends at the rapture. Therefore, the only future for believing Jews is *within the church*. This simplifies the Bible and alleviates the futurist's need for extra judgments, extra appearances, extra resurrections, extra ages, postponements, gaps, and so forth and so on. The futurist creates more problems than he solves by his insistence on a separate plan for national Israel. He must explain how only a part of the body of Christ is raptured while the other part remains on earth (either this or he must say that there are two bodies). He also has the difficulty of both the church and Israel being referred to as being married to God. Does God have two wives? Or is the bride of Christ different from the "woman" (Israel) to whom God the Father is wed? The Old Testament teaches that God is married to Israel and that he will never divorce her. The New Testament definitely refers to the church as the bride of Christ. To keep them separate is to do violence to the teachings of God concerning the sacredness of marriage. To see that they are one and the same since Calvary is to marvel at the mercies and mysteries of God. To equate the believing remnant of Israel with the Christian church does not preclude the possibility of a mass turning of Jews to Christ. Nor does it do violence to Romans 11:26. It does indicate, however, that when Jewish people are converted (whether on an individual basis or en masse) they will be added to the Christian church rather than constituting a separate *earthly* people. It also indicates that *any turning to Christ must take place before the church is raptured*, and that the destination of all believers is the same. Paul makes this fact quite clear in Romans eleven, where he uses the simile of the olive tree.

"For if thou wast cut out of that which is by nature a wild olive tree, and wast grafted contrary to nature into a good olive tree; how much more shall these, which are the natural branches, be grafted into their own olive tree?" (Rom. 11:24).

This passage agrees with the fact that our Lord built the church upon the faithful remnant of national Israel, and that Gentiles were later permitted to enter that same church—the same olive tree (Rom. 11:17; Eph. 2:11-22; 3:6). Paul very definitely teaches that Gentile Christians become members of the *same* olive tree, meaning the believing part of national Israel. Having said that *some* of the natural branches were broken off, the apostle went on to teach that these natural branches (Jews) would be grafted in again "*if they continue not in their unbelief*" (Rom. 11:23). The important point for us here is that when and if they are grafted in, the grafting will be into the same olive tree which now contains the Gentile believers. And this can only be the Christian church. This fact completely explodes the theory that God has separate future plans for national Israel and the church.

One who looks on these things as having been historically fulfilled will of course arrive at altogether different conclusions concerning eschatology than one who looks for them to occur in the future. The Scriptures as well as secular history record the fulfillment of promises made to national Israel.

*The Prophets*

Thus far we have dealt primarily with the first six books of the Bible, Genesis through Joshua. We have shown by the Word of God itself that the promises to national Israel mentioned therein have been literally fulfilled. Let the reader be reminded that many of these fulfilled passages are held by the followers of John Darby to be yet future.

Again, this is not to argue that there are not future ramifications in these first six books. Rather, it is to argue that the national promises have been fulfilled, and that the unfulfilled ones concern Christ and his church, made up of Jews and Gentiles alike (namely, the new-covenant Israel).

The same things we have proved about these six books of the Bible can be said for the majority of the futurist prooftexts. Let us continue to "rightly divide" the Scriptures section by section.

After the death of Joshua, there followed the dark period of the Judges. Few, if any, scriptures are taken from this section by Darbyites as being eschatological. Following the period of the Judges was the prophetic age, beginning with Samuel, who was the last of the judges and the first of the prophets. The greatest confusion and misunderstanding among students of the Bible seem to stem from these prophetic books of the Old Testament. Even prominent futurists are pleading now for tolerance among their people with reference to prophetic exegesis. Most of the arguments concerning Israel seem to boil down to predictions concerning their being regathered to Palestine, rebuilding the temple, and reinstituting the temple worship. The futurist makes these predictions eschatological, while the preterist sees their literal fulfillment when the Jews returned from captivity under orders from Cyrus in 536 B.C. "What saith the scripture?"

In interpreting prophecy, the futurist completely ignores well-known historical facts and chooses arbitrarily to lift the prophecies out of their historical setting and transport them on beyond the era of the Christian church. He accomplishes this to his own satisfaction by placing gaps in God's timetable, gaps about which the Bible says nothing at all.

It would not be within the scope of this book to examine each prophecy about which there is controversy. Therefore, it seems appropriate to try to fix the time of the prophecies, and also to show the historical happenings which the preterist believes to have been the fulfillment of many prophecies which the futurist holds to be eschatological.

Although the title of prophet is given to many men throughout the Bible, we have learned that what we know as the real prophetic period of the Old Testament began with Samuel and ended with Malachi. Technically, of course, John the Baptist was the last of the line of Old Testament prophets, but we are confining ourselves here to the recorded writers of the Old Testament proper. Sixteen books of the Old Testament are termed books of the prophets.

More and more, conservative scholars are realizing the importance of studying the Scriptures in the light of their historical background. Many futurists—here they join the liberals—ignore historical events in the light of prophecy.

The following would seem to be a fairly accurate chronology of the dates the books of prophecy were written:

| | | | | | |
|---|---|---|---|---|---|
| 837 | Joel | 724 | Micah | 592-570 | Ezekiel |
| 787-746 | Jonah | 640 | Zephaniah | 580-570 | Daniel |
| 760 | Isaiah | 630 | Nahum | 520 | Zechariah |
| 760 | Amos | 612 | Habakkuk | 520 | Haggai |
| 750 | Hosea | 604 | Jeremiah | 430 | Malachi |
| | | 586 | Obadiah | | |

While keeping these dates in mind, let us follow the historical events of the nation of Israel.

722 Captivity of Israel.
586 Captivity of Judah.
536 Return to Jerusalem.
516 Temple rebuilt.
458 Ezra leads another caravan of Jews to Jerusalem (second return).
445 Nehemiah becomes governor of the Jews in Palestine, begins to rebuild the wall (completes it in 52 days).

Now let us examine a chart showing these events and prophecies side by side in order that the reader may see how they dovetail, showing the hand of God in fulfilling his promises.

| APPROX. DATE | PROPHETS | PROPHECY | FULFILLMENT |
|---|---|---|---|
| 837 B. C. | Joel | | |
| 787-46 | Jonah | | |
| 760 | Isaiah, Amos | Isaiah 51:11; 5:5,6;14:1 | |
| 750 | Hosea | | |
| 724 | Micah | II Kings 20:16,17 | |
| 722 | ——— | | Captivity of Israel II Kings 25:8-11. |
| 640 | Zephaniah | | |
| 630 | Nahum | | |
| 612 | Habakkuk | | |
| 604 | Jeremiah | Jeremiah 24:6; 25:11;29:10; 30:18 and chapter 39 | |
| 586 | Obadiah | | Judah carried into captivity. |
| 592-70 | Ezekiel | Ezekiel 36:24, 33-36 | |
| 580-70 | Daniel | Zephaniah 3:20 | |
| 536 | ——— | | Return of Jews to Jerusalem. Ezra 1:1-3; 3:1f. |
| 520 | Zechariah, Haggai | Isaiah 44:28; 45:13;61:4 | |
| 516 | ——— | | TEMPLE REBUILT Ezra 6:15; II Chron. 36:23; Zech. 6:13. |
| 458 | ——— | | Ezra leads second return to Jerusalem. |
| 445 | ——— | | Nehemiah rebuilds wall of Jerusalem. |
| 430 | Malachi | | |

Although some of the dates of writing of prophecies are not known with certainty, the fulfillments are recorded, not only in the Bible, but can be pin-pointed by secular historians as well.

But our purpose in delineating these dates is to show the reader that all the controversial prophecies, which often have caused animosity among fellow Christians, and have hindered the cause of Christ, were prophesied *before* the return to Palestine, rebuilding of the temple, and so forth, under Zerubbabel. Cyrus, the Persian ruler, was used of God to carry out God's promises to national Israel. Compare Ezra 1:1: ". . . that the word of Jehovah by the mouth of Jeremiah [Jer. 25:12; 29:10] might be accomplished, Jehovah stirred up the spirit of Cyrus king of Persia. . . ."

Only the prophet Malachi possibly spoke *after* the literal fulfillments. The word "possibly" is used because some conservative Bible scholars place this book earlier than 430 B.C. The reader will search in vain for prophecies, in Malachi, of a regathering to Jerusalem, or a rebuilding of the temple. Why? Because these had been fullfilled literally by the time of that writing. When a vessel has been filled full (the literal meaning of fulfill) it is impossible to add more in that vessel.

What is the heart of Malachi's message? Not a pilgrimage to Palestine—that had already happened in 536 B.C. Not a rebuilding of the temple—that happened in 516 B.C. But rather his message concerns the messenger of Messiah (John the Baptist) and an inclusion of Gentiles! (Mal. 1:11,14). In speaking of Malachi's reference to the heathen religions in 1:11, Samuel A. Cartledge makes this statement in his book (*A Conservative Introduction to the Old Testament,* p. 165): "This is probably the finest anticipation of the universality of the true religion that can be found in the Old Testament."

Here again the futurist does violence to the Scriptures by teaching that Malachi predicts God will include all Israel when he makes up his jewels. This is based on Malachi 3:17. Let the Word speak for itself. Not once is this prediction made! On the contrary, Malachi reprimands his nation and predicts that when Messiah makes up his jewels only believers will be included. Verse 17 of this third chapter should be read in its context.

"Then they that feared Jehovah spake one with another; and Jehovah hearkened, and heard, and a book of remembrance was written before him, for them that feared Jehovah, and that thought upon his name" (Mal. 3:16). "But unto you that fear my name shall the sun of righteousness arise with healing in its wings; and ye shall go forth, and gambol as calves of the stall" (Mal. 4:2).

Those who "fear Jehovah" are quite a different matter from "all Jews."

One is saddened as one sees many making some prophecies of Malachi yet future when they have already come to pass. He predicted the coming of Elijah, and we have the word of our Lord himself that John fulfilled this (and spiritually, no less). Compare Malachi 4:5 with Matthew 11:14; 17:13; and Luke 1:17. Malachi predicted Messiah, and that happened literally at the first advent of our Lord. How unfortunate that these brethren live in the shadows when the real substance is here.

Let us hasten to say, as we said concerning other prophecies, that this is not to say there are not future predictions yet to be fulfilled. It is just to say that many which are *counted* future are now *past*. "He came unto his own . . . as many [of his own] as received him, to them gave he the right to become children of God" (John 1:11,12).

When the prophecies are permitted to say what they mean, and mean what they say, it is found that the Old Testament closed out with God's promises to national Israel having been fulfilled faithfully, except for the coming of Messiah, who was to usher in the new covenant. Today that, too, has come to pass. These promises were made concerning his first (not second) coming (compare Heb. 7:22; 8:6,13; 10:9,10).

By way of summary on national Israel in the Old Testament, let us recapitulate on the promises of God and the fulfillments of those promises.

1.  The promises to Abraham pertaining to the land of Palestine were historically fulfilled. Biblical proof of this is found in such passages as Joshua 11:23 and 21:43.

    a) The proofs that Israel historically became a great nation in fulfillment of God's promise to Abraham are too numerous and well known to need mentioning.

b) The promise to Abraham that his descendants would be as numerous as the sand and stars has been historically fulfilled. Biblical proof is found in passages such as Nehemiah 9:23.

c) The promise to Abraham concerning the Messiah included all nations of the earth (Gen. 12:3) and was historically fulfilled at the incarnation of Christ.

2. Following the return from bondage in Egypt under Moses and Joshua, other prophecies were made to the effect that Israel would return to Palestine, rebuild the temple, and reinstitute the blood sacrifices. While futurists hold these to be eschatological, actually they involved the captivities and return, which are a matter of biblical record as well as secular history. Both the captivity and return were prophesied, and both have been historically fulfilled. The temple was literally rebuilt in 516 B.C. We have this recorded in God's Word in such books as Ezra, Nehemiah, Haggai, and Zechariah.

3. All prophecies concerning the return to the land, rebuilding of the temple, etc., were made *prior* to 516 B.C. Since the rebuilding of the temple at that time — following a return to Palestine — *there have been no prophecies concerning a return to the land or a rebuilding of the temple.* Malachi, who probably prophesied after that date, made no mention of such things, nor are they referred to in any book of the New Testament as being future. There is one very simple reason why these things were never again prophesied after 516 B.C. *They had been literally fulfilled and therefore God's plan had moved beyond that stage.*

4. Following the literal and historical fulfillments of the above-mentioned promises, the next phase of God's plan called for the *first* coming of Messiah and the establishment of the new covenant, which included *all believers in our Lord Jesus Christ.* We have already alluded to a whole host of New Testament scriptures that show conclusively that this new covenant prophesied by Jeremiah (31:31) was established *with the church,* made up of both Jews and Gentiles, without distinction.

To insist upon these events having another fulfillment after the second coming of Christ to the earth is, we feel, to return to the "weak and beggarly elements" and to put Christ to open shame by returning to the bondage of the law.

*How the New Testament Interprets Israel*

"The Christian Church at large has from the beginning believed that this promise (Jer. 31:31-34) was fulfilled at the coming of Christ, and for this reason very early wrote over its own collection of sacred writings the collective title: 'He Kaine Daithke,' The New Covenant" (Albertus Pieters, *The Seed of Abraham*, p. 61).

"It was abundantly clear that the brotherhood, in claiming Jesus as the Messiah, asserted itself to be God's Israel, able to speak of the patriarchs and the prophets as its own, seeing in the new society the fulfillment of God's promise to Abraham" (George Johnston, *The Doctrine of the Church in the New Testament*, pp. 61,62).

Someone has pointed out that the Holy Spirit who inspired the Old Testament writers to write concerning Israel was the same Holy Spirit who inspired the writers of the New Testament, and that he certainly would have the authority to interpret those same scriptures. It is abundantly clear that many of the passages from the Old Testament, which the futurists interpret literally and eschatologically, were interpreted by the Holy Spirit in the New Testament in a symbolical manner and presented as fulfilled already.

Examples of this are found throughout the New Testament. In Acts 2:16 Peter maintains that Pentecost is "that which hath been spoken through the prophet Joel. . ." and goes on to quote Joel 2:28-32 in the next verse:

"And it shall be in the last days, saith God, I will pour forth of my Spirit upon all flesh: And your sons and your daughters shall prophesy, And your young men shall see visions, And your old men shall dream dreams: Yea and on my servants and on my handmaidens in those days will I pour forth of my Spirit; and they shall prophesy. And I will show wonders in the heaven above, And signs on the earth beneath; Blood, and fire, and vapor of smoke: The sun shall be turned into darkness, And the moon into blood, Before the day of the Lord come, That great and notable day: And it shall be, that whosoever shall call on the name of the Lord shall be saved" (Acts 2:17-21).

Hosea 1:10 and 2:23 are said in I Peter 2:10 to have been fulfilled *in Christians* (the church). In Hosea 1:10 we read: "Yet the number of the children of Israel shall be as the sand of the sea, which cannot be measured nor numbered; and it shall come to pass that, in the place where it was said unto them, Ye are not my people, it shall be said unto them, Ye are the sons of the living God." We find in Hosea 2:23: "And I will sow her unto me in the earth; . . . and I will say to them that were not my people, Thou art my people; and they shall say, Thou art my God." Now, turning to I Peter 2:10, we observe: "Who in time past were no people, *but now are* the people of God: who had not obtained mercy, but now have obtained mercy." In other words, Peter quotes these passages as fulfilled in his day, i.e., the first century A.D.

The Holy Spirit certainly inspired the writer of Hebrews to teach that Jeremiah 31:31 was fulfilled in the church. This is quite evident when one reads the two passages together:

"Behold, the days come, saith Jehovah, that I will make a new covenant with the house of Israel, and with the house of Judah" (Jer. 31:31).

"And the Holy Spirit also beareth witness to us; for after he hath said, This is the covenant that I will make with them after those days, saith the Lord: I will put my laws on their heart, and upon their mind also will I write them; then saith he, And their sins and their iniquities will I remember no more. Now where remission of these is, there is no more offering for sin. Having therefore, brethren, boldness to enter into the holy place by the blood of Jesus, by the way which he dedicated for us, *a new and living way,* through the veil, that is to say, his flesh; . . ." (Heb. 10:15-20).

In Luke 4:16-21 Jesus reads from Isaiah 61, and closing the book says, "*Today* hath this scripture been fulfilled in your ears" (vs. 21). It is interesting to note that the verses quoted by our Lord were specific promises to *Israel,* including preaching deliverance to the captives (vs. 18) and the "acceptable year of the Lord" (vs. 19). Futurists make this passage eschatological, but Jesus said it was fulfilled *today.*

In Acts 2:29-36 Peter quotes from the 16th Psalm and related scriptures and says in verse 31 that these scriptures were fulfilled by the resurrection of Christ:

"Brethren, I may say unto you freely of the patriarch David, that he both died and was buried, and his tomb is with us unto this day. Being therefore a prophet, and knowing that God had sworn with an oath to him that of the fruit of his loins *he would set one upon his throne; he foreseeing this spake of the resurrection of the*

*Christ,* that neither was he left unto Hades, nor did his flesh see corruption. This Jesus did God raise up, whereof we all are witnesses. Being therefore by the right hand of God exalted, and having received of the Father the promise of the Holy Spirit, he hath poured forth this, which ye see and hear. For David ascended not into the heavens: but he saith himself, The Lord said unto my Lord, sit thou on my right hand, till I make thine enemies the footstool of thy feet. Let all the house of Israel therefore know assuredly that God hath made him both Lord and Christ, this Jesus whom ye crucified."

It is worth noting that one thing which Peter teaches was thus fulfilled was *Christ sitting on the throne of David.*

In reading the content of Acts 15 one is struck by the fact that James, the brother of Christ, quotes Amos 9:11 and says that this scripture was fulfilled when Gentiles (Cornelius' household) were saved. The scripture in Amos to which James referred is a very definite futurist prooftext: "In that day will *I raise up the tabernacle of David that is fallen,* and close up the breaches thereof; and I will raise up its ruins, and I will build it as in the days of old" (Amos 9:11).

### The Apostle Paul

There was one man in the New Testament who, more than any other, spoke many times concerning Israel and their relationship to the Christian church. This person was Paul, that great apostle to the Gentiles, to whom God revealed mysteries which he had kept hidden even from the prophets (Eph. 3:4-6). This is very significant in as much as Paul lays an unchallenged claim to being the theologian *par excellence* for the Christian church.

Paul wrote thirteen epistles, and it is hard to find one which does not deal with the theology of the Jew, and his relationship to the Gentile. It is a poor "searching of the scriptures" that ignores Paul's statements (which are made unequivocally plain), and builds a "scheme" of eschatology upon the metaphorical language like that used by John in Revelation. Yet this is what the futurist chooses to do.

The New Testament makes a distinction between *national Israel* and *spiritual Israel.* Paul, more than any other person, accentuated this difference.

Examples of these distinctions can be seen from the following scriptures, although these by no means exhaust the references found in the New Testament.

### a) National Israel

"But when the Jews saw the multitudes, they were filled with jealousy, and contradicted the things which were spoken by Paul, and blasphemed. And Paul and Barnabas spake out boldly, and said, It was necessary that the word of God should first be spoken to you. Seeing ye thrust it from you, *and judge yourselves unworthy of eternal life, lo, we turn to the Gentiles*" (Acts 13:45,46).

"And think not to say within yourselves, We have Abraham to our father: for I say unto you, that God is able of these stones to raise up children unto Abraham. And even now the axe lieth at the root of the tree: *every tree therefore that bringeth not forth good fruit is hewn down, and cast into the fire*" (Matt. 3:9,10).

"And seeing a fig tree by the way side, he came to it, and found nothing thereon, but leaves only; and he saith unto it, *Let there be no fruit from thee henceforward for ever.* And immediately the fig tree *withered away*" (Matt. 21:19). (Note that the fig tree is said to represent Israel. If this be so, then Jesus said that Israel would never again be a fruitful nation.)

"Jesus saith unto them, Did ye never read in the scriptures, The stone which the builders rejected, The same was made the head of the corner; This was from the Lord, And it is marvelous in our eyes? Therefore say I unto you, *The kingdom of God shall be taken away from you, and shall be given to a nation bringing forth the fruits thereof*" (Matt. 21:42,43).

"Behold, your house is left unto you desolate" (Matt. 23:38).

"For I say unto you, that none of those men that were bidden shall taste of my supper" (Luke 14:24).

"Beware of the dogs, beware of the evil workers, *beware of the concision*" (Phil. 3:2).

"For he is not a Jew who is one outwardly; neither is that circumcision which is outward in the flesh: *but he is a Jew who is one inwardly;* and circumcision is that of the heart, in the spirit not in the letter; whose praise is not of men, but of God" (Rom. 2:28,29).

"But it is not as though the word of God hath come to nought. *For, they are not all Israel, that are of Israel*" (Rom. 9:6).

b) Spiritual Israel

"*But he is a Jew who is one inwardly*: and circumcision is that of the heart, . . ." (Rom. 2:28,29).

"(As it is written, A father of many nations have I made thee) before him whom he believed, even God, who giveth life to the dead, and calleth the things that are not, as though they were" (Rom. 4:17).

"And so all Israel shall be saved. . ." (Rom. 11:26). (Here I believe Paul speaks of national Israelites, but only of the believing remnant, or "spiritual Jews.")

"And Jesus said unto them, Verily I say unto you, that *ye who have followed* me, in the regeneration when the Son of man shall sit on the throne of his glory, ye also shall sit upon twelve thrones, judging the twelve tribes of Israel" (Matt. 19:28).

"Wherefore remember, that once ye, the Gentiles in the flesh, who are called Uncircumcision by that which is called Circumcision, in the flesh, made by hands; that ye were at that time separate from Christ, alienated from the commonwealth of Israel, and strangers from the covenants of the promise, having no hope and without God in the world. *But now in Christ Jesus ye that once were far off are made nigh in the blood of Christ.* For he is our peace, who made both one and brake down the middle wall of partition, having abolished in his flesh the enmity, even the law of commandments contained in ordinances; *that he might create in himself of the two one new man,* so making peace; and might reconcile them both in one body unto God through the cross, having slain the enmity thereby" (Eph. 2:11-16).

". . . that the *Gentiles are fellow-heirs*. . ." (Eph. 3:6).

"Know therefore that they that are of faith, the same are sons of Abraham. And the scripture, foreseeing that God would justify the Gentiles by faith, preached the gospel beforehand unto Abraham, saying, *In thee shall all the nations be blessed. So then they that are of faith are blessed with the faithful Abraham*" (Gal. 3:7-9).

". . . and upon *the Israel of God*" (Gal. 6:16).

"For we are the circumcision, *who worship by the Spirit of God, and glory in Christ Jesus* [which national Jews do not do], and have no confidence in the flesh [which natural Jews do]" (Phil. 3:3).

### c) Paul's Summary on Israel

1. *Israel had definite advantages, which made her all the more responsible.* "But if thou bearest the name of a Jew, and restest upon the law, and gloriest in God, *and knowest his will,* and approvest the things that are excellent, *being instructed out of the law*" (Rom. 2:17,18).

"What advantage then hath the Jew? or what is the profit of circumcision? *Much every way: first of all, that they were intrusted with the oracles of God*" (Rom. 3:1,2).

"Who are Israelites; *whose is the adoption, and the glory, and the covenants, and the giving of the law, and the service of God, and the promises; whose are the fathers, and of whom is Christ as concerning the flesh,* who is over all, God blessed for ever. Amen" (Rom. 9:4,5).

2. *Israel had obligations, but failed to keep the covenant with God.* "But Israel, following after a law of righteousness, did not arrive at that law. Wherefore? Because they sought it not by faith, but as it were by works. *They stumbled at the stone of stumbling:* even as it is written, Behold, I lay in Zion a stone of stumbling and a rock of offence: and he that believeth on him shall not be put to shame" (Rom. 9:31-33).

"*For being ignorant of God's righteousness, and seeking to establish their own they did not subject themselves to the righteousness of God. For Christ is the end of the law unto righteousness to every one that believeth*" (Rom. 10:3,4).

"And reckonest thou this, O man, who judgest them that practice such things, and doest the same, that thou shalt escape the judgment of God?" (Rom. 2:3).

"Now we know that what things soever the law saith, it speaketh to them that are under the law; that every mouth may be stopped, and all the world may be brought under the judgment of God" (Rom. 3:19).

"For ye, brethren, became imitators of the churches of God which are in Judea in Christ Jesus: for ye also suffered the same things of your own countrymen, even as they did *of the Jews; who both killed the Lord Jesus and the prophets, and drove out us,* and please not God, and are contrary to all men" (I Thess. 2:14,15).

3. *Calvary tore down the partition which separated Jew and Gentile.* "And the scripture, foreseeing that God would justify the Gentiles by faith, preached the gospel beforehand unto Abraham, saying, In thee shall *all the nations be blessed.* So then they that are of faith are blessed with the faithful Abraham" (Gal. 3:8,9).

"For ye are all sons of God, through faith, in Christ Jesus. For as many of you as are baptized into Christ did put on Christ. There can be neither Jew nor Greek, there can be neither bond nor free, there can be no male and female; for ye all are one man in Christ Jesus. *And if ye are Christ's, then are ye Abraham's seed, heirs according to promise"* (Gal. 3:26-29).

"Wherefore remember, that once ye, the Gentiles in the flesh, who are called Uncircumcision by that which is called Circumcision, in the flesh, made by hands; that ye were at that time separate from Christ, alienated from the commonwealth of Israel, and strangers from the covenants of the promise, having no hope and without God in the world. *But now in Christ Jesus ye that once were far off are made nigh in the blood of Christ.* For he is our peace, *who made both one,* and *brake down the middle wall of partition,* having abolished in his flesh the enmity, even the law of commandments contained in ordinances; *that he might create in himself of the two one new man, so making peace;* and might reconcile them both in one body unto God through the cross, having slain the enmity thereby: . . . *So then ye are no more strangers and sojourners, but ye are fellow-citizens with the saints, and of the household of God"* (Eph. 2:11-19).

"There is one body, and one Spirit, even as also ye were called in one hope of your calling; one Lord, one faith, one baptism, one God and Father of all, who is over all, and through all, and in all" (Eph. 4:4-6).

"Now to Abraham were the promises spoken, and to his seed. He saith not, And to seeds, as of many; but as of one, And to thy seed, *which is Christ"* (Gal. 3:16).

"Where there cannot be Greek and Jew, circumcision and uncircumcision, barbarian, Scythian, bondman, freeman; but Christ is all, and in all" (Col. 3:11).

4. *Salvation depends not on ancestry, but on God's choosing.* Note that Jews, then and today, boasted of three things primarily: (1) law, (2) circumcision, and (3) nationality. Paul deliberately tears these down in chapter 2 of Romans:

a) God is no respecter of persons (2:11).
b) Salvation is not gained by Law (2:14).
c) Salvation is not gained by circumcision (2:26).
d) Salvation is not gained by ancestry (2:28,29).

After all, God's covenant people are not those of the flesh (see Rom. 2:28; 9:6-8; Matt. 3:9,10), but those who, like Abraham and Jacob, have had an experience (conversion) with God. Compare John 8:39,40 and Galatians 3:6-9,16-18,22-29.

Every Christian is a "Jew" (spiritual Israelite) (Rom. 2:29). Compare Romans 4:17; 9:6-8; Galatians 3:6-9; 5:6; 6:16; Ephesians 2:11-15; Colossians 2:11-14.

5. *Every descendant of Abraham is not assured salvation, but only those who, like Abraham, believe the promises of God.* "But it is not as though the word of God hath come to nought. For they are not all Israel, that are of Israel: neither, because they are Abraham's seed, are they all children: but, in Isaac shall thy seed be called. *That is, it is not the children of the flesh that are children of God, but the children of the promise are reckoned for a seed*" (Rom. 9:6-8).

"Even as Abraham believed God, and it was reckoned unto him for righteousness. Know therefore that *they that are of faith, the same are sons of Abraham*" (Gal. 3:6,7).

"Beware of the dogs, beware of the evil workers, beware of the concision: *for we are the circumcision, who worship by the Spirit of God, and glory in Christ Jesus, and have no confidence in the flesh*" (Phil. 3:2,3).

"Now it was not written for his sake alone, that it was reckoned unto him; but for our sake also, unto whom it shall be reckoned, who believe on him that raised Jesus our Lord from the dead, *who was delivered up for our trespasses, and was raised for our justification*" (Rom. 4:23-25).

"Tell me, ye that desire to be under the law, do ye not hear the law? For it is written, *that Abraham had two sons*, one by the hand-maid, and one by the freewoman. Howbeit *the son of the handmaid is born after the flesh; but the son by the freewoman is born through promise.* Which things contain an allegory: *for these women are two covenants*; one from mount Sinai, bearing children unto bondage, which is Hagar. Now this Hagar is mount Sinai in Arabia, and answereth to the Jerusalem that now is: for she is in bondage with her children. But the *Jerusalem that is above* is free, *which is our mother.* For it is written, Rejoice, thou barren that bearest not; break forth and cry, thou that travailest not: *For more are the children of the desolate than of her that hath the husband. Now we, brethren, as Isaac was, are children of promise.* But as then he that was born after the flesh persecuted him that was born after the Spirit, so also it is now. Howbeit *what saith the scripture?* Cast out the handmaid and her son: *for the son of the handmaid shall not inherit with the son of the freewoman. Wherefore, brethren, we are not children of a handmaid, but of the freewoman*" (Gal. 4:21-31).

It is difficult to see how any scripture could be plainer than the above passage from Galatians 4 in distinguishing between "Israel of the flesh," whom Paul likens to Hagar the bondwoman, and "Israel of the spirit," whom he likens to the free son, Isaac. Perhaps it would be well to remind the reader that Paul was writing to a Christian church made up predominantly of Gentile Christians. It would be difficult to explain this teaching away as being a "Jewish book," or saying that Paul was speaking of a future event involving Jews only. This scripture is well worth the second reading if there be any doubt that Paul has said there was no hope for those who were merely physical descendants; and that the inheritance is for those who are *children of promise and who are interested in the Jerusalem which is above*, rather than the earthly Jerusalem. *"What saith the scripture?"*

6. *The Gentile was included in God's plan, according to prophecy. This made him equal with the Jew.*

"For this cause it is of faith, that it may be according to grace; *to the end that the promise may be sure to all the seed; not to that only which is of the law, but to that also which is of the faith of Abraham, who is the father of us all* (as it is written, *A father of many nations have I made thee*). . ." (Rom. 4:16,17).

"Even us, whom he also called, *not from the Jews only, but also from the Gentiles?* As he saith also in Hosea, I will call that my people, which was not my people; and her beloved, that was not beloved. And it shall be, that in the place where it was said unto them, Ye are not my people, there shall they be called sons of the living God" (Rom. 9:24-26).

This passage, which Paul quotes from Hosea, is a favorite text of the futurist, the only difference being that whereas Paul refers it to Gentiles and says it has been fulfilled, they make it yet future, and apply it to Israel!

"Christ redeemed us from the curse of the law, having become a curse for us; for it is written, Cursed is every one that hangeth on a tree: *that upon the Gentiles might come the blessing of Abraham in Christ Jesus; that we might receive the promise of the Spirit through faith*" (Gal. 3:13,14).

"But now apart from the law a righteousness of God hath been manifested, *being witnessed by the law and the prophets;* even the righteousness of God through faith in Jesus Christ *unto all them that believe; for there is no distinction; for all have sinned, and fall short of the glory of God*" (Rom. 3:21-23).

"And he received the sign of circumcision, a seal of the righteousness of the faith which he had while he was in uncircumcision: *that he might be the father of all them that believe, though they be in uncircumcision, that righteousness might be reckoned unto them; . . .*" (Rom. 4:11,12). Compare also Ephesians 3:8-12.

7. *It is the remnant, not the entire nation, which is predestined to be saved.*

"For what if some were without faith? Shall their want of faith make of none effect the faithfulness of God? God forbid: yea, let God be found true, but every man a liar; . . ." (Rom. 3:4).

"And Isaiah crieth concerning Israel, If the number of the children of Israel be as the sand of the sea, *it is the remnant that shall be saved:* for the Lord will execute his word upon the earth, finishing it and cutting it short. And, as Isaiah hath said before, Except the Lord of Sabaoth had left us a *seed* [remnant], *we had become as Sodom, and had been made like unto Gomorrah*" (Rom. 9:27-29).

"Even so then at this *present time* also there is a remnant according to the election of grace" (Rom. 11:5).

*Paul's Conclusion*

a) God has superseded the *natural* ancestry of Abraham, and called out a seed of Abraham whose circumcision is "of the heart and not of the flesh." The law, circumcision, and national Israel were *shadows* (compare Col. 2:17; Heb. 10:1), but since Calvary they have been replaced by the real *substance* — the church.

"And he put all things in subjection under his feet, and gave him to be head over all things *to the church, which is his body, the fulness of him that filleth all in all"* (Eph. 1:22,23).

b) *God is no respecter of persons. Since Calvary, Jew and Gentile are treated as equals, all being sinners and all needing salvation through the blood of Jesus Christ.*

"Tribulation and anguish, upon every soul of man that worketh evil, *of the Jew first,* and also of the Greek; but glory and honor and peace to every man that worketh good, to the Jew first, *and also to the Greek: for there is no respect of persons with God"* (Rom. 2:9-11).

*"Or is God the God of Jews only? is he not the God of Gentiles also? Yea, of Gentiles also:* if so be that God is one, and he shall justify the circumcision by faith, and the uncircumcision through faith" (Rom. 3:29,30).

*"For there is no distinction between Jew and Greek: for the same Lord is Lord of all, and is rich unto all that call upon him: for, Whosoever shall call upon the name of the Lord shall be saved"* (Rom. 10:12,13).

c) This is not to say that God changed his plan. On the contrary, Paul proves that this has always been God's plan. However, God has been unfolding this plan to man through a progressive revelation; it was Paul who had the privilege of "revealing" it in detail (Eph. 3:4-6). Read carefully Romans 3:21,26,31; Genesis 3:15; Galatians 3:8,16.

*Romans 11:26*

"And so all Israel shall be saved: even as it is written, There shall come out of Zion the Deliverer; he shall turn away ungodliness from Jacob."

To make this verse apply to every Jew living when Christ returns, as the futurists do, is to have Paul contradicting himself. No person who believes the Bible to be infallible can conscientiously agree that such a contradiction exists.

The context clearly indicates that Paul is referring to national Jews. However, a great mind like Paul's does not contradict itself, nor would the Holy Spirit permit a contradiction to be written in the Sacred Word. This passage, and the entire chapter, must be interpreted with reference to all that has gone before. Paul taught in Romans 11 that God had definite plans for a remnant in Israel. However, Paul never mentioned a return to Palestine, rebuilding of a temple, return to Jewish ritual, and so on. Nor is this mentioned anywhere in the New Testament.

Paul spoke of a turning to Christ, not Palestine, and this involved not the entire nation, but the remnant. Nor will Paul's theology allow even the remnant to be saved *after the rapture of the church*.

Undue stress has been placed on this one verse of Scripture (Rom. 11:26). There is not another verse in the entire New Testament that will substantiate the interpretation placed upon it.

The futurist exegetes the apostle's statement thus: "And *therefore*, all Israel *shall* be saved—at a later date." This interpretation does violence to the entire Roman epistle. It is extremely important to keep the verse within the context; and the context certainly will not allow such a meaning.

The great apostle has labored under the guidance of the Spirit to show which Israelites would be (were being) saved (compare 2:9-11,14,26; 3:19,21-23,28-30; 9:6-8,15-18,27-29; 10:12,13; 11:5-7). To show that he was dealing with the present rather than the future, Paul included himself in the Israel that was being saved.

The Roman epistle deals with the *how* of salvation and argues that the Jew has the same standing as the Gentile, as well as the same need of the same salvation. When Romans 11:26 is exegeted in this light, the word "so" does not have the force of "therefore"; rather it means "similarly" or "in like manner." And examples are too numerous to mention in rhetoric as well as in the Scriptures—which show that "shall" does not always denote a future fulfillment.

The futurist attempts to strengthen his argument for a future connotation by building on the words "in part" of verse 25. These words are taken to mean "for awhile." What the apostle actually said was that blindness had come on "a part of" Israel. Paul himself was a member of the part (remnant) of Israel on which blindness did not come (Rom. 11:1).

The proper exegesis of Romans 11:25,26 would seem to be: ". . . God permitted a part of Israel to be blinded to the gospel, in order that the full number of elected Gentiles would be saved. And in the same manner all the elect of Israel [see 11:5] are also being saved, just as God prophesied in Isaiah 59:20—'And the Redeemer shall come to Zion, and unto them that turn from transgression in Jacob, saith the Lord.' " The futurist errs on this quotation from Isaiah by making it apply to Jesus' second coming. Paul refers to the earthly ministry of Jesus. A deliverer *did* come to Zion and with "as many [of his own] as received him" he made a new covenant. Read Isaiah 59:21; Romans 11:27; Jeremiah 31:31; Matthew 26: 28; Hebrews 8:8; 10:16.

It would seem that one is faced with the alternative of either accepting this interpretation or taking a hyperliteral face value rendering. If taken literally at face value, Romans 11:26 says that every Israelite—past, present, and future—is assured salvation. The futurist interprets the verse by adding words, i.e., ". . . all Israel [living at a certain future date] shall be saved." However, a reading of scripture *with* scripture will show up this as being unbiblical teaching. Rather than wresting Romans 11:26 from its setting, the student of the Bible should compare it with other New Testament scriptures, such as John 8:39,40; Galatians 3:6-9, 16-18,22,29; Romans 2:28, 29; and 9:6-8, which deal with the same subject.

The only way to interpret Romans 11:26 in line with all the rest of Paul's teachings is to take "all Israel" to mean *all* the *believing remnant,* that is, all Jews who are predestined to accept Christ, during this present age, will be saved. Any other interpretation does violence to Paul as well as to the entire New Testament.

The futurist either ignores or explains away such passages as these found in the New Testament, and insists on interpreting the New Testament by the Old. We feel that this is a serious mistake, as the New Testament would obviously have more revelation in its favor than would the Old. This fact is proved conclusively by such passages as I Corinthians 10:11, where Paul, after speaking about some experiences of the Israelites recorded in the Old Testament, said, "Now these things happened unto them by way of example [types]; and they were written for our admonition, upon whom the ends of the ages are come."

As a matter of fact, the futurists are going contrary to the teaching of at least one of Darby's followers when they get their hermeneutics from the Old rather than the New Testament. J. G. Bellett, a staunch follower of Darby's teachings, is quoted as saying that when he found a text of the Old Testament recited or referred to in the New Testament, he felt as if the Holy Spirit had put a lamp in his hand, wherewith to explore afresh the earlier revelation. If futurists would follow this rule of exegesis, our differences would be resolved immediately. However, our difficulties stem from the fact that they ignore most of the New Testament and insist on garnering their hermeneutics from the Old Testament.

Examples of how futurists interpret the New Testament by the Old Testament are found throughout their writings, but we shall offer only one or two to point up the fact. One man has said that Daniel furnished the frame and John (in Revelation) fills in the details. If we separate the two, he said, prophecy becomes an insoluble enigma. Alva J. McLain, in a pamphlet on Daniel, said that the only obvious and sensible thing to do is to use Daniel's prophecy of the seventy weeks as a point of departure and *the inspired key* to the interpretation of the book of Revelation.

It seems sheer nonsense to say that such men as John, who wrote the Revelation after studying at the feet of Jesus himself and who was then inspired by the Holy Spirit, would be shackled by the yoke of the old dispensation. As a matter of fact, Paul uses the fourth chapter of Romans and other passages to prove that there never was one plan of salvation for the Jew and another for the Gentile, but rather that God had one eternal plan, which was intended to include the Gentile (compare Gen. 17:5 and Rom. 4:11,12,16,17,23,24).

*How the Church Fathers Viewed Israel*

a) Justin Martyr

"Since God announced that He would send a new covenant . . . we will not understand this of the old law and its proselytes, but of

Christ and His proselytes, namely us Gentiles" (*Ante Nicene Fathers*, Vol. I, p. 260).

"As, therefore, Christ is the Israel and the Jacob, even so we who are quarried out from the bowels of Christ are the true Israelitish race" (*ibid.*, p. 267).

### b) Irenaeus

"But, . . . the king has actually come . . . and has bestowed upon men the good things which were announced beforehand . . . by His advent He Himself fulfilled all things, and still does fulfill in the church the New Covenant foretold by the law" (*ibid.*, p. 511).

"Now I have shown a short time ago that the church is the seed of Abraham" (*ibid.*, p. 563).

### c) Hippolytus

(Having quoted from Isaiah) "For it is not of the Jews that he spake of old, nor is it of the city of Zion, but of the Church" (*ibid.*, Vol. V, p. 243).

It seems that the futurist (and I once was a strong one) has just a few scattered pegs on which he rests his entire scheme of eschatology. He takes just a few verses from Daniel concerning the seventy weeks, then jumps to Matthew 24, which is taken out of context, as is also Romans 11, and from there he is off to the book of Revelation, where he picks out the numbers, symbols, etc., which fit into his futuristic theory. The strange part of it is that he ignores numerous other symbols and numbers in Revelation because they do not help his cause. In order to get the church and the present kingdom out of the way, the futurist arbitrarily divides books of the Bible into "church age" (an expression which is not found in the Bible) and messianic kingdom age. Jesus speaks so much about the present kingdom in the first half of Matthew that they cannot explain it away; therefore, they say (very arbitrarily) that Matthew 13 begins the "mystery form" of the kingdom.

Nor can they get the church completely out of the book of Revelation, since the first three chapters are taken up with the conversation between Jesus and John concerning the seven churches of Asia. Therefore, determined to make most of this book a "Jewish book," such men as M. R. DeHaan and the late C. I. Scofield take the first verses of the fourth chapter, where Jesus expressly calls *John* to come up to heaven, and say he was really saying to the church to come up higher, i.e., come up out of the world (rapture), and thus they say from 4:1 to the end, the book of Revelation is a "Jewish book." This sort of reasoning may please for awhile, but, once one takes a good sober look at such hermeneutics, it becomes amusing.

By the same line of reasoning, the futurist arbitrarily places a gap between the sixty-ninth and seventieth weeks of Daniel's prophecy. He does this without one verse of Scripture or one iota of historical data to back up his argument. Also, the kingdoms of heaven and of God are said by the futurist to be two altogether different things. This again is convenient in getting rid of some "irritating" Scripture verses in their "Jewish book." However, just a cursory glance at such passages as Matthew 11:12; 13:24; Luke 16:16; Colossians 1:13; Matthew 4:17; 10:6,7; 19:23,24; Mark 1:15; Luke 9:2, ad infinitum, will show that although the kingdom is to be *perfected* at the second coming of our Lord, *he very definitely established a present kingdom on earth*; also that the *kingdom of God and the kingdom of heaven were synonymous terms.*

"And from the days of John the Baptist until now the *kingdom of heaven* suffereth violence, and the men of violence take it by force" (Matt. 11:12); "Another parable set he before them, saying, *the kingdom of heaven* is likened unto a man that sowed good seed in his field" (Matt. 13:24); "The law and the prophets were until John: from that time the gospel of the *kingdom of God* is preached, and every man entereth violently into it" (Luke 16:16); "Who delivered us out of the power of darkness, *and translated us into the kingdom of the Son of his love*" (Col. 1:13). "From that time began Jesus to preach, and to say, Repent ye; for the *kingdom of heaven* is at hand" (Matt. 4:17); "And he sent them forth to preach the *kingdom of God,* and to heal the sick" (Luke 9:2). Need the other references listed above be quoted? Let the earnestly inquiring reader read them from his own Bible.

The dangers of relying on prooftexts can be seen by examining a few scriptures. Take, for example, Romans 5:18: "So then as through one trespass the judgment came unto all men to condemnation; even so through one act of righteousnees the free gift came unto *all men* to justification of life." This scripture, if taken alone, would warrant universalism. "And Peter said unto them, Repent ye, and be baptized every one of you in the name of Jesus Christ unto the remission of your sins; and ye shall receive the gift of the Holy Spirit" (Acts 2:38). This, taken alone, would indicate baptismal regeneration. "And so all Israel shall be saved: even as it is written, There shall come out of Zion the Deliverer; he shall turn away ungodliness from Jacob" (Rom. 11:26). If used alone, this teaches that *all Jews*, regardless of actions, will be saved. "Ye see that by works a man is justified, and not only by faith" (James 2:24). In this we see salvation by works. ". . . for I will no more have mercy upon the house of Israel, that I should in any wise pardon them" (Hos. 1:6). Here we seemingly have no hope for Israel from Hosea's time on.

Needless to say, very few futurists believe any of the above doctrines, and would belittle any who based a doctrine on such handling of the Scriptures. Many scriptures appear to mean a certain thing until they are examined in the light of the whole Bible. The futurists are opposed also to the doctrines held by Jehovah's Witnesses, which allow for stages of opportunity after death. And yet, regardless of how vehemently they deny it, the futurists teach a second chance for the Jews. According to their teachings, the church will be raptured, and then, three and one-half years later (halfway through the seven-year tribulation), thousands will be given another opportunity, and will accept Christ when he returns to earth (when he raptures the church, they say, he comes only "in the air"). These must of necessity be the same people who were living on earth at the time of the rapture, and up to that time had rejected Christ. Now these same people, who rejected him during the so-called church age, are given a second chance and are saved, according to futurist teachings.

Another need along this line, as we have intimated already, is to distinguish between national Israel and spiritual Israel. The New Testament definitely speaks of both, and a great deal of intellectual honesty is needed on the part of Bible students to determine whether a particular passage is speaking of the one or the other.

At least one other problem facing the holder of the futurist view, is the problem of time. According to the dispensational view, which is involved in the futurist view, we are now living in the sixth dispensation of time, and the seventh dispensation will not begin until after the rapture of the church; and during the seventh dispensation much of God's work of redemption will be carried on. This is adverse to the teachings of Christ and all of *the New Testament, which knows only the present age and the "coming age."* This "coming age" is characterized only by rewards and punishments. It does not answer the description of an earthly millennium. It answers only one description, and that is the Eternal State wherein a general resurrection and general judgment is followed only by eternal bliss for all the righteous while all the wicked will suffer in an eternal hell.

### Futurist Assumptions

Up to this point we have established the fact that Darby's theory, the futurist view of Israel, is contrary to the entire New Testament, contrary to the church fathers, contrary to historical facts, contrary to the theology of the reformers, even to many of Darby's contemporaries, as well as contrary to most present contemporary students of the Bible. One might ask, then, how is this theory perpetuated?

In order to justify Darby's theory, the futurist must make arbitrary divisions in the Scriptures, such as contending that the first twelve chapters of Matthew were to the Jews, while chapter 13 to the end of the book was intended for Christians. Another arbitrary and ruthless division is to say that the first three chapters of Revelation apply to the church, while all the remainder of the book is for Jews. This division is "proved" by saying that Revelation 4:1 is saying *to the church,* "Come up higher." Any person reading Revelation 4:1, without prejudice, would see that it is *John* who is being told to come up to heaven, and that *the church is not even mentioned.*

Space will not permit a discussion of all the inconsistencies of the futurist's handling of Scripture, but let us look at a few of the ways in which they beg the question in order to hang on to this man-made doctrine. While it should be pointed out that all futurists do not subscribe to all the statements listed, it is nevertheless true that these are general characteristics of the futurist school of thought.

1. *The coming of Messiah* predicted in the Old Testament referred to his *second* coming (eschatological).

*Answer*: Most of these scriptures which they use clearly refer to Christ's first advent and were fulfilled during his earthly ministry.

2. *The fig tree* refers to Israel throughout the Bible. According to W. L. Pettingill: "It is agreed among enlightened Bible scholars that the fig tree is a symbol of the nation of Israel" (*Bible Questions Answered*, p. 127).

*Answer*: Although many Bible scholars agree with the futurist on this point, i.e., that the fig tree does represent Israel, the futurist fails to see the logical outcome of this conclusion. In Matthew 21:19, Jesus said to the fig tree, *or symbolically to Israel*, ". . . let there be no fruit from thee henceforward for ever." This ties in nicely with Matthew 3:9,10, and many other scriptures referring to Israel's future as a nation.

3. *There is a gap* (which has already lasted more than 1900 years) between the sixty-ninth and seventieth weeks of Daniel's prophecy (Dan. 9:25-27). In the words of the late H. A. Ironside: "The prophetic clock stopped at Calvary. Not one tick has been heard since. From the moment Christ bowed his head and yielded up his Spirit to the Father, all the glories of the kingdom spoken of by Old Testament seers and prophets have been held in abeyance" (*The Mysteries of God*, p. 50).

*Answer*: Here again the futurist *assumes* this gap without a single shred of scriptural basis, and simply begins to speculate on what will happen *after* the gap. Colossians 1:13 alone refutes the idea of a postponed kingdom.

Daniel divided the seventy weeks into three periods. All are agreed that the first two periods followed in succession and ended with the beginning of Christ's ministry at age thirty. Since the first two periods passed without a gap in between, and since neither Daniel nor anyone else made any mention of a gap, it seems logical to assume that the third period would follow in order.

A cursory reading of the book of Daniel will reveal that he predicted four kingdoms and placed the seventieth week within the fourth kingdom. Again, all conservative scholars are agreed that the fourth kingdom referred to the Roman Empire. It is clearly recorded in history that this empire came to an end in A.D. 476. Since the seventieth week was prophesied to happen during a kingdom which has ceased to exist, it follows logically that the seventieth week had to have been fulfilled *prior to* A.D. 476. It seems absurd to ignore a historical fact and say that the event is still future.

4. *The kingdom of heaven* is altogether future and does not exist today. This assumption takes a number of scriptural gymnastics because of the frequent teachings in the New Testament. In order to protect this assumption they say (1) that the kingdom of God and the kingdom of heaven are two separate kingdoms, and (2) that the abundance of teaching in Matthew's Gospel represents a "mystery form" of the kingdom from chapter 13 to the end of the book.

*Answer*: We know that the terms "kingdom of God" and "kingdom of heaven" are used interchangeably in the New Testament. And of course there is no scriptural mention of a "mystery form" of the kingdom.

A great majority of the teachings concerning the kingdom throughout the New Testament present it in a present form. We believe that the kingdom, which is now a present reality, will be perfected or consummated at the second coming of Christ to earth.

5. *The "secret rapture"* of the church. This is another invention of the mind to give the Jews a second chance to accept Christ while at the same time keeping them separate from the Christian church.

*Answer*: All of the scriptures relating to the rapture present it as anything but secretive. On the contrary, there is to be a shout which will be heard throughout the world, the trumpet will sound, and every eye shall see him (compare I Thess. 4:16,17 and Rev. 1:7).

6. *The "time of Jacob's trouble"* (Jer. 30:7) is eschatological and will take place during a tribulation period after the rapture of the church.

*Answer*: This is another case of making passages from the Old Testament "fit in with" New Testament hermeneutics, and the futurist offers no basis other than to say that it is so.

Like most of the Old Testament passages used by this school of thought, this prediction could have had its fulfillment many times over in the past, as the Jews suffered the wrath of God. Many diligent students of the Bible believe it had its main fulfillment during the destruction of Jerusalem in A.D. 70.

7. *Daniel 9:27* is said to refer to antichrist and the *second coming* of Christ.

*Answer*: Upon a closer reading, the passage lends itself to an altogether different interpretation. Rather than the second coming, it refers to the first advent of Jesus; and, rather than "he" referring to antichrist, it points back to verse 26, where Daniel was speaking of Messiah. It seems more than coincidence that Jesus was cut off in the middle of a week (Daniel's heptad, or week of years, being a seven-year period). In other words, Daniel predicted that Messiah would be cut off in the middle of a seven-year period, and Jesus was nailed to the cross (cut off from life) after approximately three and one-half years of earthly ministry.

8. *The Jews will return to Palestine*, rebuild the temple, and reinstate the blood sacrifices, and so forth.

M. R. DeHaan, in a series of radio messages entitled "Dry Bones in the Valley of Ezekiel" (which was later distributed in printed form), contends that during a seven-year period of tribulation following the rapture of the church, God will regather Israel into Canaan, have them rebuild the temple, and re-establish the Old Testament forms of worship and sacrifices. Then, according to DeHaan, Christ will appear, destroy antichrist, and set up an earthly kingdom with Jerusalem as its capital.

*Answer*: There is not a single verse in the New Testament predicting a return to Palestine, or anywhere else, by national Israel. Again, the passages quoted for this presupposition are from the Old Testament; each passage was prophesied before or during the captivity, and each prophecy concerning a return to Palestine, rebuilding of the temple, or restoration of the blood sacrifices was literally fulfilled in 536 B.C. and thereafter, when Cyrus gave permission for the captive Jews to return to Palestine. The temple was rebuilt under Zerubbabel, and actual accounts are given by prophets like Nehemiah and Haggai.

9. *The twelve literal tribes of Israel*, plus the Roman Empire, will be revived.

*Answer*: Here again they ignore history, because there are no longer twelve pure Israelite tribes, since ten of these tribes lost their identity through intermarriage after their captivity in 722 B.C. Also they ignore the fact that a remnant from each of those ten tribes returned to Palestine under Zerubbabel in 536 B.C. The apostle Paul was a descendant of one of those ten tribes (Phil. 3:5).

It is worth repeating that the Roman Empire has been extinct since A.D. 476. To be sure, God can do all things and could, if he chose, reinstate the ten lost tribes as well as a Roman Empire. It does not seem logical, however, that God will violate history. This is as far-fetched as the theory held by some futurists that Judas Iscariot will be reincarnated as the man of sin.

Concerning all the above assumptions, the futurist strangely offers not a single verse of conclusive New Testament Scripture. He simply says, "This is so because it is so," and then proceeds to build upon these shaky foundations.

Let us be reminded that Israel was a type of the Christian church. A cursory reading of the book of Hebrews will leave no doubt in the unbiased mind that this is true. One should especially read Hebrews 8:5; 9:9,24; 10:9,16,19-21; 11:9-16,39,40; 12:18-24; 13:10-14. These and other passages reveal that Israel was a type of the church, the land was a type of heaven (the present phase of the kingdom is an immediate foretaste of heaven), circumcision is a type of the new birth, the law is a type of the gospel, and the temple foreshadowed the body of Christ—the Christian church.

Paul says that every believer (Jew and Gentile alike) is a spiritual descendant of Abraham. "And if ye be Christ's, then are ye Abraham's seed, and heirs according to promise" (Gal. 3:29). And in Romans 9:33 Paul refers to all believers as the elect of God— elect being a term used of national Israel (or rather of the faithful remnant of Israel)—in the Old Testament. Old Testament saints are referred to, in Acts 7:38, as *the church* in the wilderness.

It is interesting to note that leading dispensationalists, including Darby and Scofield, taught that Israel was indeed a type of the church. Darby states, on pages 14 and 15 of *The Hopes of the Church of God,* that Israel was *a perfect type* of the church. He goes on to say, however, that this was one — the only one — type in the Bible that was never meant to have an antitype, or fulfillment. Is this reasonable? Can there be a perfect type without an antitype?

Was the church prophesied in the Old Testament? It certainly was. "Your father Abraham rejoiced to see my day; and he saw it,

and was glad" (John 8:56). Just what was Jesus' *day,* for which
Abraham looked? Was it the day of an earthly materialistic millen-
nium lasting one thousand years? Was it a day of animal sacrifices?
A day of salvation by works? No, the day foreseen by Abraham
began at the first advent, at which time Christ manifested his church.
And this church was made up of Jew and Gentile alike, thus proving
Abraham to be the father of all the righteous.

Nor was Abraham the only Old Testament saint who foretold
the church age: "*Moses* indeed said, A prophet shall the Lord God
raise up unto you from among your brethren, like unto me. . .
Yea, and all the prophets from Samuel and them that followed after,
*as many as have spoken,* they also told of these days" (Acts 3:22-24).

Wherever the church was predicted in the Old Testament it was
naturally depicted in the language of the age during which the
prophets lived. It was described in terms of animal sacrifice, altars,
temples, priests, Jerusalem, and so forth. Otherwise, the people of
that day would have been nonplused. To have described it in the
language of New Testament days would have been tantamount to
describing a modern jet plane to the people who lived in the days of
the Wright brothers at Kitty Hawk. Or tantamount to describing the
skyscrapers of New York to people who had never seen anything
other than a tent city. God inspired his Old Testament prophets to
foretell the church age in language familiar to the people of that day.
When these prophecies were fulfilled it was in the language of the
New Testament.

A law of mathematics states that things equal to the same thing
are equal to each other. With this thought in mind, it is interesting
to note that the New Testament refers to the church (made up of
Jews and Gentiles) in language reserved in the Old Testament for
national Israel. This means that the believing remnant of national
Israel and the true Christian church are synonymous terms.

Let us look at some scriptural proofs that the church superseded Israel, as is evidenced by the fact that terms descriptive of
national Israel (the believing remnant thereof) are used in addressing the church. "But ye are an elect race, a royal priesthood, a
holy nation, a people for God's own possession. . ." (I Peter 2:9).

Whether Peter addressed Jews or Gentiles is immaterial at this
point. The important point here is that he addressed *Christians.*
And the apostle said to these Christians, in the first century: *Ye*

are all of these things that go to make up Israel (the true Israel; the Israel of God); *ye* are a chosen people, a royal priesthood, a holy nation, a peculiar people. These words uttered by Peter were taken almost verbatim from the Old Testament—only there they were addressed to national Israel: "Now therefore, if ye will obey my voice, indeed, and keep my covenant, then ye shall be a peculiar treasure unto me above all people: for all the earth is mine: and ye shall be unto me a kingdom of priests, and an holy nation. These are the words which thou shalt speak unto the children of Israel" (Exodus 19:5,6). Compare also Hebrews 2:12 and Psalm 22:22.

### Christ the Hope of Israel

"There is no other name under heaven given among men whereby we must be saved, except through the name of Christ." These words apply to every person living, in any generation. They apply to Jew as well as to Gentile. And coupled with this verse is an equally important one, which also applies equally to Jew and Gentile: "Today is the day of salvation. . . ." Christ was, and is, the only hope of the Jew; and their salvation will be realized only if they accept him during this age of salvation. There will be no second appearance to them once the last trump has sounded. Once Christ begins his descent to the earth the unsaved Jews and the unsaved Gentiles will cry for the rocks to fall on them; they will seek death and be unable to find it.

Dispensational premillenarians do not agree with this historic Christian teaching. They teach that the Jews, as a nation, will be given a second chance and will be saved after the last trump sounds. They teach that Jews who have rejected Christ to the very end will have a special appearance by Jesus and that these living Jews — who will have rejected his offer during this day of salvation — will then be saved en masse. They also teach that during an earthly materialistic millennium, following the second coming, people will continue to be born and that these people will be saved through legal obedience during this alleged millennium.

John Nelson Darby, founder of modern dispensational premillennialism, taught that Jesus' earthly ministry finished Israel's *redemption*, but not her *inheritance* (*The Hopes of the Church of*

*God*, p. 15). Here, Darby was trying to carry water on both shoulders; he did not want to be accused of belittling the cross; yet he wanted to teach his pet theory that Israel's hopes have not been realized. Dispensationalists teach that Israel's real hope, her real *inheritance*, is a thousand year earthly millennium. They say this was offered, rejected, and postponed at the first advent. This alleged millennium will reinstitute — this time without imperfections — the kingdom of David, and Christ will rule with a rod of iron from Jerusalem, seated on the earthly throne of David.

This teaching flies in the face of plain scriptural teachings that *first* comes the natural and that the natural is followed by the spiritual (I Cor. 15:46). Premillenarians teach the following sequence: (1) natural kingdom (inheritance), (2) spiritual kingdom (inheritance), (3) natural kingdom (inheritance).

Abraham was the father of national Israel, and Abraham was saved through faith in Christ (read Romans 4). Paul labors to prove that Abraham's conversion came by hearing the same gospel that Paul preached to Gentiles. Would it not be passing strange indeed if Abraham's descendants should be saved through legal obedience? "Even as Abraham believed God, and it was reckoned unto him for righteousness. Know therefore that they that are of faith, the same are sons of Abraham. And the scripture, foreseeing that God would justify the Gentiles by faith, preached the gospel beforehand unto Abraham, saying, In thee shall all the nations be blessed. So then they that are of faith are blessed with the faithful Abraham" (Gal. 3:6-9). "For what saith the scripture? And Abraham believed God, and it was reckoned unto him for righteousness. . . Even as David also pronounceth blessing upon the man, unto whom God reckoneth righteousness apart from works, saying, Blessed are they whose iniquities are forgiven, and whose sins are covered. . ." (Rom. 4:3-7).

Let us return now to Darby's statement that Christ's first advent did not complete Israel's inheritance. Just what was to be her inheritance? Abraham was promised an inheritance for Israel. The New Testament informs us, however, that this inheritance was not the land of Palestine. Palestine was a mere shadow, a type, of Israel's real inheritance. "By faith Abraham, when he was called, obeyed to go out unto a place which he was to receive for an inheritance; . . . These all died in faith, *not having received the promises,*

*but having seen them and greeted them from afar*, and having con-
fessed that they were strangers and pilgrims on the earth. For they
that say such things make it manifest that they are seeking after a
country of their own. And if indeed they had been mindful of that
country from which they went out, they would have had opportunity
to return. But now they desire a better country, that is, a heavenly:
wherefore God is not ashamed of them to be called their God; for
he hath prepared for them a city . . . and these all, having had witness
borne to them through their faith, received not the promise, God
having provided some better thing concerning us, *that apart from us
they should not be made perfect*" (Heb. 11:8,13-16,39,40).

The New Testament reveals that there is no blessing to come
to any of the natural seed of Abraham as such but only through the
Seed, which is Christ. Paul clearly teaches that natural descent
alone does not guarantee salvation. "But it is not as though the word
of God hath come to nought. For they are not all Israel, that are
of Israel: neither, because they are Abraham's seed, are they all
children, but: In Isaac shall thy seed be called. That is, it is not
the children of the flesh that are children of God; but the children of
the promise are reckoned for a seed" (Rom. 9:6-8). "Now to Abraham were the promises spoken, and to his seed. He saith not, And to
seeds, as of many; but as of one, And to thy seed, which is Christ"
(Gal. 3:16). When John preached to the Pharisees (Matt. 3) he
cautioned them not to fall back on their Abrahamic ancestry. John
said that God could raise up from the stones descendants as worthy
as they! I wonder if John was not comparing those stones to the
stony hearts of the self-righteous Jewish leaders who rejected Christ.

What is Israel's inheritance? Peter mentions it: "Unto an inheritance incorruptible, and undefiled, and that fadeth not away, reserved in heaven for you" (I Peter 1:4). And who makes possible
this inheritance? Peter gave the answer in the verse preceding this
one. "Blessed be the God and Father of our Lord Jesus Christ, who
according to his great mercy begat us again unto a living hope by
the resurrection of Jesus Christ from the dead" (vs. 3). Contrary to
what dispensationalists say, it was the resurrection of our Lord — and
not his second coming to establish an earthly millennium — which
ushered in Israel's inheritance.

Paul taught (Rom. 10:4) that Christ is the end of the law
unto all who believe. That is to say that Jesus is that to which the

law pointed. The law was a schoolmaster to bring men to Christ. To accept Christ is to come out from under the curse of the law's penalty still over them. For the Israelite to reject Christ is to reject the very end, or fulfillment, of the law.

Luke had no mistaken notions about when Israel's hope would come. He spoke in the past tense, stating that God had already fulfilled his promises to send Israel's Hope: "He hath given help to Israel his servant, that he might remember mercy (As he spake unto our fathers) Toward Abraham and his seed for ever" (Luke 1:54, 55). "Blessed be the Lord, the God of Israel; For he hath visited and wrought redemption for his people, and hath raised up a horn of salvation for us in the house of his servant David (as he spake by the mouth of his holy prophets that have been from of old), Salvation from our enemies, and from the hand of all that hate us; To show mercy towards our fathers, And to remember his holy covenant; The oath which he sware unto Abraham our father, To grant unto us that we being delivered out of the hand of our enemies should serve him without fear" (Luke 1:68-74).

Israel's Hope has come. He has purchased her redemption *and* her inheritance. Israel's only hope was, and is, Jesus Christ who came and inherited the throne of David, and whose reign over Israel (the Israel of God) shall never end.

We may conclude that the first advent of Christ completed Israel's redemption — "As many as received him to them gave he power to become the sons of God" — and manifested the Israel of God, which is the church. At the cross Israel came to include all believers (Jew and Gentile). A new covenant replaced the old one (Heb. 7:18,22; 8:6,13; 10:9,10). Through his death on the cross Christ tore down the middle wall of partition standing between national Israel and the Gentiles. "Wherefore remember, that once ye, the Gentiles in the flesh, who are called Uncircumcision by that which is called Circumcision, in the flesh, made by hands; that ye were at that time separate from Christ, alienated from the commonwealth of Israel, and strangers from the covenants of the promise, having no hope and without God in the world. But now in Christ Jesus ye that once were far off are made nigh in the blood of Christ. *For he is our peace, who made both one*, and brake down the middle wall of partition, having abolished in his flesh the enmity, even the law of commandments contained in ordinances; *that he might create in himself of the two one new man,* so making peace; and might *reconcile them both in one body* unto God through the cross, having slain the enmity thereby" (Eph. 2:11-16).

Could scriptures be plainer than those just quoted? Is there need for further scriptural proof that all believers are now included in the spiritual Israel of God? And that this Israel of God has superseded national Israel which was a type of the church? "For ye are all sons of God through faith in Jesus Christ. For as many of you as were baptized into Christ did put on Christ. There can be neither Jew nor Greek, there can be no male and female; *for ye all are one man in Christ Jesus.* And if ye be Christ's, then are ye Abraham's seed, heirs according to promise" (Gal. 3:26-29).

Section I, "The Church," of the Westminster Confession, sums up the historic Christian teaching with reference to the constituents of the Christian church: "The catholic or universal Church, which is invisible, consists of the whole number of the elect that have been, are, or shall be, gathered into one, under Christ the head thereof; and is the spouse, the body, the fulness of Him that filleth all in all." The Confession gives the following scriptures as proof of this point: Ephesians 1:10,22,23; 5:23,27,32; Colossians 1:18.

The Confession is not speaking here of the Roman Catholic Church, but rather of the aggregate of all whom God has predestined to eternal life — of both the Old and New Testaments; of Jew and Gentile.

In their efforts to keep Israel separate from the church, dispensationalists teach that Christ instituted what they call "a Gentile church." This is a very erroneous, very unscriptural teaching. Indeed, Jesus manifested a Jewish-Gentile church. (I like this word "manifested" better than the word "instituted," since the church actually was a continuation of the faithful remnant of national Israel, rather than being a new institution.) And so far as numbers are concerned, it was more Jewish than Gentile at the beginning. Jewish leaders today estimate that there were over one million converts to Christianity during the first century A.D. We need to keep in mind that the apostles were Jews; every New Testament writer was a Jew — with the possible exception of Luke, and some scholars believe that even he was a Hellenistic Jew. Those in the Upper Room were Jews, as were all those converted on the Day of Pentecost.

In fact, there were no Gentile members until Peter preached to the house of Cornelius.

This is a far cry from a *Gentile* church. Jesus took the remnant, which is the only part of Israel that has ever belonged to the spiritual family of God (Rom. 2:28,29; 3:3,4; 9:6-8,27,29; 11:15), and added Gentile believers to this same olive tree. This constituted the Christian church. The Twelve were Jews; the Seventy were Jews; and the first deacons were Hellenistic Jews. The early chapters of the Acts are a history of a *Jewish* church, into which Gentiles had not yet entered.

The reader will recall the historic Christian teaching that all unfulfilled promises to Israel will be fulfilled in the church. All earthly promises to Israel have been either literally fulfilled or invalidated through unbelief. The Jewish state came to an end in A.D. 70. Since Christ tore down the middle wall of partition all unfulfilled spiritual promises are being bestowed upon *all* believers. "For through him we both have our access in one Spirit unto the Father. So then ye |Gentiles| are no more strangers and sojourners, but ye are fellow-citizens with the saints, and of the household of God, being built upon the foundation of the apostles and prophets, Christ Jesus himself being the chief corner stone" (Eph. 2:18-20). ". . . the Gentiles are fellow-heirs, and fellow members of the body, and fellow-partakers of the promise in Christ Jesus through the gospel" (Eph. 3:6). Compare also Galatians 3:6-9,28,29.

None of the points we have made concerning Israel and the church constitute a change in God's plans. It was decreed before the foundation of the earth that Israel would undergo changes; that she would come under a new covenant; and that her borders would be enlarged to include Gentiles. Not change of plan, but progressive revelation, is reflected in the church as the Israel of God (Gal. 6:16). "Having therefore obtained the help that is from God, I stand unto this day testifying both to small and great, *saying nothing but what the prophets and Moses did say should come*; how that the Christ must suffer, and how that he first by the resurrection of the dead *should proclaim light both to the people |Israel| and to the Gentiles*" (Acts 26:22,23). "Christ redeemed us from the curse of the law . . . that upon the Gentiles might come the blessings of Abraham in Christ Jesus. . ." (Gal. 3:13,14). Compare also Romans 4:17; 10:10-13.

# VI

## THE MEANING OF EVERLASTING

Many students of the Bible refuse to believe the church super-seded Israel because of their fear of denying the *literal* promises, many of which read "forever," or "eternal," or "everlasting." At first blush this truly is a problem. Yet these same persons seem per-fectly reconciled to the fact that physical circumcision (which also was given as an everlasting ritual, according to Genesis 17:13) has been succeeded by a "circumcision of the heart" (Col. 2:11). Nor are they troubled by the fact that the law, which was given through Moses as an *everlasting* covenant, has been replaced by the "law of Christ," according to the New Testament. "For ye are not under law, but under grace" (Rom. 6:14). "Wherefore, my brethren, ye also were made dead to the law through the body of Christ. . ." (Rom. 7:4). The sabbath (Saturday) also was given as an *everlasting* observance; and yet, would any person deny that after the resurrec-tion the apostles instituted Sunday as the day of worship?

If physical circumcision can be replaced by spiritual circum-cision by Christ, and if the sabbath can be changed by the resur-rection of Christ, and if the law can be superseded by a greater law of Christ (all this without denying that the old ones were *eternal* promises), then why can we not permit Christ to work out the plan of God for his people, which now is the church, "the *fulness* of him that filleth all in all"? (Eph. 1:22,23).

If the physical body of Christ can replace the law, according to Romans 6:14 (the law which was *eternal*), then why cannot the spiritual body of Christ (the church) replace Israel without being contradictory? In other words, why cannot God reveal his real meaning to this mystery which says that Israel, which had a physical beginning, was destined all along to have a spiritual culmination, and include Gentiles?

"And that he might make known the riches of his glory upon vessels of mercy, *which he afore prepared unto glory,* even us, whom he also called, *not from the Jews only, but also from the Gentiles?*

As he saith also in Hosea, I will call that my people, which was not my people; and her beloved, that was not beloved" (Rom. 9: 23-25).

"Whereby, when ye read, ye can perceive my understanding in the mystery of Christ; which in other generations was not made known unto the sons of men, as it hath now been revealed unto his holy apostles and prophets in the Spirit; to wit, *that the Gentiles are fellow-heirs, and fellow-members of the body, and fellow-partakers of the promise in Christ Jesus through the gospel"* (Eph. 3:4-6).

"Everlasting" or "eternal" as used in the Scriptures must be interpreted according to the radius of time included in a particular promise. In other words, like all other scriptures, these words must be interpreted according to their context. A promise was "eternal" or "everlasting" for the duration of time God decreed to use a given method of dealing with his people.

Certainly no one would deny that God's methods have changed with different generations. For example, the same rules are not mandatory today that were used by God under the law of Moses; nor were the same rules applied in all cases during, for example, the age of the prophets as compared with the period of the judges. Our point is that if God gave an *everlasting* promise to his people who at the time were governed by the law, and if Christ was the *end* of the law (Rom. 10:4), then that promise was everlasting only until that period was finished. With the coming of Christ into the world, the period covered by the promise came to an end, and, therefore, the promise was no longer binding upon God.

In II Chronicles 7:16 it is recorded that God promised to live in Solomon's house forever; yet that house was destroyed and does not exist today. Did God break his promise? No. "Forever" meant for as long as the house stood.

The same is true with reference to the priesthood as instituted during the Old Testament era. In many passages — of which Exodus 40:15 and Numbers 25:13 are examples — we are told that the house of Aaron constituted an *everlasting* priesthood. All Protestant Christians are agreed that the old priesthood came to an end and was replaced by Jesus, who became our High Priest. The book of Hebrews makes this fact clear. So the priesthood of law was everlasting *only as long as the law was in effect.*

In dealing with Genesis 13:15, which reads, "For all the land which thou seest, to thee will I give it, and to thy seed *for ever*," *Clarke's Commentary* has this comment: ". . . and this was always the design of God, not that Abram himself should possess it, but that his posterity would, till the manifestation of Christ in the flesh. And this is chiefly what is to be understood by the words for ever, *ad olam*, to the end of the present dispensation, and the commencement of the new. Olam means either eternity, which implies the termination of all time or duration, such as is measured by the celestial lumination; or a hidden, unknown, period, such as includes a completion or final termination, of a particular era, dispensation, etc.; therefore the first is its *proper* meaning, the latter its accommodated meaning" (Vol. I, p. 99).

In dealing with Genesis 17:8, which reads: "And I will give unto thee, and to thy seed after thee, the land of thy sojournings, all the land of Canaan, for an *everlasting* possession; and I will be their God," Clarke has this comment: "Here olam appears to be used in its *accommodated meaning*, and signifies the completion of the Divine counsel in reference to a particular period or dispensation. And it is literally true that the Israelites possessed the land of Canaan till the Mosaic dispensation was terminated in the complete introduction of that gospel. . ." (*Clarke's Commentary*, Vol. I, p. 114).

According to Clarke, and other scholars, these words have a *proper* meaning and an *accommodated* meaning. Using this as a guide to understanding the promises of the Bible and their meaning, one could say:

## 1. Everlasting Circumcision

a) Circumcision had an *accommodated* eternalness, which was in force until Christ instituted, by his death, the "circumcision of the heart." The literalist would have a difficult time proving that physical circumcision (as a rite) did not come to an end with the birth of the church at Pentecost. And yet, according to the type of reasoning the literalist uses with reference to the promises concerning Israel, *how could* physical circumcision have come to an end, seeing as how it was given as an *everlasting* covenant?

"And the uncircumcised male who is not circumcised in the flesh of his foreskin, that soul shall be cut off from his people; he hath broken my covenant" (Gen. 17:14).

b) Circumcision also has a *literal* eternalness, which includes all believers in God's covenant, Old Testament believers as well as believers of the New Testament dispensation. These are the circumcised in heart (Deut. 30:6; Col. 2:11; Rom. 2:28,29; Phil. 3:3). This spiritual circumcision shall never end.

2. Everlasting Law

a) Law had an *accommodated* eternalness, which was in force until the death of Christ instituted the "law of Christ," and brought to an end (for all believers) the old law (Rom. 10:4). Let us be reminded again that this law of which Jesus became the end was instituted as an *eternal* or *everlasting* law. Will any hyperliteralist deny that Jesus did replace this law in the hearts of his followers after Calvary? Paul said to the Christians at Rome (a mixed congregation, which, all scholars agree, included Jews), ". . . *for ye are not under law, but under grace*" (Rom. 6:14).

b) Law also has a *literal* eternalness in that God's commands, both those of the Old Testament and of the New, are ever binding upon the circumcised in heart.

3. Everlasting Israel

a) Israel, as the people of God, had an *accommodated* eternalness, which bound the believing remnant of Israel to God until the death of Christ tore down the middle wall of partition and caused Israel to include believing Gentiles (Eph. 2:14-16).

"But now in Christ Jesus ye that once were far off are made nigh in the blood of Christ. For he is our peace, who made both one, *and brake down the middle wall of partition*, having abolished in his flesh the enmity, even the law of commandments contained in ordinances; *that he might create in himself of the two one new man, so making peace; and might reconcile them both in one body unto God through the cross,* having slain the enmity thereby" (Eph. 2:13-16).

b) Israel also has a *literal* eternalness, which includes *all the Israel of God,* of both the Old and New Testament, both Jew and Gentile (Gal. 6:16). This spiritual Israel will reign forever.

If this type of exegesis be branded by the hyperliteralist as "spiritualizing" then suffice it to say that Jesus as well as the New Testament writers did the same type of "spiritualizing," and "the servant is not greater than his master." Compare Malachi 4:5 as interpreted by Jesus in Matthew 17:12,13. Also turn to Acts 15:16 and see the interpretation placed upon Amos 9:11. Is this not "spiritualizing"?

*Hyperbole*

Perhaps we should begin this section by defining the word we are about to use. *Webster's New International Dictionary* defines "hyperbole" as "a statement exaggerated fancifully through excitement, or *for effect."*

Futurists argue that the promises to Israel have not been literally fulfilled because of the word "all," as in "all the land," etc. This is wrong for at least two reasons. First of all, it denies the plain teachings of Scripture — "So Joshua took *the whole land,* according to *all* that Jehovah spake unto Moses; and Joshua gave it for an inheritance unto Israel according to their divisions by their tribes . . ." (Josh. 11:23). Compare also Joshua 1:6; 21:43; Deuteronomy 1:8; 6:23.

Secondly, this argument is wrong because it refuses to recognize hyperbole, which is used throughout the Bible. We feel that exaggerated statements (hyperboles) are used by the Holy Spirit, not in order to make untrue statements, but rather to gain effect, as Webster defines the word for us. To attempt to hold a hyperliteral interpretation in every incidence where the word "all" is used in the Bible is to court hermeneutical disaster.

Space will permit only a few examples of the use of the word "all" as hyperbole.

"And the Midianites and the Amalekites and *all the children of the east lay along in the valley like locusts for multitude; and their camels were without number*, as the sand which is upon the sea-shore for multitude" (Judges 7:12). To be without number is an utter impossibility. Therefore, the Spirit inspired this writer to use hyperbole in order to emphasize the fact that there were many, many camels.

"Saul and Jonathan . . . they were swifter than eagles, they were stronger than lions" (II Sam. 1:23).

"And there are also many other things which Jesus did, the which if they should be written every one, *I suppose that even the world itself would not contain the books that should be written*" (John 21:25).

Did John literally mean that all the world could not hold the books which would be filled if all the deeds of Jesus were recorded? Or was John simply using the freedom of hyperbole for effect? Let each reader judge for himself as he reads the above verse.

Milton S. Terry has this to say concerning the use of hyperbole in the Bible: "Hyperbole is a rhetorical figure which consists in exaggeration, or magnifying an object beyond reality. . . . Such exaggerated expressions, when not overdone, or occurring too frequently, strike the attention and make an agreeable impression on the mind" (*Biblical Hermeneutics*, Vol. II, p. 165).

Bible students are agreed that Luke 2:1 refers only to the Roman Empire. Yet the statement says "all the world." We also read in the New Testament that the Gospel had been preached in "all the world" (Col. 1:6,23; see also II Tim. 4:17). Is this not hyperbole, meaning that the gospel had been preached far and wide?

All men must guard against giving words one meaning when it suits their purpose and another meaning when otherwise it would go contrary to their school of thought. For example, the futurists — if they held consistently to a literal use of the word "all" — would have to accept passages such as Joshua 11:23, which says that God gave Israel "all the land" promised to their fathers. Another passage ignored by them is Luke 18:31, where Jesus said that he was going up to Jerusalem and that at that time "*all things that are written by the prophets concerning the son of man shall be accomplished*" (KJV; italics added). When they are confronted with clear passages such as these, however, they find it necessary to "interpret" — the very thing they castigate other Christians for doing.

As one studies scriptures like those above one soon sees that the meaning of a word must be judged according to its context. The word "all" is certainly used many places where it is to be taken as meaning every iota, as when Paul says that *all have sinned* (Rom. 3:23). It must also be realized, however, that this word is used often as hyperbole.

# VII

## TRIBULATION

Preceding the second coming of Christ there is to be a time of severe tribulation for the church. This tribulation has, in fact, already begun. It began with the first coming and will be terminated by the second advent of Christ.

This is not to be confused with the great tribulation predicted by our Lord in Matthew 24:21, which is also called "the time of Jacob's trouble," or "the abomination of desolation." These prophecies concerned national Israel and were fulfilled in A.D. 70, when Titus overran Jerusalem and abominated the temple by riding horses up the steps and placing a Roman emblem in the holy of holies. Jesus referred to this as the greatest tribulation ever known or ever to be. Bible scholars generally agree that our Lord meant this was to be the greatest tribulation ever to come upon Israel *as a nation.* Since the Jewish state came to its prophesied end in A.D. 70, an even greater tribulation could come to pass — involving, not Israel, but the church — and still not be contradictory to the words of our Lord.

It should be recalled that the great tribulation of A.D. 70 was visited specifically upon national Israel, upon the Jewish state. We have already given excerpts from eyewitness historians concerning the severity of God's wrath at that time. However, that was strictly a punishment for non-believing national Israel. The true church, both Jew and Gentile, escaped that calamity by doing what the Lord had instructed them to do.

"Mark 13:14: The ecclesiastical historian, Eusebius, early in the fourth century, tells us that the Christians fled to Pella, at the northern extremity of Persia, being 'prophetically directed. . .' " (Jamieson, Fausset, Brown, *Commentary Critical and Explanatory on the Whole Bible*, p. 87).

While approximately one and one-half million non-believing Jews were killed by the armies of Titus during the Jewish Wars, all believers fled to Pella, fifty miles away, and escaped harm.

The great difference between the sufferings of national Israel and those of the church (the new Israel) is not so much a difference in degree, but rather a difference in the very nature of the suffering. Israel's was physical; the church's is primarily spiritual. Paul said, in speaking to the church, "For our wrestling is not against flesh and blood, but against the principalities. . ." (Eph. 6:12).

Some students of the Bible believe that the great tribulation spoken of by our Lord in Matthew 24:21 began in A.D. 70 under Titus, but that it actually continues until the end of history. This belief is based upon the statement of our Lord that "*immediately* after the tribulation of those days," his second coming would take place (Matt. 24:29,30). Certainly there is merit in this thought, since the second coming has not taken place, and since it would be difficult to construe "immediately" as meaning two or three thousand years after the event. That our Lord spoke primarily of the destruction of Jerusalem is obvious. A study of parallel passages leaves no room for doubt on this fact. "When therefore ye see the abomination of desolation, which was spoken of through Daniel the prophet, standing in the holy place . . . then let them that are in Judaea flee unto the mountains. . ." (Matt. 24:15-31). "But when ye see Jerusalem compassed with armies, then know that her desolation is at hand. Then let them that are in Judaea flee unto the mountains. . ." (Luke 21:20-27).

Many prophecies have a dual meaning, which is to say that there is a primary fulfillment in the historical setting in which the prophecy is made, then a secondary fulfillment which usually has more of a spiritual (though deeper) fulfillment. Perhaps the prophecy of Matthew 24 comes under this category.

We know that the great tribulation of A.D. 70 brought the Jewish state to its complete and final end. We know too that the kingdom was taken from the Jews and given to the church (Matt. 21:43). So then here was a transition period in the history of God's people; one group — having forfeited their covenant relationship with God — were having the accumulation of God's wrath visited upon them. The other group were taking up the mantle which by its very nature carried with it suffering and tribulation.

That the new-covenant Israel was to be bathed in persecution (tribulation) there can be no doubt as one reads the Bible. The prophets of old foresaw and predicted a golden age during which

God would reign in the hearts of his people. This golden age is the present kingdom wherein God's laws are written on the hearts of his people (compare Jer. 31:31-34). Paradoxically, this golden age was to be also a time of God's judgment. His new people were to be pilgrims in the present world, but citizens of a distant land (heaven). This golden age was to be a time of the refiner's fire, during which the true metal of every believer was tempered and made ready for that new country.

John the Baptist was a pivotal figure in biblical history. He came announcing both the golden age and the visitation of judgment on the world. "And in those days cometh John the Baptist, preaching in the wilderness of Judaea, saying, Repent ye; for the kingdom of heaven is at hand" (Matt. 3:1,2). "Bring forth therefore fruit worthy of repentance" (Matt. 3:8). "And even now the axe lieth at the root of the tree: every tree therefore that bringeth not forth good fruit is hewn down, and cast into the fire" (Matt. 3:10). "whose fan is in his hand, and he |Jesus| will thoroughly cleanse his threshing-floor; and he will gather his wheat into the garner, but the chaff he will burn up with unquenchable fire" (Matt. 3:12).

Not only was tribulation foretold in the New Testament, it was also looked upon as the badge of a genuine believer. Paul recounted his own hardships, then warned that ". . . all that would live godly in Christ Jesus shall suffer persecution" (II Tim. 3:12). That persecution is the lot of every Christian is evident from such passages as Revelation 7, where John describes every believer in heaven as one who came out of (through) great tribulation. Other scriptures teach this same lesson; the following are but a small sampling of them.

"A disciple is not above his teacher, nor a servant above his lord. It is enough for the disciple that he be as his teacher, and the servant as his lord. If they have called the master of the house Beelzebub, how much more them of his household!" (Matt. 10:24,25).

"So that we ourselves glory in you in the churches of God for your patience and faith in all your persecutions and in the afflictions which ye endure; which is a manifest token of the righteous judgment of God; to the end that ye may be counted worthy of the kingdom of God, for which ye also suffer" (II Thess. 1:4,5).

"I John, your brother and partaker with you in the tribulation and kingdom and patience which are in Jesus. . ." (Rev. 1:9).

"The kingdom of heaven is likened unto a certain king . . . and the rest laid hold on his servants and treated them shamefully and killed them" (Matt. 22:2-6).

"Beloved, think it not strange concerning the fiery trial among you, which cometh upon you to prove you, as though a strange thing happened unto you: but insomuch as ye are partakers of Christ's sufferings, rejoice; that at the revelation of his glory also ye may rejoice with exceeding joy. If ye are reproached for the name of Christ, blessed are ye; because the Spirit of glory and the Spirit of God resteth upon you. For let none of you suffer as a murderer, or a thief, or an evil-doer, or as a meddler in other men's matters: but if a man suffer as a Christian, let him not be ashamed; but let him glorify God in this name. For the time is come for judgment to begin at the house of God: and if it begin first at us, what shall be the end of them that obey not the gospel of God? And if the righteous is scarcely saved, where shall the ungodly and sinner appear? Wherefore let them also that suffer according to the will of God commit their souls in well-doing unto a faithful Creator" (I Peter 4:12-19).

"If the world hateth you, ye know that it hath hated me before it hated you. If ye were of the world, the world would love its own: but because ye are not of the world, but I chose you out of the world, therefore the world hateth you. Remember the word that I said unto you, a servant is not greater than his lord. If they persecuted me, they will also persecute you; if they kept my word, they will keep yours also" (John 15:18-20).

"These things have I spoken unto you, that in me ye may have peace. In the world ye have tribulation: but be of good cheer; I have overcome the world" (John 16:33).

The following quotations also speak to this subject. "It is taken for granted throughout the New Testament that affliction is the normal lot of Christians; it is, in fact, an evidence of the genuineness of their faith and an earnest of their part in the coming glory. Cf. Acts XIV. 22; Rom. VIII. 17f.; 2 Tim. II. 12. It is noteworthy that the inevitability of tribulation had formed part of the apostle's instruction to the Thessalonian Christians as to others. What had been an acute problem to faith in Old Testament times—the suffering of the righteous—had come to be recognized as an essential element in God's purpose for His people. Since their Lord Himself had suffered, they need expect nothing else; let them rather glory in tribulation (cf.

John XV. 20, XVI. 33; Rom. V. 3)" (Davidson, Stibbs and Kevan, *The New Bible Commentary*, p. 1055).

"In the present life they not only share the common trials, afflictions, and sufferings of life, but in addition to that they also become partakers of the sufferings of Christ. They are involved in the world's hatred of Christ. The Saviour's prophetic utterance, 'they have hated me, they will also hate you,' is a prediction that is fulfilled in every age. David spoke the language of experience when he said, 'Many are the afflictions of the righteous' (Ps. 34:19); and Paul reminded his converts of the fact that 'through many tribulations we must enter into the kingdom of God' (Acts 14:22). The eleventh chapter of the Epistle to the Hebrews also bears eloquent testimony to that fact. According to Romans 8:17 it is even one of the conditions on which the future inheritance of believers depends. Paul reminds his spiritual son Timothy of the many persecutions which he suffered and then says in II Timothy 3:12, 'Yea, and all that would live godly in Christ Jesus shall suffer persecutions' " (L. Berkhof, *The Second Coming of Christ*, p. 97).

Jesus, our Lord, suffered from the moment he began his ministry. In fact, even as a child he was so threatened that it became necessary for his parents to flee with him to Egypt. Our Lord taught his disciples that all who follow him should be prepared to accept the ridicule and persecution of the world. Indeed, the first requirement for a genuine Christian is that he shoulder a cross. The cross is the emblem of Christianity and symbolizes a struggle to the death between the forces of good and the forces of evil.

John, in the twelfth chapter of the Revelation, recounts, in apocalyptic language, the birth and earthly ministry of our Lord. He states that Satan — having failed to exterminate the Christ — began to persecute the followers of Christ (Rev. 12:17). That persecution continues and waxes worse.

A glance at history reveals that at least three outstanding periods of persecution have come upon the church. The first of these was the bitter persecution of Christians by non-believing Jews of the first century. Jews were primarily responsible for the crucifixion of Christ; Jews were Paul's worst enemies; John the Revelator spoke of a group of Jews as "a synagogue of Satan" (Rev. 2:9). The second wave of persecution against the church was carried on by the

Roman Empire. The third onslaught — and this one still continues — is that by the papacy of Rome.

These three persecutions — like all others — have been headed up by men, acting on orders from Satan. However, there is to be a final battle, and this will be led by the antichrist himself. This time of increased persecution or tribulation may well be what John called the Battle of Armageddon. He refers to it again in Revelation 20, referring to the evil forces as Gog and Magog. Paul deals with this same battle in II Thessalonians 2. Our next chapter deals more fully with the antichrist.

Tribulation is a natural by-product of genuine Christianity. This was prophesied in the Old Testament, announced by the forerunner of Christ, attested to by the Lord himself, taught by his disciples, and has been experienced by every true follower of Christ.

The *fact* of tribulation is self-evident; its *nature* is primarily spiritual; its *purpose* is to refine; and its end will be the appearing the second time unto salvation by the Lord Jesus Christ.

The tribulation of the church began with the first advent of our Lord as he entered the arena to fight Satan in his own territory (Matt. 12:29). Our Lord's persecution was climaxed at Calvary. There he defeated Satan in fulfillment of Genesis 3:15.

The church has already witnessed many persecutions. However, these persecutions will grow progressively worse until finally they culminate in the appearance of the antichrist himself.

Individual believers are to accept persecution as a seal of their genuine conversion experience. This does not mean that we are to have a martyr complex. Rather it should be looked upon as a joy to share in the sufferings of Christ and his cause. Paul left a Christian philosophy for every Christian to emulate. For he reckoned that the sufferings of this life are not even to be compared with the joy which awaits the Christian. Paul rejoiced in the fact that suffering was but for a little season, and that the church militant was destined to become the church triumphant.

# VIII

## THE ANTICHRIST

God's people have always been a persecuted group. This could be said concerning Israel of the old covenant and it is especially true of the Israel of God under the new covenant. In fact, history reveals that the church has grown more under persecution than when things were at ease in Zion. Tribulation seems to play a major role in the permissive will of God. This persecution is to grow increasingly worse until antichrist himself assumes personal leadership.

Antichrist might be defined as a demonic-human adversary of Christ who will appear before the second advent as the last oppressor and persecutor of Christians. Preceding antichrist there have been legions of demons (lesser antichrists). John pointed up the fact that many antichrists already were in the world at the time of his writing (I John 2:18).

The Old Testament records some outstanding prototypes of the antichrist. In Ezekiel 38 and 39 the prophet foresees a great cleansing-persecution by Gog and Magog. Apparently Gog referred to a prince or leader, while Magog was to be his people. The prophet predicts a golden age for his people (chapters 33-37) during which there will be no need for protective walls, etc. This golden age is to be followed by the persecutions of antichrist, who in turn is to be put down by the very power of God (39:6).

Daniel also prophesies a prototype of the antichrist. And, like Ezekiel, Daniel uses language so descriptive of antichrist and of the end of the world that the type does not fully satisfy all that is prophesied. Antiochus Epiphanes (175-164 B.C.) no doubt was a type and fulfilled a part of the prophecy; however, the full reference was to antichrist who is to appear at the end of the golden age of the New Testament.

"The interpretation which may be called traditional Church is to regard these verses as referring to the Antichrist. Antiochus who first persecuted the Church shortly before the first advent of Christ may be regarded as typical of the Antichrist who will persecute the

Church before the second advent of Christ" (Davidson, Stibbs, and Kevan, *The New Bible Commentary*, p. 681).

It is interesting to compare these Old Testament types with the antitype. It is said of all three — Gog, Antiochus, and antichrist — that (1) they will oppose the people of God, and (2) they will be ultimately destroyed by the intervention of the Lord himself (cf. Ezek. 39:6; Dan. 8:25; II Thess. 2:8; Rev. 20:9).

In the New Testament, too, we see types or forerunners of the antichrist. John said that many antichrists were already active in his day. The unbelieving Jews of New Testament times certainly were antichristian. Titus is looked upon as being a type of antichrist, as is the papacy of Rome. All these, however, are mere shadows and fall short of complete fulfillment.

Satan is a great imitator. God has his holy angels, Satan has his angels; God places his mark upon his people (Rev. 7:3), Satan also marks his followers (Rev. 13:16); God rewards obedience with life, Satan also rewards his followers for their obedience to him ("the wages of sin is death"); even in the arrangement of his forces Satan imitates God. For on the one hand we have God, angels, Christians; on the other hand we have Satan, demons, wicked followers.

Satan will be an imitator to the end. Since Christ has predicted his second advent, Satan too must have a counterpart. In II Thessalonians 2 Paul teaches that antichrist will be "revealed" (vss. 6-8), and speaks, in verse 9, of the "coming" of antichrist. As Christ will appear the second time as God incarnate, the antichrist will appear (imitating the second advent) as Satan incarnate. Here we have the real significance of the word "antichrist." According to Greek lexicons "anti" not only means to oppose Christ, it also means "for, instead of" Christ (the anointed One). When antichrist comes he will claim that he is the Messiah and that this is his (Messiah's) second advent. He will oppose Christ while acting *as* Christ.

Ironically, many will believe and follow antichrist. For by that time the stored-up wrath of God will have reached the overflow level and he will allow such a stupor to come over the wicked that they will believe the big lie of Satan (II Thess. 2:11,12). By the time antichrist appears, his followers will have such an allegiance to him that they will follow him regardless of the cost or consequences. They will follow him even into the second death, defying God to the very end (Rev. 16:9-11). These and other scriptures make it appear doubtful that any will be saved once the final antichrist appears. This leads the present writer toward the belief that the Holy Spirit is spoken of in II Thessalonians 2:7 as being the One who now restrains antichrist but who will be "taken out of the way" during the "little time" of antichrist's rule. After all, the paramount work of the Holy Spirit at present is to convict men of sin and to point them to Jesus as Savior. During antichrist's reign the unsaved are to have a spiritual blindness sent upon them (II Thess. 2:11,12). According to this, the saving function of the Holy Spirit will have finished its course. There would therefore be no need for him to remain.

The little season during which the lawless one is loosed would seem to be a time of testing and refining for God's people. It will be a time which separates the mere professors from the genuine believers. Though many will have a form of godliness, one who stands for the true faith will be greatly persecuted.

Lawlessness is portrayed as being perhaps the outstanding characteristic of the "little time" during which antichrist is loosed. An interesting comparison may be made between the description in II Thessalonians 2 and that in Revelation 20. Paul refers to antichrist as "the lawless one" while John says that Satan will be "loosed for a little time" (Rev. 20:3). In both these word pictures one gains the impression of unrestrained disregard for law and authority. Since God is the author of law and order, this looseness or lawlessness is in direct opposition to the known will of God. This is antichrist's ultimate aim, i.e., to exalt himself above God (II Thess. 2:40).

One thought relating to the antichrist is usually overlooked. Scripture nowhere states that he will be recognized for what he is. Rather, he will appear much as did the serpent in Eden — cunning and deceiving. He will appear as a religious leader!

In view of present circumstances, antichrist might well be already on the scene, even though not yet in his final form. The ecumenical movement is made to order for one person (antichrist) to assume the leadership of an apostate super "church." This person could well be the Pope of Rome. Leading ecumenists are bowing more and more in that direction. The last decade has witnessed a Romish flavor of ritualism in many major denominations. Many altar-centered churches were, until recently, Bible-centered. If anti-christ has not been the architect in Protestantism in recent years he could scarcely find a more opportune atmosphere in which to launch his program!

The New Testament teaches that certain things are to precede the second advent. Among these are apostasy, self-love, persecution, and the antichrist. That the first three of these abound today seems self-evident. We have indicated our suspicion that antichrist has already appeared and is leading a spiritual warfare against the king-dom of God.

The Bible teaches that this warfare between Christ and Satan began at the birth of Christ, that it has reached climaxes at certain points in history — examples are the destruction of Jerusalem in A.D. 70, the fall of Rome in A.D. 476, the Inquisitions, and so forth — and that it will end with Satan himself personified as the antichrist. When antichrist has taken personal leadership of all satanic forces, and when it looks as if he will actually overcome the Christian church, then the trumpet will sound and Christ will appear.

That antichrist will be persecuting the church when Christ ap-pears is learned from such scriptures as the following.

". . . it is a righteous thing with God to recompense affliction to them that afflict you, and to you that are afflicted rest with us, at the revelation of the Lord Jesus from heaven with the angels of his power in flaming fire, rendering vengeance on them that know not God. . ." (II Thess. 1:6-8).

". . . touching the coming of our Lord Jesus Christ, and our gathering together unto him . . . it will not be, except the falling away come first, and the man of sin be revealed, the son of perdition, he that opposeth and exalteth himself against all that is called God or that is worshipped; so that he sitteth in the temple of God, setting himself forth as God . . . and then shall be revealed the lawless one whom the Lord Jesus shall slay with the breath of his mouth, and bring to nought by the manifestation of his coming" (II Thess. 2:1-8).

"And when the thousand years are finished, Satan shall be loosed out of his prison, and shall come forth to deceive the nations which are in the four corners of the earth, Gog and Magog, to gather them together to the war: the number of whom is as the sand of the sea. And they went up over the breadth of the earth, and compassed the camp of the saints about, and the beloved city: and fire came down out of heaven, and devoured them. And the devil that deceived them was cast into the lake of fire and brimstone, where are also the beast and the false prophet: and they shall be tormented day and night for ever and ever" (Rev. 20:7-15).

In these passages Paul and John speak of the same event. Both speak of a persecution of the church immediately preceding the second advent, both refer to the persecutor and to his final end. And both refer, poetically, to the second coming of Christ as "fire from heaven."

This great and final battle between God's forces and those of Satan will signal the second coming of Christ to earth, since his coming will put down the antichrist and bring final victory to the church, the Israel of God (II Thess. 2:8). "And at that time shall Michael stand up, the great prince who standeth for the children of thy people; and there shall be a time of trouble, such as never was since there was a nation even to that same time: and at that time thy people shall be delivered, every one that shall be found written in the book. And many of them that sleep in the dust of the earth shall awake, some to everlasting life, and some to shame and everlasting contempt" (Dan. 12:1,2).

". . . for it [the second coming] will not be, except the falling away come first, and the man of sin be revealed, the son of perdition, he that opposeth and exalteth himself against all that is called God or that is worshipped; so that he sitteth in the temple of God, setting himself forth as God. . . . For the mystery of lawlessness doth already work: only there is one that restraineth now, until he be taken out of the way. And then shall be revealed the lawless one, whom the Lord Jesus shall slay with the breath of his mouth, and bring to nought by the manifestation of his coming; even he, whose coming is according to the working of Satan with all power and signs and lying wonders, and with all deceit of unrighteousness for them that perish; because they received not the love of the truth, that they might be saved. And for this cause God sendeth them a working of error, that they should believe a lie: that they all might be judged who believed not the truth, but had pleasure in unrighteousness" (II Thess. 2:1-12).

"And I saw another sign in heaven, great and marvellous, seven angels having seven plagues, which are the last, *for in them is finished the wrath of God*" (Rev. 15:1).

"And men were scorched with great heat: and they blasphemed the name of God who hath the power over these plagues; and they repented not to give him glory. And the fifth angel poured out his bowl upon the throne of the beast; and his kingdom was darkened; and they gnawed their tongues for pain, and they blasphemed the God of heaven because of their pains and their sores; and they repented not of their works. And the sixth poured out his bowl upon the great river, the river Euphrates; and the water thereof was dried up, that the way might be made ready for the kings that come from the sunrising. And I saw coming out of the mouth of the dragon, and out of the mouth of the beast, and out of the mouth of the false prophet, three unclean spirits, as it were frogs: for they are spirits of demons, working signs; which go forth unto the kings of the whole world, to gather them together unto the war of the great day of God, the Almighty. (Behold, I come as a thief. Blessed is he that watcheth, and keepeth his garments, lest he walk naked, and they see his shame.) And they gathered them together into the place which is called in Hebrew Armageddon. And the seventh poured out his bowl upon the air; and there came forth a great voice out of the temple, from the throne, saying, It is done; and there were lightnings, and voices, and thunders: and there was a great earthquake, such as was not since there were men upon the earth, so great an earthquake, so mighty. And the great city was divided into three parts, and the cities of the nations fell: and Babylon the great was remembered in the sight of God, to give unto her the cup of the wine of the fierceness of his wrath. And every island fled away, and the mountains were not found. And great hail, every stone about the weight of a talent, cometh down out of heaven upon men: and men blasphemed God because of the plague of the hail; for the plague thereof is exceeding great" (Rev. 16:9-21).

"And when the thousand years are finished, Satan shall be loosed out of his prison, and shall come forth to deceive the nations which are in the four corners of the earth, Gog and Magog, to gather them together to the war: the number of whom is as the sand of the sea. And they went up over the breadth of the earth, and compassed the camp of the saints about, and the beloved city: and fire came down out of heaven, and devoured them. And the devil that deceived them was cast into the lake of fire and brimstone, where are also the beast and the false prophet; and they shall be tormented day and night for ever and ever" (Rev. 20:7-10).

When these scriptures are collated, they teach the following:

1. The wicked as well as the righteous will suffer tribulation.

2. The wicked will not repent during this time of spiritual warfare.

3. Tribulation was already going on in Paul's day, but Paul predicted a worse time when the antichrist would be released.

4. During the time of tribulation, the wicked, led by antichrist himself, will oppose the righteous.

5. The time of this warfare — this time of increased tribulation — is to be one of the last historical events to take place in this present world.

6. The coming of Christ will put down the antichrist, thereby ending all tribulation for the saints.

7. It is nowhere stated that Christians will recognize antichrist when he appears. This being so, we may well be going through the "little time" already. Current events certainly favor such a conclusion.

John says antichrists are those who deny that Jesus is the Christ. This, according to John, is to deny God the Father. We have said that antichrists of John's day were henchmen or demons of the main antichrist who was yet to come. When he comes he will not be satisfied merely to deny Christ—he will represent himself as being the Christ.

Antichrist imitates just about every act of Christ's. Both had a first advent into the world. Both have angels serving them. Both have missionaries. Each will reward his followers: "For the wages of sin is death; but the free gift of God is eternal life in Christ Jesus our Lord" (Rom. 6:23). And, since the Lord is destined to return a second time to the earth, Satan too is planning a second appearance, in the form of the antichrist. In every case he imitates Christ.

Antichrist's stay on the earth will be short-lived, as God counts time. There is not a shadow of doubt as to which side will win the battle of Armageddon. Although Satan will even appear to overcome the church, and will be at his height of persecuting the righteous when Christ appears, that appearing will put Satan down with finality. He will then be cast into the lake of fire where he will remain to suffer throughout eternity (Rev. 20:10).

Since it looks as though antichrist may already be abroad in the land, every genuine believer should rest heavily on the promises of God, and count it a joy to suffer for the cause of Christ. This suffering, says Paul, could not even be compared with the blessings awaiting God's people at the second coming.

# IX

## THE SECOND ADVENT

Our generation has witnessed many marvelous things. More physical and scientific advancements have been made in the last half century than were made in the preceding two thousand years. Since the turn of the century man has split the atom, broken the sound barrier, perfected many disease cures, plumbed the depth of the seas, and orbited the earth, to name but a few of his accomplishments.

However, the most stupendous phenomenon ever witnessed is yet future. It is definitely fixed on God's agenda, and the exact time is known only to him. We speak of the second coming of Christ to the earth. Let the reader envision a day when routine activities go on as usual (read Matt. 24:37-39). People are buying, selling, working, resting, sinning, worshiping —when suddenly a sound is heard from heaven like that of a trumpet. Every gaze will be drawn heavenward (Rev. 1:7) to see Jesus Christ — attended by a heavenly host — descending upon a cloud.

According to the Scriptures, the second advent is to be literal, bodily, visible. This statement is based upon such scriptures as the following.

". . . as they were looking, he was taken up; and a cloud received him out of their sight. And while they were looking stedfastly into heaven as he went, behold, two men stood by them in white apparel; who also said, Ye men of Galilee, why stand ye looking into heaven? this Jesus, who was received up from you into heaven, shall so come in like manner as ye beheld him going into heaven" (Acts 1:9-12).

"For the Lord himself shall descend from heaven, with a shout, with the voice of the archangel, and with the trump of God. . ." (I Thess. 4:16).

The angels taught that Jesus — the same Jesus whom they watched go, in a bodily form, into heaven — would come again to the earth *in like manner*. And Paul was emphatic in saying the Lord *himself* shall descend from heaven.

### Defining Our Terms

Not every mention of a "coming" or "appearing" of our Lord refers to the second advent. Confusing doctrines have grown out of the attempt of some to apply too many scriptures to the second coming of Christ. Let us take as an example the words of Jesus recorded in Matthew 10:23: ". . . Ye shall not have gone through the cities of Israel, till the Son of man be come." Although many have used this verse to prove a point with reference to the second coming, actually it has no reference to it at all. The Lord was sending out the Twelve on an earthly mission, and promised them that he would personally join them before they finished the assignment.

Another example of misapplication of Scripture on this doctrine would be our Lord's prediction of his transfiguration. In Matthew 16:28 we find these words: "Verily I say unto you, there are some of them that stand here, who shall in no wise taste of death, till they see the Son of man coming in his kingdom." Although many apply this prediction to the second advent, the verses which follow immediately after give the true fulfillment of the prophecy. For Matthew goes on to say that "after six days Jesus . . . was transfigured before them. . ." (Matt. 17:1,2).

In Matthew 24, our Lord very definitely speaks on two different subjects — the destruction of Jerusalem, which took place in A.D. 70, and the end of the world. Some make the mistake of applying this entire chapter to the second coming. It is only natural that these folk end up with conflicting doctrines.

### a) Synonymous Terms

The Greek language portrays two distinct types of action. One is linear action and could be illustrated by a line drawn by a pencil. The other is called punctilliar action, and this is illustrated by a single dot made by pressing the pencil lead against a sheet of paper.

The second advent is to be a punctilliar type action, i.e., a single event, rather than something coming in different stages.

Throughout the New Testament many terms are used to describe the second coming of Christ. Such terms include: "the day of the Lord" (Acts 2:20; II Thess. 2:2; II Peter 3:10), "the day of the Lord Jesus" (I Cor. 5:5; II Cor. 1:14), "the day of our Lord Jesus Christ" (I Cor. 1:8), "the day of Jesus Christ" (Phil. 1:6), "the day of Christ" (Phil. 1:10; 2:16), "the day of God" (II Peter 3:12; Rev. 16:14), "that day" (Matt. 7:22; 14:36; 26:29; Luke 10:12; II Thess. 1:10; II Tim. 1:18), "the last day" (John 6:39,40,44,54; 11:24; 12:48), "his day" (Luke 17:24), "the revelation of Christ" (II Thess. 1:7; I Peter 1:7; etc.), "the appearing of Christ" (I Tim. 6:14; II Tim. 4:1,8), "the coming of Christ" (I Cor. 15:23; I Thess. 2:19; James 5:7).

Since each "day" quoted above refers to the same event, the terms relating to the second advent actually may be reduced to four— appearing, revelation, coming, and day.

Dispensationalists attempt to make these four terms refer to many separate steps or stages in the second coming of Christ, with a lapse of time and other events separating each step. However, one need not even have a knowledge of Greek in order to disprove this claim. For the lexicons and Bible dictionaries generally agree that these terms have the following meanings.

*Parousia*: "arrival," "presence." This word is translated "coming" in the New Testament.

The parousia (of Christ) occurs in the following passages: I Corinthians 15:23; I Thessalonians 2:19; 3:13; 4:15; 5:23; II Thessalonians 2:1,8.

"The word expresses two closely connected ideas of arrival and presence. *Parousia* signifies 'becoming present' and 'being present.' Somewhat of an analogy would be our English word 'visit' " (Geerhardus Vos, *The Pauline Eschatology,* p. 74).

*Epiphanias*: "appearing," "a manifestaton," "brightness." This is from a root word meaning to "shine upon," "give light," "become visible."

*Apokalupto*: "disclosure," "appearing," "coming," "lighten," "manifestation," "be revealed," "revelation." This is from a root word meaning to "take the cover off," i.e., "disclose," "reveal."

"Coming" is a derivation of the same root as "revelation," and means "arrival," "presence," "visit." *Parousia* was used in classical and Koine Greek in the general sense of "presence," but also of "arrival" or "coming."

*Hemera*: "day." "fig. a period (always defined more or less clearly by the context)" (*Greek Dictionary of the New Testament*, p. 35; James Strong, *The Exhaustive Concordance of the Bible*).

One can readily see that these four terms — coming, appearing, revelation, day — portray synonymous concepts, and that they refer to a singular event. These different terms are used, not to depict different occasions, but rather to draw attention to unique aspects of that one great occasion. Each is simply a different facet of a single gem. In one context the inspired writer intended to emphasize the certainty of Jesus' *coming*; another writer wished to elucidate the fact that our Lord's majesty — which is presently hidden from view — will be *revealed* at his second coming; another text will bring comfort to the believer as he is reminded that our Lord will some day be bodily *present* and that his appearing will be visible for all to behold.

This is no different from the four accounts of the life of our Lord recorded in the four Gospels. Certainly no one would suggest that the Gospels record four different lives of Christ, each taking place at a different time in history. Still there are four different emphases there; one writer brings out the kingship of Christ, another his manhood, another his miracles, and yet another his eternality. Here again are four sides of one personality, four facets of one great jewel. And so it is with the different aspects of the one second coming of Christ to the earth. It is to be multi-dimensional and each term simply views it from one certain angle. Dr. Harold Ockenga says: "No exegetical justification exists for the arbitrary separation of the Coming of Christ and the Day of the Lord" (quoted from Norman F. Douty, *Has Christ's Return Two Stages?*, p. 75).

A careful analysis of the following scriptures will make it self-evident that different terms used with reference to the second coming of Christ actually refer to a single event.

"And the Lord make you to increase and abound in love one toward another, and toward all men, even as we also do toward you;

to the end he may establish your hearts unblameable in holiness before our God and Father *at the coming of our Lord Jesus with all his saints*" (I Thess. 3:12,13).

". . . waiting for the revelation of our Lord Jesus Christ" (I Cor. 1:7).

". . . that ye may be sincere and void of offense unto the day of Christ" (Phil. 1:10).

"Be patient therefore, brethren, until the coming of our Lord . . ." (James 5:7).

". . . we should live soberly and righteously and godly in this present world; looking for the blessed hope and appearing of the glory of the great God and our Saviour Jesus Christ" (Titus 2:12,13).

Both Paul and James presuppose that some Christians will remain on the earth until Jesus' appearing. This can only mean that all these terms refer to one and the same event. The dispensationalists, on the other hand, contend that these terms refer to distinct and separate events and that only some of them will involve Christians while some will involve only the unrighteous.


b) Day versus Days

Much confusion has grown from the erroneous teaching that the last day and the last days are synonymous. Actually, each of these terms has a meaning distinct from the other. One refers to a duration of time covering a number of happenings, while the other refers to a single event.

In defining our terms, we gave Dr. Strong's definition of "day" as it is used in the New Testament. Dr. Strong correctly points out that the length of time involved in the period denoted by the word "day" is always defined for us by the context itself. With this thought before us, I wish to point out that the word "day," wherever it refers to the second coming, is always in the singular (punctilliar) vein. An extended period of time, when referred to in the New Testament, is always distinguished by the plural, i.e., *days* as distinguished from *day*. The reader is never left in doubt as to whether any given passage has reference to an extended period (linear action) or a given point in time (punctilliar action).

c) In These Last Days

The New Testament makes clear the fact that the birth of Christ ushered in the last days (plural). This has been true at least since the Day of Pentecost, for at that time the apostle Peter made the following statement: ". . . this is that which hath been spoken through the prophet Joel: And it shall be *in the last days*, saith God, I will pour forth of my Spirit upon all flesh: And your sons and your daughters shall prophesy, And your young men shall see visions, And your old men shall dream dreams: Yea and on my servants and on my handmaidens *in those days* Will I pour forth of my Spirit; and they shall prophesy. And I will show wonders in the heaven above, And signs on the earth beneath; Blood, and fire, and vapor of smoke: The sun shall be turned into darkness, And the moon into blood, Before the day of the Lord come, That great and notable day: And it shall be that whosoever shall call on the name of the Lord shall be saved" (Acts 2:16-21 — Peter quoted from Joel 2:28-32).

Peter said that those people on the Day of Pentecost witnessed events that had been predicted by the prophet Joel to happen in the last days. The fact that they happened was ample proof that the predicted time and events were present. So that the *last days* began with the first advent of our Lord and we are still in them.

The writer of Hebrews also informs us that the last days have already begun. Note the past tense in the following verses:
"God, having of old time spoken unto the fathers in the prophets by divers portions and in divers manners, *hath at the end of these days* spoken unto us in his Son. . ." (Heb. 1:1,2).

". . . but now once at the end of the ages hath he been manifested to put away sin by the sacrifice of himself" (Heb. 9:26). This is a clear reference to Christ and states that God has spoken directly through Jesus to the world. Only one event corresponds to a time when God spoke directly through a Son, and that event was the earthly ministry of our Lord. Therefore, the last days began with the first advent.

In Paul's writings it is not difficult to see that the great apostle to the Gentiles taught that the people of his generation were already living in the eleventh hour of time.

"Now these things happened unto them by way of example; and they were written for our admonition upon whom the ends of the ages are come" (I Cor. 10:11).

The apostle Peter places the first advent of our Lord in the end of time as evidenced by his statement in I Peter 1:20: "Who was foreknown indeed before the foundation of the world, but was manifested at the end of the times for your sake."

John is specific in saying, "Little children, it is the last hour . . ." (I John 2:18).

Since we have seen that the Bible clearly teaches that we are in the last days, then it is a wresting of the Scriptures to picture the last days as being altogether future. And, since we are already in the last days, it follows that any event predicted for that period is either history, or else is in the process of being fulfilled during our present age.

When the New Testament speaks of then current or past periods, these are always in the plural. It speaks of the days of Herod (Matt. 2:1), the days of John the Baptist (Matt. 3:1; 11:12), the days of the prophets (Luke 4:25; Matt. 23:30), the days of tribulation (Matt. 24:19-22,29), the days of Noah (Matt. 24:37), the days of Jesus' earthly ministry (Mark 1:9; Heb. 5:7). All these persons mentioned did certain things on a given day (singular), but the *periods* of their ministries are always in the plural (days).

### d) The Coming Last Day

The last day (singular), on the other hand, is still future, according to the teachings of the New Testament. In the New Testament one never reads, with reference to the second coming, of the days of judgment, the days of the Lord, the days of Jesus Christ, the days of the resurrection, the revelations, the comings, the appearings, or the like. This event is always spoken of in the singular — the *day*, the *judgment*, the *resurrection*, the *coming*.

"Many will say to me in that day, Lord, Lord, did we not prophesy by thy name. . ." (Matt. 7:22).

"Verily I say unto you, It shall be more tolerable for the land of Sodom and Gomorrah in the day of judgment, than for that city" (Matt. 10:15).

"For as the lightning, when it lighteneth out of the one part under the heaven, shineth unto the other part under heaven; so shall the Son of man be in his day" (Luke 17:24).

"After the same manner shall it be in the day that the Son of man is revealed. In that day, he that shall be on the housetop, and his goods in the house, let him not go down to take them away . . ." (Luke 17:30,31).

"And this is the will of him that sent me, that of all that which he hath given me I should lose nothing, but should raise it up at the last day" (John 6:39). Also read verses 40, 44, and 54.

"Martha saith unto him, I know that he shall rise again in the resurrection at the last day" (John 11:24).

". . . the word that I spake, the same shall judge him in the last day" (John 12:48).

"The sun shall be turned into darkness, and the moon into blood, before the day of the Lord come, that great and notable day" (Acts 2:20).

"But after thy hardness and impenitent heart treasurest up for thyself wrath in the day of wrath and revelation of the righteous judgment of God" (Rom. 2:5).

These and many other scriptures point up the fact that the second coming will take place on a given day rather than being extended over more than one day. The second coming, in other words, will occur on the last day of these last days. We are already in these last days and ever drawing nearer to the last day.

e) The Two Terms — Day and Days — Used Together

One can hardly fail to see the contrast in the New Testament use of day versus days. This contrast is pointed up even more sharply in passages wherein the words are used together. An example follows.

"And as it came to pass in *the days* of Noah, even so shall it be also in *the days* of the Son of man. They ate, they drank, they married, they were given in marriage, until *the day* that Noah entered into the ark, and the flood came, and destroyed them all. Likewise even as it came to pass in *the days* of Lot; they ate, they drank, they bought, they sold, they planted, they builded; but in *the day* that Lot went out from Sodom it rained fire and brimstone from heaven, and destroyed them all: after the same manner shall it be in *the day* that the Son of man is revealed. In *that day*, he that shall be on the housetop, and his goods in the house, let him not go down to take them away: and let him that is in the field likewise not return back" (Luke 17:26-31).

Here Luke compares the ministry of our Lord with the ministries of Noah and Lot. He also likens the climax of the second coming with the climaxes of the other men. The entire period included in Noah's time on earth is referred to in the plural, i.e., "the *days* of Noah." Then, says Luke, on a certain *day* during Noah's days on earth, he entered the ark. Lot likewise on a certain *day*, during his *days* on earth, went out from Sodom and on that *day* an eventful thing happened. Then, using these well-known events as examples, Luke says that during the days of Christ things are just as they were during the days of Noah, i.e., people go on eating, drinking, getting married, being generally unconcerned about the things of God. Then, says Luke, there will come a day (singular) when people will be called to account. Luke speaks of three persons in history — Noah, Lot, Jesus — and in the case of each one he uses a plural ("in the days of") and a singular ("in the day," "in that day").

### Characteristics of the Second Coming

God has reserved some knowledge concerning the second coming to himself. For example, no man knows the time it will take place. Only God knows that (Matt. 24:36). However, the Bible does tell us many things concerning the second advent. We know, for example:

1. It will come suddenly (Rev. 22:29; Luke 17:24).

2. It will come unexpectedly (Matt. 24:39; Luke 12:40; I Thess. 5:2; Rev. 16:15).

3. It will be seen by all (Rev. 1:7).

4. It will be heard by all (Matt. 16:27; Mark 13:26; II Thess. 1:7).

5. It will be accompanied by angels and clouds (Matt. 16:27; 24:30,31; 25:31,32).

*Some Results of the Second Coming*

1. *It will complete the first advent* (Heb. 9:28). Actually, the first and second advents of Christ complement each other. One is not complete without the other. Nor does this contradict our earlier statement that the second coming itself will not be in stages. The second coming is itself a complete and singular stage in God's plan.

Our Lord set eschatology in motion by his first advent into the world. He established the new covenant, and threw open the door of salvation to all peoples by tearing down the middle wall of partition existing between Jew and Gentile (Eph. 2:11-16). The first advent also manifested the kingdom, and began the judgment of the world. However, none of these will be consummated until the second coming.

2. *Complete salvation will be realized.* One of the best illustrations of the twofold nature of our salvation is found in Hebrews. "So Christ, also, having been once offered to bear the sins of many, shall appear a second time, apart from sin, to them that wait for him, unto salvation" (Heb. 9:28).

Jesus came, in the fullness of time, and became the perfect sacrifice to purchase a perfect salvation for all who will believe in him. And each person who has accepted Christ as Savior has been saved eternally and can never be condemned with the world (John 4:14; 10:28; Rom. 5:1; 8:1). He has already been delivered from the wrath to come (I Thess. 1:10). Still, there is a tension between what the believer is and what he is to become. Our immortal souls are still housed in mortal bodies which will remain mortal until our Lord returns a second time (Rom. 8:23).

Peter speaks of the different aspects of salvation. He points out that the resurrection of Christ assured believers an incorruptible inheritance. Yet he says that the complete enjoyment of this inheritance is reserved in heaven and that we are "guarded through faith unto a salvation ready to be revealed in the last time" (I Peter 1:3-5). So the Christian has been saved, he is being saved, and he is waiting to be saved from the wrath to come. This is illustrated in passages such as Romans 5:9-11.

3. *The second coming of Christ will bring about an eternal separation.* Today there is intercourse between the living saved and living unsaved. When the Lord returns, the great gulf between them will be eternally solidified. The standing of each person when the Lord returns will be his standing throughout eternity. The lost person — Jew and Gentile — will have sinned away his last opportunity. And the Christian will have had his last opportunity to witness to the lost with a view toward winning souls for Christ. The day of salvation will have ended, the door of mercy will have been closed (Matt. 24:37-39). In drawing this comparison between the flood in Noah's day and the second coming, our Lord points up a lesson that is inescapable. ". . . Noah entered into the ark, and they knew not until the flood came, and took them all away; so shall be the coming of the Son of man" (Matt. 24:38,39).

We know — and the Lord here reminds his listeners of this fact — that, once the flood came, not another soul entered the ark. Jesus said, "So shall be the coming of the Son of man." We find this same analogy in Matthew 25:1-13, "And they that were ready went in with him. . . ." All others were turned away because the separation had been made final, once the bridegroom appeared — or once the door of the ark had been closed at the appearance of the flood waters.

"But when the Son of man shall come in his glory, and all the angels with him, then shall he sit on the throne of his glory: and before him shall be gathered all the nations: and he shall separate them one from another, as the shepherd separateth the sheep from the goats; and he shall set the sheep on his right hand, but the goats on the left. Then shall the King say unto them on his right hand,

Come, ye blessed of my Father, inherit the kingdom prepared for you from the foundation of the world: . . . Then shall he say also unto them on the left hand, Depart from me, ye cursed, into the eternal fire which is prepared for the devil and his angels: . . . And these shall go away into eternal punishment: but the righteous into eternal life" (Matt. 25:31-46).

". . . so shall be the coming of the Son of man. Then shall two men be in the field; one is taken, and one is left; two women shall be grinding at the mill; one is taken, and one is left" (Matt. 24:39-41).

"Again, the kingdom of heaven is like unto a net, that was cast into the sea, and gathered of every kind: which, when it was filled, they drew up on the beach; and they sat down, and gathered the good into vessels, but the bad they cast away" (Matt. 13:47,48).

"So shall it be in the end of the world; the angels shall come forth, and sever the wicked from among the righteous, and shall cast them into the furnace of fire: there shall be the weeping and the gnashing of teeth" (Matt. 13:49,50).

"Let both grow together until the harvest: and in the time of the harvest I will say to the reapers, Gather up first the tares, and bind them in bundles to burn them; but gather the wheat into my barn. . . . the harvest is the end of the world. . ." (Matt. 13:30,39).

When this separation takes place the saints will be rewarded and the wicked will be judged (II Thess. 1:10; Phil. 3:20,21; II Tim. 4:8; I Peter 1:13; 5:4; II Thess. 1:8).

4. *The kingdom of God will be consummated.* Jesus manifested the kingdom at his first coming. At the second advent it will be perfected, then turned over to God the Father by God the Son (I Cor. 15:24), so that God may be all in all. At this time the earth will be cleansed (Rom. 8:20,21; II Peter 3:7), all evil elements will be removed and cast into hell. Then God's will truly will be done on earth as it is now done in heaven (I Cor. 15:24). Sin will then not exist outside of hell.

5. *The defeat of Satan will be completed, or consummated.* This was begun at the Lord's first advent, but will be completed at his second coming. The Scriptures clearly teach that Satan was defeated when Christ died on the cross. There the head of the serpent was bruised in fulfillment of Genesis 3:15. However, Satan still goes

around like a roaring lion seeking whom he may devour; and he would deceive even the elect "*if it were possible*." This is not possible, however, since the Savior bound Satan, i.e., limited his power so that he could no longer deceive the nations (Rev. 20:3). Satan, though defeated, still has not had his sentence executed. It has been pronounced, but not yet executed. Even Satan himself knows full well that his time is short (Rev. 12:12). Satan acts now under a suspended sentence. When Christ comes again that sentence will be executed and Satan will be cast eternally into the lake of fire (II Thess. 2:8; Rev. 20:10).

6. *History will be brought to its close, and the final state will be ushered in.* Although men divide time into two periods, with the dividing line at the birth of Christ, actually, the New Testament knows but two ages — the present age and the age to come (Matt. 12:32; Mark 10:30; Luke 20:34,35).

In reference to this world, the New Testament mind looked on it as that which had existed from the creation (Matt. 25:34), and which would end at the second coming of Christ (Matt. 13:39). The New Testament looked on the birth of Christ as marking the end-time of this present world (Heb. 9:26, etc.). The coming world is not to be a millennium which will end after 1000 years, but the eternal state which has no end.

## Progressive Doctrinal Development

Each doctrine referred to above shows a progressive development. This can be said of many, perhaps most, doctrines dealt with in the New Testament. First the blade, then the ear, next the full grain in the ear (Mark 4:28,29). Just about any doctrine of the New Testament could be used to illustrate this biblical rule of growth.

Paul was alive in Christ and looked forward only to an eternity with his Lord. Yet Paul taught that we are saved in hope; if we *had* a thing, Paul said, it would be incongruous to go on hoping for it (Rom. 8:24,25). In these areas we are dealing with divine paradoxes; and we need to keep in mind that a paradox is not a contradiction but merely a seeming contradiction. Man cannot comprehend every law of God.

*Related Events*

In both his Thessalonian epistles Paul shows the relatedness of the second coming to the rewarding of the righteous as well as to the punishing of the wicked. In both these epistles, too, men have made unfortunate chapter divisions. In I Thessalonians parts of chapters 4 and 5 form a unit, while in II Thessalonians chapters 1 and 2 belong together.

Whenever Paul, the foremost Christian theologian of all time, was inspired to write, many thoughts crowded in upon his great mind. One gains the impression from his thirteen epistles that this learned man thought faster than his hand could write, or faster than he could dictate. In the two sections we have just mentioned, Paul (1) began dealing with the second coming of Christ; (2) brought in, parenthetically, some thoughts on Christian living, etc.; (3) then returned to his main subject of the second coming. Upon returning to the subject, Paul uses different terminology in dealing with the same event — thus showing that these are synonymous terms.

". . . we that are alive, that are left unto *the coming of the Lord* shall in no wise precede them that are fallen asleep. For the Lord himself shall descend from heaven, with a shout, with the voice of the archangel, and with *the trump of God:* and *the dead in Christ shall rise first;* then we that are alive, that are left, shall together with them be caught up in the clouds, to meet the Lord in the air: and so shall we ever be with the Lord. Wherefore comfort one another with these words.

"But concerning the times and the seasons, brethren, ye have no need that aught be written unto you. For yourselves know perfectly that *the day of the Lord so cometh as a thief in the night.* When they are saying, Peace and safety then *sudden destruction cometh upon them,* as travail upon a woman with child; and they shall in no wise escape. *But ye, brethren, are not in darkness, that that day should overtake you as a thief"* (I Thess. 4:15-5:4).

Upon studying the above passage, one learns the following:

1. The coming of the Lord and the trump of God both describe the same event, seeing that Paul used them interchangeably.

2. At the coming of Christ (at the trump of God), the Christian dead will be raised and, along with the Christians then living, will be raptured to meet the Lord in the air.

3. So far as the unsaved are concerned, Jesus will come like a thief in the night, i.e., when least expected.

4. "That day" (here used interchangeably with the "coming of the Lord," and "the trump of God") will not come as a surprise to the faithful.

5. At the coming of the Lord (the last trump, that day), the unsaved will be destroyed. Also at the coming of the Lord (the last trump, that day), Christians will be resurrected. This being so, then both groups will remain together until the second coming.

"And to you that are afflicted rest with us, at the revelation of the Lord Jesus from heaven with the angels of his power in flaming fire, rendering vengeance to them that know not God, and to them that obey not the gospel of our Lord Jesus: who shall suffer punishment, even eternal destruction from the face of the Lord and from the glory of his might, when he shall come to be glorified in his saints, and to be marvelled at in all them that believed (because our testimony unto you was believed) in that day. . . .

"Now we beseech you, brethren, touching the coming of our Lord Jesus Christ, and our gathering together unto him; to the end that ye be not quickly shaken from your mind, nor yet be troubled, either by spirit, or by word, or by epistle as from us, as that the day of the Lord is just at hand" (II Thess: 1:7–2:2).

Paul is obviously speaking here (using first one term then another) of a single event. His subject does not change during the course of these verses. In these verses he speaks of "the revelation of the Lord Jesus," "the coming," "the glorification of the saints," which is to take place "in that day," at "the rapture," and "the day of the Lord." These all are used here by the apostle as synonymous terms. Paul also points out, in this same passage, that the saints will be glorified at the same time the unsaved are punished. Those who know not God "shall suffer punishment, even eternal destruction from the face of the Lord . . . when [at the time] he shall come to be glorified in his saints . . . in that day."

In I Corinthians 1:7,8, Paul uses "the revelation of our Lord Jesus Christ" and "the day of our Lord Jesus Christ" interchangeably.

In I John 2:28, the "manifestation" of Christ, and his "coming" are used as synonymous terms.

| | End of World | Manifestation | Appearing | Trump | Revelation | Coming | Day |
|---|---|---|---|---|---|---|---|
| Saints Resurrected | | I Peter 5:4; Col. 3:4. | | I Cor. 15:51, 52; I Thess. 4:15, 16. | I Peter 1:13. | I Cor. 15:23; I Thess. 4:15. | Acts 17:31; I John 4:17; II Peter 2:9; 3:7. John 6:39, 40, 44, 54. |
| General Judgment | | | II Tim. 4:1. | | | Matt. 16:27. | |
| Saints Rewarded | Matt. 13:40, 43. | Col. 3:4; I John 2:28; 3:2. | II Tim. 4:8; Heb. 9:28. | I Thess. 4:15-17. | I Peter 1:13; II Thess. 1:7-10. | II Thess. 1:10; 2:1; I John 2:28; I Thess. 3:13; 4:15-17. | I Cor. 3:13-15; II Thess. 1:10. |
| Wicked Punished | Matt. 13:49, 50. | II Thess. 2:8. | | | II Thess. 1:7-10. | II Thess. 1:10; 2:8. | II Thess. 1:10; Rom. 2:5; Matt. 7:22,23; Jude 6. |
| Separation | Matt. 13:40-43; 47-50. | | | Matt. 24:30, 31. | Luke 17:29, 30, 34, 35. | Matt. 24:37, 40; 25:31-46; Mark 13:26, 27. | |
| General Resurrection | | | | | | | John 11:24. |

A study of this chart will reveal that these events all are to be fulfilled at approximately the same time. Certainly no scriptural justification may be found for allowing long intervals of time between these events.

The chart shows, too, that the second coming of Christ is to be one event, though it is called by different names. This can be proved from the fact that many of the terms listed — such as "coming," "appearing," "manifestation," etc., are quoted from the same verses of Scripture.

When Jesus returns, both the wicked and the righteous will still be living on the earth. Both will witness his second coming, and both will be involved in it. A comparison of scripture with scripture makes this fact forceably clear.

Many events are to find their fulfillment at the second coming of Christ. Among these are:

1. The resurrection, rapture, judgment, and rewarding of the saints.
2. The resurrection, judgment, and punishment of the wicked.
3. The close of history and ushering in of the final state.
4. The consummation and turning over of the kingdom to God the Father.
5. The punishment of Satan.

Each of these events has already been set in motion by the first advent, death, burial, and resurrection of our Lord. Each, however, awaits final fulfillment at the second advent.

# X

## RESURRECTION

Here we come to one of the key doctrines of the Bible. The resurrection was at the center of the message of the early church. Paul, the apostle to the Gentiles, staked the validity of his entire ministry on the fact of the resurrection. Without it, he said, all would be vain.

Two types of resurrection are dealt with in the New Testament, and both are stressed. There are both a spiritual resurrection and a bodily resurrection. The first of these is the new birth, while the second is to take place at the *parousia*. Every Christian has already experienced the first resurrection; this took place the moment he surrendered his heart completely to Christ as Savior and Lord. Until that time the person was dead. ". . . ye were dead through your trespasses and sins" (Eph. 2:1). Paul, the theologian *par excellence*, teaches in the same verse that those who once were dead have been made alive (resurrected, brought from the dead) through Christ: "And you did he make alive. . . ."

Paul elaborates upon this teaching in other passages, such as the following.

". . . even when we were dead through our trespasses, *made us alive* together with Christ (by grace have ye been saved), *and raised us up* with him, and made us to sit with him in the heavenly places, in Christ Jesus" (Eph. 2:4-6).

"And you, being dead through your trespasses and the uncircumcision of your flesh, you, I say, did he make alive together with him, having forgiven us all our trespasses" (Col. 2:13).

"If then ye were raised together with Christ, seek the things that are above, where Christ is, seated on the right hand of God" (Col. 3:1).

This apostolic teaching was concurred in by such outstanding church fathers as Origen and Augustine, and was the teaching of most if not all of the Protestant reformers. John Calvin and Martin Luther preached it strongly.

In chapter 5 of John's Gospel, Christ speaks of two resurrections. These are the only two types of resurrection ever mentioned by Jesus. He covered the entire subject in these verses. Therefore, every mention of resurrection in the Bible must harmonize with one of these two. He spoke clearly and to the point. Here, as in all Bible study, the obscure passages must be interpreted by the clear ones.

Upon examining these two resurrections (John 5:24-29), one sees their different characteristics.

1. One is present, the other is future.
2. One is spiritual, the other is physical.
3. One is restricted to believers, the other includes everyone.

"Verily, verily, I say unto you, He that heareth my word, and believeth him that sent me, hath eternal life, and cometh not into judgment, but *hath passed out of death into life*" (John 5:24).

Having made this general statement, Jesus went on to explain this doctrine. "Verily, verily, I say unto you, *the hour* cometh, and *now is*, when the dead shall hear the voice of the Son of God; and they that hear shall live" (John 5:25).

It would be difficult to imagine language plainer than this concerning what constitutes the first resurrection of the Christian. Jesus said that in that generation dead people would hear his voice and thereby be caused to live (be resurrected). His words, "The hour . . . *now is*. . ." could not refer to the future. Therefore, we must seek another meaning for these words. The biblical answer is given in passages such as Ephesians 2:1,5,6 and I John 3:14, where the new birth is spoken of as a resurrection from the dead.

"And you did he make alive, when ye were dead through your trespasses and sins, . . . even when we were dead through our trespasses, made us alive together with Christ. . ." (Eph. 2:1-5. "We know that we have passed out of death into life, . . ." (I John 3:14).

As a result of the first resurrection, and his part in it, the believer has spiritual life (John 5:24); old things are passed away, behold all things have become new (II Cor. 5:17); he is now a citizen of heaven (Phil. 3:20; Heb. 13:14); he has begun already to reign with Christ (Eph. 2:6; Col. 1:13; Rev. 1:6); he has already been delivered from the power of the second death (I Thess. 1:10; Rev. 20:6). All these blessings will reach fruition at the second resurrection; however, each has already begun as a result of the believer's participation in the first resurrection, i.e., his becoming a joint-heir with Christ (through the new birth) who is himself the First Resurrection (John 11:24; I Cor. 15:20).

We have said of the first resurrection that it is present, spiritual, and that it involves only believers. Let us examine verse 25: "Verily, verily, I say unto you, the hour cometh, *and now is*, when the dead shall hear the voice of the Son of God; and they that hear shall live." Our Lord's words "and now is" let us know that he was speaking of an event to take place at the time he spoke. Further, our Lord said the hour "now is" when dead people were to hear his voice and that those who heard would live.

We are interested here in the spiritual resurrection, which we take to be the new birth. Since the fall of Adam and Eve, all are spiritually dead. God said to Adam: "In the day you eat thereof you shall surely die." Adam lived physically a few hundred years after eating the forbidden fruit. However, God's word was none the less true; Adam did die that same day. He died a spiritual death. He lost the image of God in which he had been created. Since Adam died spiritually — and since he was the federal head of mankind — every person who has reached the age of accountability has become spiritually dead. Jesus, through the cross, made possible a resurrection from this spiritual death. When he arose from the grave our Lord conquered death. Actually, then, our Lord himself is the First Resurrection. Let us reconcile this statement with our previous statement that the new birth is the first resurrection for the Christian. Before conversion every person is spiritually dead (cf. Eph. 2:1,5,6 and I John 3:14). Paul teaches that the believer is partaker with Christ in the crucifixion and also in his resurrection (Rom. 6:6; Col. 3:3). Thus, to be born again is to have part in the first resurrection.

Commenting on scriptures such as Colossians 3:3,4 and Ephesians 2:6, Ridderbos makes an enlightening statement: "Here the mystical, spiritual interpretation is an utter failure. One must rather say that Paul, when applying to the Church not only the Cross and death of Christ but also His exaltation until the parousia, is thinking in categories quite different from mystical ones. It is not true that Christ first died for those who are His, who only afterwards also die and rise with Him, spiritually, mystically or ethically. No, when He died on Golgotha, they also died with Him, and when He arose in the garden of Joseph of Arimathea, they were raised together with Him. Paul actually says it himself in so many words in 2 Corinthians 5:14: 'We thus judge, that one died for all, therefore all died.' Consequently, when he says in another place: 'For ye died' (Col. 3:3), or, 'We who died to sin, how shall we any longer live therein?' (Rom. 6:2); the apostle does not appeal to the conversion of the faithful, but to their being included in Christ's death. And the same holds true for the resurrection, the exaltation in heaven, the coming back of the Church with Christ. Whatever happened to Christ, happened to the Church, not only analogously or metaphorically, but in the historical sense of the word. She was included in Him, was, and is, present in Him throughout all the phases of the great history of salvation" (Herman N. Ridderbos, *When the Time Had Fully Come, Studies in New Testament Theology*, p. 55).

In this same sense, the Christian has already had part in the first resurrection. For Christ is the Resurrection (John 11:25); and since the first resurrection has happened to Christ, it has also happened to every genuine convert. Our resurrection, like our dying to sin, took place at our conversion — both being retroactive through the saving power of Christ. And — since every Christian is a joint-heir with Christ — the second death can have no more power over us than it can have over him. This statement must be made reverently; nevertheless, it is scripturally true

Having spoken of the spiritual resurrection, our Lord went on to speak of a general physical resurrection. "Marvel not at this [see vs. 25]: for the hour cometh, in which all that are in the tombs shall hear his voice, and shall come forth; they that have done good, unto the resurrection of life; and they that have done evil, unto the resurrection of judgment" (John 5:28,29).

Whereas the first resurrection was to begin taking place during Jesus' earthly ministry, this general resurrection was predicted as being future from that day. This second resurrection is also future from our present day.

The general resurrection — which includes all the dead of all time — is foreshadowed in the Old Testament. Usually, these Old Testament glimpses are rather vague until we come to Daniel.

"And at that time shall Michael stand up, the great prince who standeth for the children of thy people; and there shall be a time of trouble, such as never was since there was a nation even to that same time: and at that time thy people shall be delivered, every one that shall be found written in the book. And many of them that sleep in the dust of the earth shall awake, some to everlasting life, and some to shame and everlasting contempt" (Dan. 12:1,2).

We note here that Daniel's prophecy of the resurrection is in perfect harmony with the accounts given in the New Testament. He pictures the resurrection as following a time of great persecution of God's people, and points out that it will bring about a separation of the righteous from the wicked.

Many passages in the New Testament illustrate the fact that the righteous and the wicked will be resurrected at the same time. The bodily resurrection which is to occur when Christ returns the second time to earth is always, without exception, spoken of in the singular. Martha fixes the singularity and the setting for the resurrection in her conversation with her Lord: "I know that he shall rise again in the resurrection *at the last day*" (John 11:24). And Jesus answered that *he was the resurrection* (vs. 25).

The early church knew and preached but one resurrection. ". . . they taught the people, and proclaimed in Jesus the resurrection from the dead" (Acts 4:2).

When Paul's theology was brought into question by his Jewish enemies he stated specifically, "that there shall be *a* resurrection both of the just and unjust" (Acts 24:15). Paul also stated that this was an Old Testament belief held in common by the Jews: "having hope toward God, *which these also themselves look for*, that there shall be a resurrection both of the just and unjust" (Acts 24:15). It is a reflection upon Paul's use of grammar to say, as some do, that he believed in more than one bodily resurrection. It is also a reflection upon one's theory of inspiration to think that the Holy Spirit would inspire such a statement.

It is difficult to understand how so many persons can ignore these plain verses while they take an obscure passage from Revelation (20:5,6) and build a doctrine of two or more bodily resurrections upon it. Truly, the letter kills, but the spirit gives life!

Paul condemns those who say the resurrection (singular) is past already (II Tim. 2:18).

If there were more than one physical resurrection, then many of our Scripture passages would not make sense in their present form. It would have been necessary for Paul to have said, "I believe in resurrections, one for the just and one for the unjust." Martha would have found it necessary to have specified *which* resurrection she had in mind when stating that her brother would rise in the last day. And the early church would not have taught "a resurrection," but resurrections (plural). It would not have sufficed to say of the Sadducees, "They say there is no resurrection" (Matt. 22:23). If there were to be more than one bodily resurrection, then it would be said of the Sadducees, "They say there are no resurrections."

Dispensationalists reject the doctrine of one general resurrection of both the righteous and the wicked simply because they are not always dealt with together in Scripture. They argue that since the Bible speaks, for example, of "the resurrection of the just," then there must of necessity be a separate resurrection of the unjust." They also argue that since resurrection chapters such as I Corinthians 15 do not even mention the unsaved dead, then it must follow that the wicked will not be present when the righteous are raised.

First of all, this is to argue from silence, which is always poor exegesis. And, more important, these are by no means the only passages of Scripture which deal with only one side of a subject. A similar example may be gained by comparing the four Gospels with reference to the scene at the empty tomb following the resurrection of Christ. Each Gospel writer emphasizes a different fact concerning the angels at the tomb. Matthew 28:2 mentions one angel; Mark 16:5 speaks of a young man; Luke 24:4 refers to two young men: John 20:12 tells of two angels being present.

No problem exists concerning the terms "angels" and "men," for these are used interchangeably elsewhere in Scripture. However, using the same argument used with reference to I Corinthians 15, one could contend — seeing that Matthew and Mark mentioned only one angel (or young man) —the second one was not present at that same time. Therefore, one could contend, these four Gospels do not speak of the same events.

Reason dictates, naturally, that Matthew and Mark saw fit to mention only a part of those present, while Luke and John mentioned the full scene. Reason also dictates this same conclusion with reference to I Corinthians 15 when it is compared with the many other scriptures dealing with the resurrection. Paul, for example, lumps the two together in Acts 24:15 and also in II Thessalonians 1 and 2.

In all his epistles Paul deals in practical things, often in answer to questions from the churches. Thus he does not deal specifically with the resurrection of the wicked, because that would not serve his purpose. He deals at length, however, with their punishment, since that would encourage the Christians by letting them know that right will eventually triumph over evil.

Further proof that the righteous and the wicked will be resurrected at the same time lies in the fact that both remain together until the very end of the world (Matt. 13:30,39,49,50). It is difficult to see how the millennialists find one thousand or more years lying between the resurrection of the righteous and that of the wicked. And without this alleged interval, their entire theory goes begging.

When we say the righteous and wicked are to remain together, we do not speak of the souls of the dead, but rather of those persons living when Christ returns. When a Christian dies, his soul goes immediately into the presence of God, while his body returns to the earth (Ecc. 12:7). When a sinner dies, his body also returns to the earth, but his soul goes to a place of conscious torment, where it is imprisoned to await the final judgment (Luke 16:19-31; II Peter 2:9). Both will remain in these states of existence until the trump sounds at the end of the world. Then both will be raised together, along with all those who remain alive until the second coming.

Having stated that both the righteous and the wicked are to remain together until the second coming, let us look to the Scriptures for proof of this statement.

"Let both grow together *until the harvest:* and in the time of the harvest I will say to the reapers, Gather up first the tares, and bind them in bundles to burn them; but gather the wheat into my barn" (Matt. 13:30). "So shall it be *in the end of the world:* the angels shall come forth and sever the wicked from among the righteous, and shall cast them into the furnace of fire: there shall be the weeping and the gnashing of teeth" (Matt. 13:49,50).

Paul says, in I Corinthians 15:26, that death will be the last enemy destroyed. Paul goes on to say, beginning with verse 51 of this same chapter, that all Christians will be changed from mortal to immortal *at the last trump.* This resurrection, says Paul, will be the sign that "Death is swallowed up in victory" (vs. 54). Now if the last enemy is to be destroyed at the resurrection of the just, then it is incongruous to picture other enemies still being present one thousand years from that time! Turning to Revelation 20:13-15, we find John the Revelator telling of other things which are to happen at the time death is destroyed: "And death and Hades were cast into the lake of fire. This is the second death, even the lake of fire. And if any was not found written in the book of life, he was cast into the lake of fire."

Both Paul and John are dealing here with the last enemy. Paul says specifically that death will be the last enemy dealt with. Then Paul says that at the time the last enemy *is* dealt with, the saints will be resurrected and rewarded. John, dealing with the destruction of this same last enemy, teaches that at the same time the last enemy is dealt with the wicked also will be punished. The reader should note that John describes the second death as taking place *after* Satan has made his final battle against the people of God and that Satan has, in fact, been cast into hell (Rev. 20:10). Note, too, that this final battle which Satan leads takes place *after the millennium* (Rev. 20:7).

The dispensationalist builds his entire millennial thesis on Revelation 20:1-10, just as if the rest of that chapter did not exist. An outline of Revelation 20 reveals that John actually deals with four happenings in their chronological order: (1) the binding of Satan (vss. 1-3), (2) the millennium (vss. 4-6), (3) the battle of Armageddon, fought between Gog and Magog on the one hand and the followers of Christ on the other (vss. 7-10), (4) the final judgment and destruction of the final enemy, death (vss. 11-15).

In speaking of the wheat and the tares (representing the righteous and the wicked) our Lord said, "Let both grow together until the harvest: and in the time of the harvest I will say to the reapers, Gather up first the tares and bind them in bundles to burn them; but gather the wheat into my barn" (Matt. 13:30).

After the crowd had dispersed, the disciples asked Jesus to explain this parable to them. "And he answered and said, He that soweth the good seed is the Son of man; and the field is the world; and the good seed, these are the sons of the kingdom; and the tares are the sons of the evil one; and the enemy that sowed them is the devil: and the harvest is the end of the world; and the reapers are angels. As therefore the tares are gathered up and burned with fire; so shall it be in the end of the world. The Son of man shall send forth his angels, and they shall gather out of his kingdom all things that cause stumbling, and them that do iniquity, and shall cast them into the furnace of fire: there shall be the weeping and the gnashing of teeth. Then shall the righteous shine forth as the sun in the kingdom of their Father" (Matt. 13:37-43).

An explanation of this passage seems superfluous, owing to the way in which the Lord explained every detail. Yet, many weird misinterpretations have been placed on it. The millennialist teaches that the wicked will be resurrected one thousand years after the resurrection of the just. Yet the Lord teaches (Matt. 13:30) "gather up *first* the tares. . . ."

The Savior said that he spoke of the wicked and the righteous in this present world. He stated specifically — in fact, gave an order to the effect — that the good and bad were to remain together until the end of the world." "So shall it be in the end of the world." He says that the field spoken of is the world (note that the tares are not in the kingdom of God, but in the world).

Again, it is almost unbelievable that students of the Bible do such violence to these words of our Lord and teach that there will be a millennium between the resurrection of the righteous and that of the wicked. Certainly there can be no interval at all between the resurrection of the two groups if both are to grow side by side until the harvest. John's single apocalyptic passage in Revelation 20 cannot be allowed to contradict the clear teachings of the entire New Testament. All passages are equally inspired and true, but the plain must interpret the figurative.

In chapter 25 of Matthew the Lord is again recorded as having spoken concerning a separation of the righteous from the wicked. The time is fixed at the end of the world, i.e., at the second coming of Christ.

"But when the Son of man shall come in his glory, and all the angels with him, then shall he sit on the throne of his glory; and before him shall be gathered all the nations: and he shall separate them one from another, as the shepherd separateth the sheep from the goats. . ." (Matt. 25:31,32).

We shall deal in detail with this passage when we come to the chapter dealing with the judgment. Suffice it here to say that once again we are reminded that the righteous and the wicked will not be separated until the coming of Christ at the end of the world.

Another evidence that the righteous and the wicked are to remain together until the general resurrection is found in Paul's teaching. Paul definitely teaches that the wicked will be punished at the same time the righteous are rewarded, and he says that both will happen "in that day." ". . . at the revelation of the Lord Jesus from heaven with the angels of his power in flaming fire, rendering vengeance to them that know not God, and to them that obey not the gospel of our Lord Jesus: who shall suffer punishment, even eternal destruction from the face of the Lord and from the glory of his might, when he shall come to be glorified in his saints, and to be marvelled at in all them that believed . . . in that day" (II Thess. 1:7-10).

Paul leaves no doubt or room for speculation as to what he means or as to when it will take place. He says that (1) at the revelation of the Lord Jesus certain things will happen —(a) the wicked will suffer punishment and destruction (compare this with Rev. 20:14), (b) the saints will be rewarded and will escape the persecutions which they now suffer; (2) the time at which the wicked will receive this punishment is "when he |Christ| shall come to be glorified in |with| his saints." If both the rewarding of the saints and the punishment of the wicked are to take place at the same time, i.e., "at the revelation," "when he shall come," "in that day," then it stands to reason that there could not be two separate bodily resurrections, one for the righteous and one for the wicked.

A scriptural conclusion may be based upon the above-mentioned Scripture passages. (A) Death will be the last enemy abolished by Christ; (B) Christians are to be rewarded at the time this last enemy is abolished (I Cor. 15:54); (C) The wicked are to be judged and cast into hell at the time the last enemy is destroyed (Rev. 20:14). Since both events take place at the time of the second death, then both events must of necessity take place at one and the same time. Things equal to the same thing are equal to each other.

The resurrection is to be heralded by the blowing of the last trump (trumpet). This last trump will, in fact, be the signal for many simultaneous events to take place. Certainly it would be ludicrous to insist on there being more than one *last* trump connected with the end of time. We shall list some of the things to be signalled forth by the blowing of this last trumpet.

1. The last trump will be the signal for Christ to appear (Matt. 24:30,31; I Thess. 4:16).

2. The last trump will accompany the earthly phenomena surrounding the second coming of Christ (Matt. 24:29-31).

3. At the sound of the last trump, the wicked will mourn (Matt. 24:30).

4. At the sound of the last trump, the righteous will be raptured (Matt. 24:31; I Cor. 15:51,52; I Thess. 4:16,17).

5. At the last trump, the righteous will be resurrected and given their new bodies (I Cor. 15:51,52).

6. At the last trump, the kingdom will be consummated (Rev. 11:15).

7. At the last trump, the wicked will be punished (Rev. 11: 15-18).

Since all these things happen at one and the same time — and we should note they happen to the righteous and to the wicked simultaneously — it is a contradiction to separate these events by one thousand or more years. This the millennialists attempt to do.

### The Rapture

"Rapture" is from a Latin word (rapiemur) and portrays a snatching away. This doctrine is based on I Thessalonians 2:1; John 14:3; and Matthew 25:1-13. The "rapture theory" has fallen into ill repute because of the controversy growing out of the fantastic interpretations of many dispensationalist groups. Most Bible dictionaries do not even list the word.

When looked at sanely and collated with other scriptures, these verses do seem to form a teaching concerning the resurrection of the saints at Jesus' second coming. Perhaps Bible scholars have "thrown the baby out with the bath" in their attempts completely to disassociate themselves from the radicals on this doctrine. For certainly Paul does teach that the saints will be caught up (raptured) to meet the Lord in the air when he comes again. And our Lord himself seems to allude to this in Matthew 25:1-13. There he teaches a lesson concerning the present kingdom of heaven: true believers are to meet Christ on his return. "Behold, the bridegroom! *Come ye forth to meet him . . .* the bridegroom came, and they that were ready went in with him to the marriage feast. . . ." This was based upon a custom of that day to go out and meet a visiting dignitary and to escort him the rest of the way on his journey. "When a dignitary paid an official visit or *parousia* to a city in Hellenistic times, the action of the leading citizens in going out to meet him and escorting him on the final stage of his journey was called the *apantesis;* it is similarly used in Mt. XXV. 6; Acts XXVIII. 15. So the Lord is pictured as escorted to the earth by His people—those newly raised from death and those who have remained alive. . ." (Davidson, Stibbs, Kevan, *The New Bible Commentary*, p. 1057).

The rapture of the saints will include every believer from every generation. This means that both Old and New Testament saints will be raised. Then all these, along with all the living saints, will be caught up to meet the Lord in the air. His journey will not cease in mid-air, else he would be meeting the saints instead of the saints meeting him. Actually, the Lord will descend from heaven to earth, and the saints will meet him in mid-air and will escort him the rest of the way.

The rapture will take place immediately after the resurrection and just before the judgment. When the trumpet sounds, things will take place simultaneously. Our Lord will begin his descent to the earth, the brightness of this event will put down Satan, and all the graves will be opened. Instantaneously, the saints who come out of the graves will be given new bodies (I Cor. 15:51,52). The saints who are living at that time will also be given new bodies, then all the saints together will go out to meet the Lord and to escort him to the earth. We are dealing here only with the *bodies* of those who die in the Lord, since their souls will have been in the paradise of God until that instant when they are clothed upon with the new bodies. Christ will bring his *disembodied* saints with him when he comes (I Thess. 3:13; 4:14; Jude 14).

We said that *all* the graves would be opened at the sound of the trump. What, then, of the unsaved while the saints are being raptured? A number of scriptures concerning them will be fulfilled at that instant. First of all, they will witness the joy of the saints and the rapture. They will be forced to bow the knee and acknowledge that this is of a certainty the Christ (Rom. 14:11; Phil. 2:9-11). This acknowledgment will not, however, bring salvation. For the sound of the trumpet will close the door of salvation. They will see the Suffering Servant of the cross reigning now as Judge of the quick and the dead, and they will seek a place of hiding but will find none (Rev. 1:7).

Dispensationalists, and many premillennialists, use the rapture passage in I Thessalonians 4 to argue that the unsaved will not be resurrected at the time the saints are. They base this on Paul's statement in verse 16 that "the dead in Christ shall rise *first*." In this passage Paul is not even speaking in relation to the unsaved. The antecedent to the word "first" in this passage is verse 15, wherein Paul had stated that living saints would not be rewarded ahead of those who had died in the Lord. So that what the apostle said was "first" (i.e., before the living Christians are raptured) the souls of those who sleep will be reunited with the living saints; then (only after this has *first* been done) we that are alive, that are left, shall together with them be caught up (raptured) in the clouds, to meet the Lord in the air.

## XI

## THE JUDGMENT

Judgment is a natural part of God's ongoing plan. Many acts of God, dating back to the fall of man in the Garden of Eden, are classed as judgments by the Bible writers. God has judged national Israel many times. For example, Israel's many captivities are called judgments of God upon his people; and these many judgments culminated in her national destruction by Titus in A.D. 70. The church too has undergone many judgments of God throughout her history. Individual Christians were judged, and justified, at the time of their repentance and conversion. Nations too have been judged. In fact, every great catastrophe is looked upon by the Scriptures as God's intervening judgments. Both John the Baptist and Jesus announced that judgment was ushered into the world at the first advent (Matt. 3:10-12; John 12:31).

All these judgments, however, are partial and incomplete. They foreshadow a final day in history when a general judgment will bring history to its close and commence the final state. This final judgment will follow immediately after the second coming, general resurrection, and rapture.

When the last trump sounds, it will be the signal for a number of things to happen. Among them will be the following.

1. The Lord will descend from heaven accompanied by a heavenly host of angels. He will bring with him the souls of all the saints (believers) who have died, from the creation until his second coming. At death these souls left their mortal bodies; the bodies returned to the earth while the souls went immediately into the presence of God (Ecc. 12:7).

2. All the graves will open. All (both living and dead) will receive new bodies. We must *imply* this concerning the unsaved, for while the Scriptures intimate that they will have bodies matching their evil souls, nothing specific is said concerning the bodies of the wicked. It seems logical to assume that — since the righteous are

to receive immortal bodies to correspond with their immortal souls — the wicked would also have mortal bodies to match their mortal souls. We use the word "mortal" here in the sense of earthly as against the heavenly bodies of saints. Both will remain throughout eternity.

3. All saints, living and dead, having been transformed — the souls of those who have died in the Lord will unite with the new bodies coming out of the grave — will be caught up to meet the Lord in the air. However, his train will not stop in mid-air. Rather, the saints will meet him for the purpose of escorting him to the earth.

4. The Lord, upon coming to the earth "with his saints," will immediately inaugurate the general and final judgment. God the Father will judge through God the Son. The saints, owing to their being joint-heirs with Christ, will assist Christ in the judgment. In other words, our part will be in and through our relationship to our Lord. The glory will be due him.

In outlining these events in numerical order, we, in the words of Paul, "speak as a man." For, after all, God is not limited by time or space. From his perspective all things in the end of time will happen simultaneously. From our finite vantage point, however, it is necessary to record them as though they are to happen in sequence. Even a theological mind such as Paul's was limited by the use of human words. The great apostle came close to describing it though when he said that only the twinkling of the human eye would separate the sounding of the trump, the descent, the resurrection, and the rapture (I Cor. 15:51,52).

The final judgment is prefigured many times in the Old Testament. Daniel 7 is one example. It is an indication of the importance of this event when one discovers that Malachi, the last book of the Old Testament, devotes its last chapter to this subject.

"For, behold, the day cometh, it burneth as a furnace; and all the proud, and all that work wickedness, shall be stubble; and the day that cometh shall burn them up, saith Jehovah of hosts, that it shall leave them neither root nor branch. But unto you that fear my name shall the sun of righteousness arise with healing in its wings; and ye shall go forth and gambol as calves of the stall. And ye shall tread down the wicked; for they shall be ashes under the soles of your feet in the day that I make, saith Jehovah of hosts.

"Remember ye the law of Moses my servant, which I commanded unto him in Horeb for all Israel, even statutes and ordinances. Behold, I will send you Elijah the prophet before the great and terrible day of Jehovah come. And he shall turn the heart of the fathers to the children, and the heart of the children to their fathers; lest I come and smite the earth with a curse" (Mal. 4).

Several enlightening things are taught in this chapter by Malachi concerning the judgment. (1) It is to take place on a single day, (2) both the righteous and the wicked will be present on that day, (3) for the wicked it will be a time of punishment, while it will cause the righteous to rejoice, (4) that day will be preceded by a forerunner who comes in the spirit and power of Elijah, who will turn the hearts of many Israelites toward repentance so that they will not be overcome by the day of judgment. These words with reference to Elijah are used in announcing the birth and ministry of John the Baptist, and the New Testament definitely teaches that he fulfilled this prophecy (Matt. 17:13). He was forerunner to the Messiah, he turned the hearts of many Israelites to God, and he announced the coming great day of Jehovah.

While these points are stated in the Old Testament, they are crystallized and enunciated in the New Testament. Jesus stated, "For the Son of man shall come in the glory of his Father with his angels; and then [at that time] shall he render unto every man according to his deeds" (Matt. 16:27).

Every person, from Adam to the last person born on earth, will be present at the judgment. The judgment will not be for the purpose of determining men's destinies, but merely to manifest them. Paul says that all must stand before God (Rom. 14:10; II Cor. 5:10). The saved person will be there to give an account of his deeds since conversion. All things will be made manifest, and the righteous will be rewarded according to deeds done in the body. He must give account of his stewardship. This doctrine needs to be returned to by those of us who believe in eternal security! For many have used this precious doctrine — which is clearly taught in the New Testament — as a cloak for license. Christians need to be reminded that we will stand before God, and that we stand to lose rewards even though our salvation is secure (I Cor. 3:13-15). The Christian will never again be judged for salvation; however, he most definitely will be present at the judgment and will be judged to determine the amount of rewards he will receive.

Again, it would seem superfluous indeed to elaborate on the scriptures which deal with the general judgment, except for the fact that so many persons deny that all will stand before God at the same time. Fortunately, we are not left to haggle over prooftexts on this great subject; many complete sections of the Bible deal with the general judgment.

### Matthew Thirteen

We have already used this passage to point up the fact that the righteous and the wicked will remain on the earth together until the trumpet sounds. It is also appropriate, however, in bringing both groups together at the judgment.

Matthew 13:24-30 records a parable of our Lord related to the judgment. Jesus teaches that no separation is to take place until the harvest, which he later explains as being the end of the world. "Let both grow together until the harvest: and in the time of the harvest I will say to the reapers, Gather up first the tares, and bind them in bundles to burn them; but gather the wheat into my barn."

We are not left in doubt as to the meaning of this parable, for the disciples came to the Lord, after the crowds had left, and asked him for an explanation of it. The Lord obliged them, and his interpretation is recorded in verses 26-43. He said that he himself is the sower, the field is the world, the wheat is the sons of the kingdom (i.e., all believers), the tares are the followers of Satan, the harvest is the end of the world, and the reapers are angels. ". . . so shall it be in the end of the world . . . and shall cast them into the furnace of fire: there shall be the weeping and the gnashing of teeth. Then shall the righteous shine forth as the sun in the kingdom of their Father."

In verses 47-50, the Lord likens the kingdom of heaven to a net used by fishermen. His listeners would immediately visualize what the Master meant by this parable. They had often drawn fishing nets to the shore loaded with good and bad fish. They would also recognize the sorting, casting the bad fish away while keeping the good ones. Let this parable speak for itself.

"Again, the kingdom of heaven is like unto a net, that was cast into the sea, and gathered of every kind: which, when it was filled, they drew up on the beach; and they sat down, and gathered the good into vessels, but the bad they cast away. So shall it be *in the end of the world;* the angels shall come forth, and sever the wicked from among the righteous, and shall cast them into the furnace of fire: there shall be the weeping and the gnashing of teeth" (Matt. 13:47-50).

### Matthew Twenty-five

Verses 31-46 of this chapter represent another clear teaching concerning the judgment. Rather than quote this long section, we present an outline of it.

1. The time? "When the Son of man shall come in his glory."

2. Who will be present? "And before him shall be gathered all the nations."

Dispensationalists attempt to disassociate this scripture from the final judgment of the wicked. They teach that this is a separate judgment "of the nations." This, they say, is not a salvation judgment, but rather a judgment of the Gentile nations to determine which nations will be permitted to remain on earth during the millennium. According to this theory, the Jews will not be present at the judgment in Matthew 25. Nor will it be a judgment of individuals, but rather a judgment of nations.

The dispensationalist prides himself on a literal interpretation of all Scripture. When he comes to this passage, however, he throws all caution to the wind and spiritualizes it completely. "All the nations," he says, actually means "all the nations, *except Israel.*" And whereas the Lord says to the wicked, "Depart . . . into eternal fire" (vs. 41), and "And these shall go away into eternal punishment" (vs. 46), what he actually means is "Depart into an earthly millennium which will have a limited duration of one thousand years."

The dispensationalists' argument rests on their insistence that here we are dealing with nations but not with individuals. Perhaps the quickest way to refute this argument would be to turn to another passage in this same Gospel, where the Lord is again the speaker, and where he uses this same word. "Go ye therefore, and make disciples of all the nations, baptizing them into the name of the Father and of the Son and of the Holy Spirit: teaching them to observe all things whatsoever I commanded you: and lo, I am with you always, even unto the end of the world" (Matt. 28:19,20).[1]

No Protestant, to our knowledge, would attempt to baptize *a nation*, or even teach *a nation*. Rather, we would deal with individuals within each nation. And so it will be at the judgment. To say that all the nations will be there is simply another way of saying that every individual will be present. Nations are made up of individuals.

3. What will happen once the nations are gathered before the throne? "And he shall separate them one from another," placing one group on one side and the other group on the other side. Different destinies will then be assigned to the two groups.

4. What of the righteous group? "Then shall the King say unto them on his right hand, Come, ye blessed of my Father, inherit the Kingdom prepared for you from the foundation of the world."

5. What of the wicked? "Then shall he say also unto them on the left hand, Depart from me, ye cursed, into the eternal fire which is prepared for the devil and his angels" (cf. Rev. 20:10,14).

6. Conclusion? "And these [wicked] shall go away into eternal punishment: but the righteous into eternal life" (vs. 46). See John 5:29; Revelation 20:14.

The following statement by Kik is appropriate here: "The average Christian believes that Matthew 25:31-46 is a picture of the Last Judgment. And he is right. The Premillennialist has to explain this passage away because it does not fit in with his prophetic view. In his interpretation he has to forsake 'literal' interpretation of which he speaks so much. He has to explain that the 'all nations' are not 'all' nations, and that the nations that are there are there only 'representatively.' There is nothing in the passage to indicate this. It is a clear picture of the Last and Universal Judgment" (J. M. Kik, *Matthew Twenty-Four*, p. 94).

---

[1] Mark, in a parallel passage, renders this same commission, ". . . preach the gospel to *every creature*" (Mark 16:15, KJV). This proves conclusively that when the Scriptures speak of "all nations" the reference is to all individuals — including Israelites.

### John Five

Having spoken of the first resurrection (vs. 25), or the new birth, the Lord says: "Marvel not at this: for the hour cometh, in which all that are in the tombs shall hear his voice, and shall come forth; they that have done good, unto the resurrection of life; and they that have done evil, unto the resurrection of judgment" (John 5:28,29). This passage speaks for itself, and certainly leaves no room for plural judgments with intervals between.

"And he charged us to preach unto the people, and to testify that this is he who is ordained of God to be the Judge of the living and the dead" (Acts 10:42).

"Inasmuch as he hath appointed a day in which he will judge the world in righteousness by the man whom he hath ordained. . ." (Acts 17:31).

"For the Son of man shall come in the glory of his Father with his angels; and then shall he render unto every man according to his deeds" (Matt. 16:27).

### The Book of Revelation

The book of Revelation makes it clear that the judgment will be of a universal nature. One such picture is in Revelation 11:18. "And the nations were wroth, and thy wrath came, and the time of the dead to be judged, and the time to give their reward to thy servants the prophets, and to the saints, and to them that fear thy name, the small and the great; and to destroy them that destroy the earth."

Here John declares that his vision of the judgment day revealed that the wicked were punished at the same time the righteous were rewarded. John, in fact, completely interchanged the two groups in this passage. This leaves no doubt that both are to take place simultaneously. Otherwise, John reversed the order of the dispensationalists' plurality of judgments by speaking of the wicked before he spoke of the righteous. Dispensationalists teach that the righteous will be dealt with one thousand and seven years before the wicked are to be judged. Matthew 13:30 also reverses this order. "Gather first the tares. . . ."

*Revelation Twenty*

In the closing verses (vss. 11-15) of this chapter one finds a most descriptive account of the final universal judgment. John was inspired to place this drama in its chronological order; going before it is recorded the millennium, followed by the loosing of Satan, his final persecution of the church, and his overthrow by Christ. Then John records the general judgment, and follows it with a description of the final state in chapters 21 and 22.

John sees the Lord seated upon a great white throne of judgment. This coincides exactly with the prophecy of Christ recorded in Matthew 25:31, "But when the Son of man shall come in his glory, and all the angels with him, then shall he sit on the throne of his glory." The Lord also prophesied in Matthew 25:32ff that all nations would be brought before him, judged, and sent to their different destinies. John sees this too, and describes it simply, "And I saw the dead, the great and the small, standing before the throne." John saw record books at the judgment, and distinguishes one of these books as "the book of life." Certainly this places the righteous at this event, for it would be nonsensical to state that John was here describing their judgment as having taken place one thousand years earlier! In verse 15, John points out that this book of life was the factor which determined whether or not one was cast into the lake of fire. This lake of fire, John said, is the second death, and he stated in verse 6 of this chapter that this second death would have no power over those who had had a part in the first resurrection, i.e., those who had been saved.

John speaks in an inclusive sense of "the dead," and says that they are judged "according to their works" as recorded in "the books." This coincides with other clear scriptures such as Matthew 16:27. After this judgment, says John, the second death was pronounced, at which time death and Hades were cast into the lake of fire. We recall Paul's words in I Corinthians 15:26 that death would be the last enemy abolished, and that this abolishment would come to pass when Christians were resurrected. Jesus taught that the saints would not be resurrected until "the last day" (John 6:39,40, 44,54).

Throughout the Bible there is pictured a *judgment scene*. This scene recurs time and again as the different inspired writers refer here to the complete scene, there to different facets of the total scene. When all the panoramic pictures are carefully analyzed it is not difficult to piece together a total picture consistent with each different reference.

In the judgment scene, God's power and majesty are always exemplified. One time this will be a reference to God the Father, at another, God the Son. Sometimes both are brought together. This shows the great harmony with which God the Father will judge *through* God the Son.

Viewing the scriptural portrayal of the judgment scene, one is reminded of Isaiah's vision as it is recorded in Isaiah 6. There Isaiah described God as being high and lifted up above all else, his presence filling the entire temple, indicating that all was obscured from view except the majesty of God himself. Descriptive words eluded Isaiah as he attempted to recount his vision of God. Words likewise failed the inspired New Testament writers as they described the judgment scene which will appear in the last day. In John's vision of the majestic judgment scene he said the earth and the heaven fled away from it (Rev. 20:11).

Jesus is pictured in this scene as a trial judge. The judge is seated upon a throne befitting his mien. Jesus predicted this judgment scene in Matthew 25:31-46, and fixed the time at his second coming. "Then shall he sit on the throne of his glory: and before him shall be gathered all the nations" (vs. 31).

Paul mentioned the throne of judgment, referring to it as "the judgment-seat of God" (Rom. 14:10). In II Corinthians 5:10, Paul refers to the throne as "the judgment-seat of Christ." In Paul's Christology, as in the rest of the New Testament, each member of the Trinity was equal. Therefore, their titles could be used interchangeably.

John gives his account of the judgment scene in Revelation 20:11-15. He too sees a throne and speaks of it as "a great white throne." This is John's poetic way of speaking of the sovereignty and holiness of the One seated upon the throne.

There are those who attempt to make separate and distinct judgments of the above-mentioned thrones and judgment seats. As they do this, the wish is father to the thought, i.e., they are attempting to justify other, preconceived doctrines based upon an obscure passage of Scripture.

Historical Christian teaching always has been that these are but different angles of one general judgment scene. The great majority of church fathers, creeds, reformers, and commentaries could be cited to this effect.

Record books are brought forth in which perfect records have been kept. Perfect justice will therefore prevail. Certainly this is not always true of our court cases. But here each person is assured of impartial judgment based upon unquestionable records. John the Revelator points out (Rev. 20:12) that actually two sets of books will be produced at the court scene. The first set will condemn every person present as a law breaker. However, the Judge himself has voluntarily undergone punishment in order to pay the penalty demanded by the law! In order to escape the judgment penalty, however, one must have accepted the Judge as his substitution. And this acceptance must have been made before court convened. As individuals accepted this free gift their names were entered in the book of life. This book too will be brought forward at the judgment (Rev. 20:12). "And if any was not found written in the book of life, he was cast into the lake of fire" (Rev. 20:15). Also compare John 5:29 and Matthew 25:46.

The scene under consideration is definitely one of universal judgment. Jesus taught that the repentant would be present with the unrepentant at the judgment. Luke 11:31,32 records these words: "The queen of the south shall rise up in the judgment with the men of this generation, and shall condemn them: for she came from the ends of the earth to hear the wisdom of Solomon; and behold a greater than Solomon is here. The men of Nineveh shall stand up in the judgment with this generation, and shall condemn it; for they repented at the preaching of Jonah; and behold, a greater than Jonah is here."

Sodom and Gomorrah (Matt. 10:15) and Tyre and Sidon (Matt. 11:22) all will be present at the judgment along with those to whom the Lord was speaking on that occasion.

One of the clearest pictures of the last judgment found in the Old Testament is in the book of Daniel. Daniel gives an unmistakable picture of a judgment at which both the wicked and the righteous will be present. "And many of them that sleep in the dust of the earth shall awake, some to everlasting life, and some to

shame and everlasting contempt" (Dan. 12:2). This agrees completely with the New Testament accounts of the judgment scene which
we have already listed (Matt. 25:31-46; Rom. 14:10; II Cor. 5:10;
Rev. 20:11-15). It also agrees closely with John 5:28,29.

Some argue that Daniel did not have in mind a general judgment because he used the word "many" rather than speaking of "all
the dead." To this we answer: (1) Daniel has the righteous and
the wicked being raised and judged together; this regardless of the
number of persons present, outlaws a time interval between the
judgment of the two groups; (2) owing to progressive revelation,
Daniel did not know all the facts concerning the judgment. Certainly
he could not give the exact number who would be present. Daniel
saw a vision of the last judgment, and he saw that *many* were present.
"Many of them that sleep in the dust" in no way contradicts the
fact that these "many" represent "all" who sleep in the dust. Jesus
filled in the details in John 5:28,29 by teaching that all that are in
tombs shall come forth.

Daniel records another vision of the judgment in his seventh
chapter. There Daniel says that "thousands of thousands" ministered
to the judge, and that "ten thousand times ten thousand stood before
him" (Dan. 7:10). Most interpreters, considering Daniel's apocalyptic language, do not take this to be a literally exact number. It is
more likely that Daniel is attempting to point out that those present
at the judgment will be "many."

It is a mistake to apply hyperliteralism to any of the descriptive
passages which portray the judgment scene. Here, it would seem
obvious, God condescends to the level of our human understanding.
He accommodates the word pictures to our understanding. For
certainly God does not need literal books in order to know what each
person has done. The first century Christians fully understood this
language. For they were accustomed to the Bema judgment-seats of
earthly judges such as Pilate (Matt. 27:19; John 19:13) and Herod
(Acts 12:21), etc. These judgment-seats were elevated and were
throne-like. Their elaborateness would depend upon the station of
the judge.

Another measure of the universality of the final judgment is
the singular way in which it is referred to throughout the Bible. One
never reads of "days of judgment," but rather of "the day of judgment," or simply "that day." Christians are to be rewarded at

"that day." The unsaved are to be punished "at that day" (Matt. 7:22,23). The New Testament speaks with finality of "the judgment [singular] of the great day [singular]" in Jude 6.

Paul describes a single day of wrath (Rom. 2:5) during which God will "render to every man according to his works" (1) to one group, eternal life (vs. 7), (2) to another group, wrath and indignation (vs. 8). All this is to happen, says the great Christian theologian, "in the day when God shall judge the secrets of men, according to my gospel, by Jesus Christ" (Rom. 2:6). Also compare John 12:48; I Thess. 1:10; I Cor. 5:5; II Tim. 1:12; 4:1; I John 4:17.

Yes, both the righteous and the wicked are woven by Scripture into the portrait of the judgment scene. The righteous are pictured as joyous, owing to their standing in Christ. The wicked are pictured, always and without exception, as being fearful, bitter, and filled with awe at what they have rejected. As in the case of other doctrines, synonymous terms are used to describe the judgment — such terms as "the judgment seat of Christ," "the great white throne," "the judgement," "the day of judgment," "that day," and so forth. These terms do not portray several different judgments; they are merely different parts of one great mosaic.

# XII

## REVELATION TWENTY

Without agreement on some basic premises, there can never be a proper exegesis of any passage of Scripture. Therefore, before beginning the actual exegesis of Revelation 20, we make the following observations.

1. The passage itself gives no explanation of John's meaning. Therefore, one must interpret this scripture by other scriptures.

2. There is a definite rule of hermeneutics which teaches us that obscure passages of Scripture must be governed by the clear passages. To teach that this obscure passage near the very end of the Bible is the key to understanding the rest of the Bible is to fly in the face of such known rules of interpretation.

3. It is self-evident that this lone passage dealing with the millennium is couched in a book of the Bible literally filled with symbols, numerology, figures of speech, poetic language, spiritual lessons couched in Old Testament terminology, etc. Although this is true, the very word "revelation" in verse 1 of chapter 1 means "unveiling." This first verse of the Revelation also informs us that this unveiling was "signified" to John. This word means that the message, or unveiling, was given in symbols, or figures. So, there is something amiss when a symbol which was given to *unveil* God's plan becomes a *veil of obscurity* dropped over in such a manner that only a chosen few can understand its meaning.

"The youthful student of Scripture should be reminded, first of all, that its figurative language is no less certain and truthful than its plain and literal declarations. The figures of the Bible are employed not simply to please the imagination and excite the feelings, but to teach eternal verities" (E. P. Barrows, *Companion to the Bible*, p. 557).

4. Since the Revelation was written primarily to bring comfort to the Christians of John's day, who were being persecuted, it is obvious that a correct understanding must be gained by learning what these symbols and figures meant to the people of that day. A study

of that period reveals the fact that John's readers were accustomed to the Greek theatre, where everything was acted out, with the actors wearing different masks in different scenes to bring out the characters they portrayed. Therefore, it was the most natural thing for God to inspire John to portray his spiritual lessons as scenes of a drama of real life. We concur with the devoted New Testament scholars who have discovered for us that the Revelation is written as a drama and the form is apocalyptic. Two especially well-written books on this subject are *Worthy Is the Lamb*, by Ray Summers, and *The Meaning and Message of the Book of Revelation*, by Edward A. McDowell. Both books were published by Broadman Press, Nashville, in 1951.

5. Apocalyptic writings are known to have definite characteristics, such as figurative language, imagery, numerology, hyperbole, and the like. These are used for a purpose — to teach spiritual lessons to God's people. These characteristics are used much in the same way a producer uses stage props and scenery. The important thing in watching a drama is not the props, but the message they help to portray. The same is true with reference to the apocalyptic literature, including that used by inspired men of the Bible. The numerology, imagery, etc., are not meant to be ends within themselves, but rather they are used as means to an end in teaching a lesson God has for his people. Few people would think of attending a play and becoming so interested in the scenery as to substitute it for the play itself. Yet this is often done by many who study the apocalyptic books of the Bible. They become fascinated by the chin-whiskers worn by the actor and miss his lines completely. They are so enraptured by the stage setting that they fail to grasp the story itself.

6. An axiom of Bible study is that most sections demand literal interpretation unless the context or other known Scripture passages demand figurative or spiritual interpretation. In apocalyptic literature the very opposite is true; here one must interpret figuratively, unless literal interpretation is absolutely demanded. The nature of such books as Ezekiel, Daniel, and the Revelation makes understanding impossible apart from an appreciation of the tools of the artist who painted the picture.

7. Premillennialists take only a part of Revelation 20 literally, while freely "spiritualizing" most of the chapter. They also fail to harmonize the chapter, stopping short after verse 10. Every part of

the chapter should be interpreted in its context. Whereas verses 1 through 10 are said to teach a literal millennial period following the second coming of Christ and falling between two resurrections and two judgments, verses 11 through 15 definitely teach a *general* judgment, attended by *all* the dead, "small and great," *after* the millennium. These verses will be dealt with in more detail later; suffice it to say now that to find two opposing doctrines in the same chapter of the Bible is to contend that the Bible contradicts itself. Of course, no person who accepts the Bible as infallible can believe such a contradiction exists.

Revelation 20 falls into four natural divisions, each division containing a central thought. Let us get these divisions before us and interpret them as teaching spiritual truths in spiritual language, under the religious symbolism of the age in which they were written. Our conclusion must then be substantiated by clear teachings found in other sections of God's Word.


### 1. *The Binding of Satan*

"And I saw an angel coming down out of heaven, having the key of the abyss and a great chain in his hand. And he laid hold on the dragon, the old serpent, which is the Devil and Satan, and bound him for a thousand years, and cast him into the abyss, and shut it, and sealed it over him, that he should deceive the nations no more, until the thousand years should be finished: after this he must be loosed for a little time" (Rev. 20:1-3).

A close reading of these verses makes it obvious that they contain one central thought — a binding of Satan. It is also obvious that the thought is conveyed through symbolism. Even those who insist on a literal one thousand year binding of Satan hasten to say that most of the other symbols are to be interpreted *spiritually!* They admit that the key, the abyss, the chain, the sealing, etc., are obviously figures of speech; they also agree that Satan is not literally a dragon and at the same time a serpent, but that John is describing him poetically. While these folk insist on taking *part* of this chapter hyperliterally, they can see the incongruities involved in binding Satan, a spiritual being, with physical chains and keys. This is why they admit that parts of this section of Revelation are to receive a figurative interpretation.

The question arises here, as in all parts of the Revelation, as to just who is to be the judge in deciding what parts of a given verse are to be interpreted literally and which parts symbolically. Who gives the millennialist the right to decide that one word is literal while the very next word is symbolic, then to ostracize another Christian for daring to suggest that *both* words might be symbolism?

To say that Satan is to be bound after Christ comes the second time, then released again, contradicts many clear passages of Scripture. Assuming this to be so, and assuming that one Scripture passage does not contradict another, let us search out clear teachings of the New Testament concerning a binding of Satan. It is to be noted that John nowhere fixes the *time* for this event.

Only one event coincides with John's picturesque language here in Revelation 20:1-3 — this event is the defeat of Satan brought about by Christ's first advent and crucifixion. For those who object that Satan still has much power today, let it be noted that John does not picture him as obliterated, but merely imprisoned. Many a prisoner has been known to operate from inside barred windows through henchmen on the outside. And many a dog, though bound, has bitten people who came within the confines of his chain. Satan is bound, but with a long chain. Our Lord certainly overcame him and pronounced sentence upon him (John 12:31); however, the sentence will not be completely executed until the second coming (II Thess. 2:7,8). Satan was eternally doomed when, on the cross, Christ bruised the head of the serpent in fulfillment of Genesis 3:15.

Floyd E. Hamilton (*The Basis of Millennial Faith*) makes some helpful observations on the subject of Satan's being bound.

"I suppose that no one would insist that Satan is to be bound with a literal chain of iron or some other metal, for Satan is a spirit and material chains could not hold him captive for a moment. *Binding always means the limitation of power in some way.* When men bound themselves with an oath not to do something, they agreed to limit their own power and rights to the extent of their oaths. A man and wife are bound by their marriage vows, but that does not mean that they are bound in respect to other relationships in life. A slave is bound to his master, but he lives his life as a human being with freedom to do countless other things which do not interfere with his relationship as a slave to his master. So Satan's being bound does not mean that he is powerless to tempt people, and we know that he does. It is merely limitation of Satan's power in one particular respect especially, that of ability to 'deceive the nations.' During the interadventual period the gospel is to be proclaimed to all nations, and Satan is powerless to prevent it. The way of salvation has been opened to all nations and there is nothing that Satan can do to block that way" (pp. 131-32; italics added).

"In Hebrews 2:14, the writer tells us, 'that through death He might *bring to nought* him that had the power of death, that is, the devil.' Christ brought the devil to nought, that is, He limited the devil's power in such a way that all his efforts amounted to nothing, and his power was definitely frustrated. All these things show that in the New Testament Christ claimed that in a very real sense he had bound Satan, and limited his power. In Revelation 20, one particular aspect of that binding is before us, namely, the limiting of Satan's power to deceive the nations as he did before the coming of Christ. From that time forward during the whole of the interadventual dispensation Satan is defeated in fact. He can still go about like a roaring lion seeking whom he may devour, but in this particular respect he is a caged lion" (*ibid.*, pp. 132-33).

When Jesus sent the Twelve on a preaching mission (Luke 9:1) he gave them "power and authority over all demons." He also sent seventy disciples on a similar mission, and they returned rejoicing in the fact that "even the demons are subject unto us in thy name" (Luke 10:17). Then it was that Jesus said to them that he beheld Satan fall from heaven. We take this as a reference to his defeat of Satan at the cross (see Rev. 12:7-12). Our Lord went on to say to the seventy disciples, "Behold, I have given you authority . . . over all the power of the enemy" (Luke 10:19).

Matthew records a time during our Lord's earthly ministry (Matt. 12:22-29) when the enemies of Christ accused him of casting out demons in the power of Satan himself. Our Lord took this opportunity to point out that his mighty works proved (1) that he had established his kingdom (vs. 28), and (2) that he, being stronger than Satan, had come into Satan's house (this world) and *bound* him (vs. 29).

Following the Temptation, our Lord issued a command to Satan which was immediately obeyed (Matt. 4:10,11). Our Lord referred to his crucifixion as the "casting out" of Satan (John 12:31-33). Paul also refers to the cross as follows: "Having despoiled the principalities and the powers, he made a show of them openly, triumphing over them in it" (Col. 2:15). John informs us (I John 3:8): "To this end was the Son of God manifested, that he might destroy the works of the devil." Paul shows the defeat of Satan's power when he says (Eph. 4:8): ". . . When he ascended on high, he led captivity captive. . . ." The writer of Hebrews (2:14) says that through his death our Lord "brought to nought" the devil. This shows conclusively that our Lord bound Satan (i.e., limited his power) at the first advent.

We concur with Hamilton that John, in Revelation 20:1-3, refers to only one facet of that limitation, that is, Satan's power to deceive the nations by keeping them from hearing the gospel. Before Christ came, only the Jew (except for the rare instances when Gentile proselytes were circumcised and made partakers with Israel) was offered the plan of salvation. Thus Satan was able to deceive the nations (Gentiles) by keeping them from hearing the gospel and being saved. After Calvary, however, Satan's power to do this was bound. Our Lord then said: "All authority hath been given *unto me* in heaven and on earth. Go ye *therefore*, and make disciples of *all the nations*, . . ." (Matt. 28:18,19).

Having said that Satan was bound, John went on to say that he would be released at the end of the millennium "for a little time" (Rev. 20:3). Now this also is in keeping with the clear teachings of the New Testament. This loosing, I believe, corresponds with the appearing of the man of sin referred to by the apostle Paul in II Thessalonians 2:1-12. Paul's statement, "The mystery of lawlessness doth already work: only there is one that restraineth now, until he be taken out of the way," corresponds perfectly with what we have said about the limiting of Satan's present power. This restrainer is taken to be the Holy Spirit. This also points up the fact that Satan *is bound*, having only such power as God grants him. Whenever God is ready, *he* will remove the restrainer; that is, the Holy Spirit will "be taken out of the way" (II Thess. 2:7). Then, says Paul, the lawless one (man of sin) will be given full power to deceive them that perish (vs. 10). Paul goes on to say that the Lord Jesus Christ will slay the man of sin (Satan) at His second coming. Compare this teaching and order of events with John the Revelator's teaching in Revelation 20. John says that after the millennium Satan, who has been chained during that period, will be loosed for a little time (vs. 3) and that he will then go about to deceive the nations. John says, in symbolic language (vs. 9), that fire from heaven will put down Satan and his followers. A comparison of II Thessalonians 1 and 2 with Revelation 20 cannot help but reveal that Paul and John both speak of the same events. And both passages agree entirely with many other clear passages of the Bible dealing with our Lord's second coming and events preceding it.

### 2. *The Millennial Reign*

"And I saw thrones, and they sat upon them, and judgment was given unto them: and I saw the souls of them that had been beheaded for the testimony of Jesus, and for the word of God, and such as worshipped not the beast, neither his image, and received not the mark upon their forehead and upon their hand; and they lived, and reigned with Christ a thousand years. The rest of the dead lived not until the thousand years should be finished. This is the first resurrection. Blessed and holy is he that hath part in the first resurrection: over these the second death hath no power; but they shall be priests of God and of Christ, and shall reign with him a thousand years" (Rev. 20:4-6).

The main thought of this passage is the millennial reign. This reign takes place during the same period in which Satan is bound. We established from verses 1-3, compared with clear New Testament passages, that the time of Satan's binding is the interadvent period. So that to fix the time of Satan's binding is to fix, at the same time, the time of the millennium.

Keeping in mind John's use of drama, symbols, and numerology, let us examine the stage setting and "props" for this depicted event. Then let us arrive at its message in the light of other New Testament passages. John says the people of this millennial reign are seated upon thrones. He then describes those who are seated on the thrones as persons who were martyred for their faithfulness to Christ, having refused to worship the beast or his image; their faithfulness was evident by their not having the mark of the beast on either their foreheads or their hands.

Here, then, are three characteristics of those on the stage of this inspired drama: (1) they are reigning with Christ; (2) they are martyrs for the faith; and (3) they do not have the mark of the beast. Actually, this is a description (in figurative language) of every Christian of every age. Although some feel the word "soul" in this passage can refer only to those who have departed this life, this term is used throughout the Bible to refer to living people (Gen. 46:26; Ex. 1:5; 12:4; Acts 2:41; 7:14; I Peter 3:20).

As for the reign of the saints, John himself referred to the living Christians as kings and priests (Rev. 1:6). Certainly a king is one who reigns. Paul speaks in the past tense (Col. 1:13) when he pictures the present reign of the saints: "Who delivered us out of the power of darkness, and *hath translated us into the kingdom* of the Son of his love." Ephesians 2:6 also is in the past tense: "And raised us up with him, and *made* us to sit with him in the heavenly places in Christ Jesus."

As to the description of those on the thrones as martyrs, this also can be applied to every Christian, since the words "martyr" and "witness" are taken from the same root word. Every genuine believer is a witness (martyr) and is commanded to sacrifice his life for the Lord. To become a genuine believer, or follower of Christ, is to become, immediately, persecuted — martyred — for his sake. In the Gospel of John, chapter 15, verse 20, our Lord himself tells us what to expect: ". . . A servant is not greater than his Lord. If they persecuted me they will also persecute you; . . ." In John 16:33 Jesus says: "In the world ye shall have tribulation: but be of good cheer; I have overcome the world." Paul tells us in II Timothy 3:12, "Yea, and *all* that would live godly in Christ Jesus shall suffer persecution."

In Revelation 7 John saw the future of all the saints of all time (vs. 9) and described this entire multitude as those who had come through the great tribulation (vs. 13), having been washed in the blood of the lamb. The third characteristic of these saints was their not having the mark of the beast. This would immediately cause a mental picture to form in the minds of the early Christians. The Roman rulers had attempted to deify themselves. The big contest in John's day was between Christ and emperor worship. John himself was a prisoner on the Isle of Patmos because he refused to substitute "Lord Caesar" for his Lord Jesus. It is a known historical fact that Domitian had statues of himself placed in strategic places and commanded all people to bow down to them. A committee was appointed to see that each person paid homage to these statues, thus acknowledging the emperor as divine. All who complied with this order received an official seal upon a part of the body, and without this mark a person could neither buy nor sell in the Roman world. This was what John called the "mark of the beast." The first beast was the emperor, while the second beast referred to the enforcement committee.

In contrast to this "mark of the beast," each Christian receives the mark of God's approval (see II Cor. 1:22; Eph. 1:13; 4:30; Rev. 7:3,4). Thus the Christian of every generation is a martyr for his faith, while at the same time he reigns with Christ. Someone has well said that God does not take his people *around* persecution, but that he protects them through it. Here, then, is a divine paradox: God reigns spiritually in the hearts of his people even while they are persecuted in their physical surroundings. Christians indeed find their lives by losing them.

Those who reign during the millennium are said to have experienced a "first resurrection," while the rest of the "dead" lived not until the thousand years were ended. Premillennialists take this passage to indicate two bodily resurrections, separated by one thousand years. This contradicts many clear passages of Scripture and indeed contradicts the last division of this very same twentieth chapter of the Revelation.

When viewed symbolically, however, this passage coincides nicely with many clear passages from the New Testament. The new birth is spoken of in many places as a resurrection from the dead. Certainly this is the *first* resurrection. In the Gospel of John the same man who wrote the Revelation records a message of Jesus in which he spoke of *two distinct resurrections*, one of them being spiritual (the new birth), while the second is physical. This was dealt with in chapter IX.

In speaking of the first resurrection (Rev. 20:5), John said the rest of the dead lived not (the word "again" is not in the original) until the thousand years were finished. This is in perfect agreement with John 5:25, where our Lord said that only those who heard (believed) his voice would live. It is, in fact, in agreement with the entire New Testament, which teaches that all unbelievers remain dead in trespasses and sin, while all believers have already been made alive — resurrected.

Revelation 20:6 is a restatement of John 5:24, where our Lord is recorded as saying that the believer "hath eternal life, and cometh not into judgment, but hath passed out of death into life." Note the similarity of language as John says in Revelation 20:6 that he who has part in the first resurrection will escape the second death. That the second death is *spiritual* rather than physical is apparent from the fact that those cast into the lake of fire — which is the second death (Rev. 20:24) — are tormented throughout eternity. It is incongruous to have John say that a *physical* resurrection guarantees against a *spiritual* punishment. Both are spiritual, both the first resurrection and the second death. "Blessed and holy is he that hath part in the *first resurrection*: on such the *second death* hath no power . . ." (Rev. 20:6).

### 3. *The Loosing of Satan*

"And when the thousand years are finished, Satan shall be loosed out of his prison, and shall come forth to deceive the nations which are in the four corners of the earth, Gog and Magog, to gather them together to the war: the number of whom is as the sand of the sea. And they went up over the breadth of the earth and compassed the camp of the saints about, and the beloved city: and fire came down out of heaven, and devoured them. And the devil that deceived them was cast into the lake of fire and brimstone, where are also the beast and the falst prophet; and they shall be tormented day and night for ever and ever" (Rev. 20:7-10).

Everything dealt with in the first six verses of Revelation 20 is already in the process of fulfillment. Here, in verses 7-10, John is given a vision of things to happen just before and at the time of our Lord's second coming. Satan, whose power was limited (bound) by our Lord's victory on the cross, will have his complete power restored in the very end of the millennium, and will begin a full-scale warfare against the church. Paul informs us (II Thess. 2:7) that this warfare is already going on, but in a limited way. This limitation is because of the present "binding" of Satan in his power to deceive the nations concerning salvation. In calling this final battle Gog and Magog, John is following the pattern of the entire book of Revelation — he uses Old Testament terminology to teach New Testament spiritual truths.

John does not leave his hearers to speculate as to what he means by this coming battle which he calls "Gog and Magog." In verse 9 he says that the target in this battle will be the "beloved city," which is headquarters for the "camp of the saints." Contrary to those who make this battle apply to national Israel, John tells us that the beloved city is actually the church, which, of course, includes all believers. All are agreed that only the church is referred to in the New Testament as the bride of Christ. In chapter 21 of the Revelation John specifically says that the city of Jerusalem in his apocalyptic message represents the bride of Christ, or the church.

"And there came one of the seven angels who had the seven bowls, who were laden with the seven last plagues; and he spake with me, saying, Come hither, I will show thee the *bride, the wife of the Lamb*. And he carried me away in the Spirit to a mountain great and high, and showed me the *holy city Jerusalem*, coming down out of heaven from God, having the Glory of God: . . ." (Rev. 21:9-11).

The writer of Hebrews used this same symbolic language in speaking of the *present* position of the saints: "But ye are come unto Mount Zion, and unto the city of the living God, the heavenly Jerusalem, and to innumerable hosts of angels, to the general assembly and church of the firstborn who are enrolled in heaven, . . ." (Heb. 12:22,23).

John predicts how this battle will end and also the destiny of Satan who will lead it. John saw that when the battle reached its very height, then fire from heaven would destroy all the enemies of the saints (Rev. 20:9). Paul describes the same event, in II Thessalonians 1:6-2:8, and he, too, teaches that the second coming of our Lord will bring this great battle to its end. John describes it as fire from heaven, while Paul terms it the breath of Jesus' mouth at the manifestation of his coming. Paul also mentioned flaming fire in connection with the second coming (II Thess. 1:7). To make these two different events is to beg the question by haggling over word pictures.

"For the mystery of lawlessness doth already work: only there is one that restraineth now, until he be taken out of the way. *And then shall be revealed the lawless one, whom the Lord Jesus shall slay with the breath of his mouth, and bring to nought by the manifestation of his coming*; even he, whose coming is according to the working of Satan with all power and signs and lying wonders, and with all deceit of unrighteousness for them that perish; because they received not the love of the truth, that they might be saved. And for this cause *God sendeth them a working of error, that they should* believe a lie: that they all might be judged who believed not the truth, but had pleasure in unrighteousness" (II Thess. 2:7-12).

Satan's being loosed for a little time coincides with Paul's man of sin being given full sway just before the second coming of our Lord. The fact that Paul says God will send a working of error upon the unbelievers at that time also points up the fact that Satan's power to deceive is limited (bound), and that he can act only as God *permits*.

### 4. *The General Judgment*

"And I saw a great white throne, and him that sat upon it, from whose face the earth and the heaven fled away; and there was found no place for them. And I saw the dead, the great and the small, standing before the throne; and the books were opened: and another book was opened, which is the book of life: and the dead were judged out of the things which were written in the books, according to their works. And the sea gave up the dead that were in it; and death and Hades gave up the dead that were in them: and they were judged every man according to their works. And death and Hades were cast into the lake of fire. This is the second death, even the lake of fire. And if any was not found written in the book of life, he was cast into the lake of fire" (Rev. 20:11-15).

In this future scene John prophesies what is to happen following the millennium. He sees the time when the millennium will have ended, and Satan will have been released for a little time. He will have led an unprecedented warfare against the Christian church, only to have been defeated by the glorious appearing of the Christ. Then John sees that a general judgment follows.

That verses 11-15 depict a general resurrection followed by a general judgment seems so self-evident as not to require a discussion. Suffice it to say that in these verses we find: (1) all the dead are to be present at this judgment, "the great and the small"; (2) two different kinds of books will be used, the book of life containing the names of the saints, and the books containing the works of the unsaved; (3) a separation will take place, determined by the book of life (cf. Matt. 25:46 and John 5:29 with this section); and (4) death will be conquered at that time: "And death and Hades were cast into the lake of fire." Paul says elsewhere that the *last* enemy to be destroyed is death, and he definitely fixes that as the same time that Christians are to be resurrected and rewarded (1 Cor. 15:26,51-55).

It would be difficult to find a more exact description of a general judgment than that recorded in Revelation 20:11-15. We know from other scriptures that the resurrection will precede the judgment. And if one is general, both are general. To base a doctrine of *two* bodily resurrections upon a chapter containing this vivid picture of *one general resurrection* is a poor searching of the Scriptures. While dogmatism is unwarranted in any part of Revelation 20, verses 11-15 lend themselves more readily to dogmatism than do verses 4-6.

As we close this section, a definition of terms would seem to be in order. As one studies the charts which dispensationalists use so profusely, one will notice that they often depict a "first" physical resurrection followed one thousand and seven years later by the "general resurrection." This is a contradiction of terms. For the general resurrection has traditionally referred to a resurrection of all the dead of all time. If, as the premillennialists teach, all Christians are raised separately from the unsaved — then a second resurrection could not be properly called a general resurrection.

What the premillennialists actually have are two *partial* resurrections. In terming the latter of these a general resurrection they are attempting to stay within the framework of historic Christian teaching while at the same time inserting doctrines which disagree radically with the historic teachings of the New Testament, church fathers, Protestant reformers, and commentaries. This is another of those places where the chiliast cannot have his theological cake and eat it.

To believe in a general judgment is immediately to cease being a chiliast in the true sense of the word.

## Conclusion

Far from being a key, Revelation 20 is a recapitulation of many clear teachings of the Bible. While its language is apocalyptic, it does not contradict the clear passages. It reiterates those teachings.

In studying the Revelation one needs constantly to keep in mind Paul's admonition that the letter kills while the spirit gives life. One must go beyond the stage settings and chin whiskers in John's spiritual drama. The *spirit* of Revelation 20 coincides perfectly with the clear teachings of the New Testament. Here, as in John 5, the writer describes two resurrections — the first being the new birth, the second being the bodily resurrection. The first resurrection takes place when one is born from above, and, immediately, one is made a participant in the ongoing millennial reign of Christ; this is the kingdom of God, wherein God now reigns in the hearts of all true believers. The second resurrection will take place at the harvest which is the end of this present age; this will precede the general judgment (compare Matt. 25:31-46 with Rev. 20:11-15). This is to be followed only by the final state which is described in Revelation 21 and 22.

The present phase of the kingdom and the millennium are synonymous terms. The kingdom is best defined as *God reigning in the hearts of his followers*. The great majority of chiliasts — premillennialists, futurists, and dispensationalists — agree that the kingdom of God is the millennium. They argue, however, that it does not exist today, but will be established after the second coming of Christ. They distinguish between the kingdom of heaven — which they admit exists today — and the kingdom of God.

The New Testament uses the terms "kingdom of God" and "kingdom of heaven" interchangeably (compare Matt. 11:12 with Luke 16:16; and Matt. 4:17 with Mark 1:14,15). Since the kingdom and millennium are admittedly one and the same, and since the kingdom already is a reality — then the millennium of Revelation is realized eschatology. The millennium, like the kingdom, was instituted by our Lord.

Although Jesus manifested the kingdom (millennium) at his first advent, it will be consummated at his second coming, then turned over to God the Father.[1]

One cannot accept the fact of a general resurrection or universal judgment and still be a chiliast. Thus to prove from the Scriptures that there will be a universal or general judgment is to prove, *ipso facto*, that the millennium — whatever else one might believe about it — must take place *before* the judgment.

Revelation 20, the only chapter in the entire Bible which mentions the millennium, records a universal judgment (vss. 11-15) *following* the millennium.

Historic Christian teaching has always been that (1) as a result of the fall, the earth and mankind have been under Satan's spell; (2) the Old Testament prophets predicted a golden age during which Messiah would overcome Satan, write God's laws on the hearts of God's people, and reign over the earth with his people; (3) Jesus, at his first advent, overcame Satan (bound him) and instituted the golden age; (4) all believers — having been released from Satan's power — reign with Christ; (5) Jesus will return a second time to the earth, and at that time there will be a universal resurrection, universal judgment, renewing of the earth; (6) then follows the final state in which all believers will reign throughout eternity in heaven while all unbelievers will suffer punishment in hell throughout eternity.

These historic teachings represent the thinking of the great majority of church fathers, Protestant reformers, Christian educators, and recognized commentaries. They are also subscribed to by every major denomination, and no extant creed differs noticeably from them. Yet, surprisingly enough, beliefs which are foreign to these have infiltrated just about every known denomination.

These beliefs are taught throughout the Bible in a progressive revelation. They are just as surely taught in the book of Revelation. There, John uses the style he was inspired to use, i.e., apocalyptic

---

[1]Each school of thought agrees that the millennium represents a co-reigning with Jesus. The Scriptures teach that the kingdom presently belongs to Christ, but that he will turn it over to the Father once the last enemy (death) has been destroyed. In order for one to *co-reign* with Jesus, that reign would need to take place before the kingdom ceases to be under the jurisdiction of Jesus.

language. This type of language makes great use of poetry, symbols, numerology, and the like. John forewarns his readers of his intention to do this very thing. This is the meaning of the word "signify" in the very first verse of the Revelation.

Apocalyptic language does not make the book of Revelation any less true than any other part of the Bible. In fact, there is usually deeper truth in symbolic language than can be expressed in plain words. This apocalyptic language does make it extremely important that each reader bridle his imagination. Otherwise, he may place too much emphasis upon the stage and actually miss the message of the play itself.

# XIII

## THE MILLENNIUM

Millennialism must play an important role in any approach to eschatology. It has in fact shaped most of the books on the subject. Most millennial thinking begins with Revelation 20, since this is the only place in the entire Bible where the one thousand year reign is even mentioned. We feel that Revelation 20 ought to be our last stop, not our first. There are three main theories concerning the millennial period of Revelation 20. Premillennialism teaches that there will be an earthly reign of one thousand years *after* the return of Christ to the earth. Postmillennialism advocates a thousand year reign *before* the return of our Lord. Amillennialism, as we know it today, believes the one thousand years of Revelation 20 represent a perfect period of time which began at the incarnation and will last *until* the return of our Lord. It ought to be pointed out that few scholars today, of any school of millennial thought, take the one thousand years of Revelation 20 as exactly one thousand literal years; most take it to represent a perfect period of time in the plan of God. The differences of opinion concern the time when this period will take place, rather than the length of the period. An excellent book describing all three theories is *The Basis of Millennial Faith*.[1]

One who adopts any particular school of millennialism *in toto* places limiting boundaries upon his study of God's Word. For any and every passage then must have read into it one's interpretation of Revelation 20. If any passage appears to differ from that millennial thinking, then such passage must be altered to fit one's presupposition, based on this one obscure passage. This is to let the tail wag the dog.

In view of all that we know about the characteristics of apocalyptic literature — especially its use of symbolism and numerology —

---

[1] Floyd E. Hamilton, *The Basis of Millennial Faith*, Grand Rapids: Wm. B. Eerdmans Publishing Company, 1955.

it seems absurd to let one obscure passage in an apocalyptic book govern the entire Bible. It seems much more logical to read Revelation 20 *after* one has read all the scriptures preceding it, rather than making it one's starting point. Then this obscure passage ought to be made to harmonize with all clear passages of Scripture. This we have tried to do.

To use Revelation 20 as a key to the entire Bible becomes even more preposterous when one realizes that all three millennial theories are constantly undergoing changes. For example, there is very little resemblance between historic premillennialism and the premillennialism of our time. The dispensationalists have even a third brand of premillennialism. And, whereas amillennialism technically means "no millennium," all leading amillennial thinkers known to this writer very definitely do believe in a millennium, and most of them fix it as the period between the two advents of our Lord. Some amillennialists believe this reign includes all believers in Christ, while others of that school limit it to Christians who are now in heaven.

It is regrettable that all of us are expected to take an either-or position concerning the three above-mentioned theories of millennialism. If one is not "pre-mil," then it is immediately assumed that he subscribes *in toto* to the theories of either the "post-mill" or "a-mil." Indeed, some allow but two alternatives: their own school or liberalism. In this area of theology, especially, a label often becomes a libel. A man is forced to choose a title, and there are but three choices open to him. The time has arrived when all man-made theories should be discarded, and eschatology should be based upon the question, "What saith the scripture?"

In each of the three schools of thought concerning millennialism, there have been equally noble and conservative men. We might be surprised to find elements of truth in each of the camps. Theological chauvinism is dangerous. Many practice the dictum: "My school of interpretation, may she always be right, but right or wrong, my school." This is spiritual pride, and is very sinful. Until conservative men drop this attitude and ask, "What saith the scripture?" our divisions will continue. Many conservative men today are compelled to be what the sociologist terms "marginal men," that is, they do not fit into one group, and yet they do not want to be classified with the other group.

Since the Scriptures mention no specific millennial label, and since the labels we have are based upon one obscure passage of Scripture, we choose to disavow all such titles and simply seek out the scriptural teachings without any title. Perhaps the wag was not too far afield when he coined a fourth title, "pan-millennialism," which simply holds that everything will pan out the way God wants it in the end. We do hasten to say, however, that since this subject has been so well thought out and so thoroughly dealt with by men from these various schools of thought, it should not be thought at all strange if the conclusions of this book resemble the thinking of one or more of them. Indeed, it would be strange if it were otherwise. Truth, like gold, is where you find it.

The word "millennium" is based upon the mention in Revelation 20:1-10 of a period of one thousand years. This is the only place in the entire Bible where this one thousand year period is mentioned. The term, while not actually used in the Bible, is derived from two Latin words: *mille*, meaning thousand, and *annum*, meaning year.

Some students of the Bible believe these ten verses in the Revelation serve as the key to understanding the entire Bible. Now, it seems strange indeed that God would place such an important key in the most *figurative* book in the Bible, then couch it in such language that thousands of intelligent Christians would be unable to interpret it correctly! Nor does it speak well for progressive revelation to place the key to understanding at the very end of the Bible. This would mean that one who began at the book of Genesis — certainly a logical place to start — would read the entire Bible, only to come to the end of sixty-six books and discover that he had not been reading with understanding! For, without this "key" no one would ever devise a literal, earthly rule of one thousand years. As we have indicated, the millennium is not so much as mentioned in any other verse of Scripture until one arrives at the twentieth chapter of the Revelation.

We have stated that there are three main theories concerning the millennium of Revelation 20 — premillennialism, amillennialism, and postmillennialism. However, today there are three separate schools within premillennialism itself — historic premillennialism, futurism, and dispensationalism. About the only doctrine these groups hold in common is their belief that Jesus will return *before* (pre) the millennium is established. Actually, then, there are not three, but five, main schools of millennial thought — premillennial, futurist, dispensational, postmillennial, and amillennial — each having its own distinctive beliefs.

1. The historic premillennial belief originated in early post-apostolic times and flourished until the time of Augustine (A.D. 400). Augustine restudied the millennial problem and broke with the prevailing teachings. His interpretation dealt such a blow to the premillennial teaching that it was all but unheard of again until after the Protestant Reformation. During the first, short-lived existence — between post-apostolic times and the time of Augustine — historic premillennialists simply believed that a messianic reign would be set up on earth between the resurrection of the saints and the resurrection of the unsaved. Satan was to be bound during this time, and the saints — Jew and Gentile alike — were to reign with Christ during this millennial kingdom. The future of national Israel, as distinct from that of the church, was all but unheard of until the nineteenth century.

2. Futurists have earned their name by their insistence that most prophecies, taught by the Christian church to have been fulfilled, are in reality to have their fulfillment in the future. Their main emphasis is on the prophecies concerning national Israel. We have mentioned the fact that historic premillennialists had no separate plan for the Jew, but treated all believers alike in their millennial plans. The futurist, on the other hand, insists that the millennium is to be built around national Israel, with the temple being rebuilt, the Mosaic law put back into force, the blood sacrifices reinstituted, and so forth. The futurist would agree with the historic premillennialist in teaching that Jesus will return *before* the millennium is established; but from there on he has many teachings never held by historic premillennialists. Futurism, which builds all its doctrines around an alleged future program for national Israel, originated in the early nineteenth century. Although this was during the time of John Nelson Darby, it would seem to have been started by Darby's contemporaries. It remained for Darby, a Plymouth Brethren, to develop dispensationalism, which grew out of futurism. Joseph Smith put out his *Book of Mormon* in 1830. Smith taught a regathering of Israel

to Palestine. In 1831 William Miller (the founder of Adventism) began preaching his "findings." Miller set 1843 as the time the world would come to an end. Many of his followers sold their possessions and put on their robes to await the Lord's return at that time. Judge Rutherford (the leader of Jehovah's Witnesses) wrote a book entitled *Comfort for the Jews*. Rutherford was the successor to Charles Taze Russell, who founded Millennial Dawnism around 1880. It was in this type of theological climate that both futurism and dispensationalism were born.

3. Dispensationalists divide all history into seven arbitrary periods of time, which they call dispensations. These dispensations are listed on page 5 of *The Scofield Reference Bible* as innocency, conscience, human government, promise, law, grace, and kingdom. This school of thought teaches that we are now in the sixth dispensation. This is called the "church age," and is said to be characterized by grace. After God raptures the church, according to this view, the seventh dispensation will begin. This will be the kingdom, or millennial age. Like the futurists, the dispensationalists teach that during the millennium the temple will have been rebuilt, all Jews will have returned to Palestine, and all Jews living at that time will have been converted (*after* the church and Holy Spirit have been removed from the world!) and will have the place of honor in the millennium. The literal throne of David will be raised up, and Christ will sit on it while he rules the nations with a rod of iron from the temple in Jerusalem. The law and the blood sacrifices will be brought back, and people will be saved by observing them. *The Scofield Reference Bible*, which has done more than any other piece of literature to spread the dispensational teachings, states that man is tested in each of these seven dispensations by obedience to the rules laid down for that period. In each dispensation this testing is different, says Dr. Scofield. For example, during the church age man is saved by grace through faith in the cross, whereas during the dispensation of law, and again when the kingdom (millennium) is set up, the testing is by keeping the law and sacrifices. None of these teachings were held by historic premillennialists, and many of them are not held by the futurists. As stated before, the main thing held in common by the three schools is the belief that Jesus will return before the millennium is established; and, as also previously stated, John Nelson Darby originated this theory from the then-new theory of futurism. *The Scofield Reference*

*Bible* was written for the specific purpose of perpetuating Darby's beliefs after C. I. Scofield had heard Darby lecture.

4. Postmillennialists teach that Christ will not return until *after* (post) the millennium. Before the second coming the gospel will have so permeated the world that almost the entire population will have been saved. They expect the world to become better and better until the millennium is ushered in, this being a period during which a truly Christian government will be established all over the world, with a high degree of justice prevailing. There will then be a near-perfect reign of peace and prosperity. Satan will be bound during this period.

The general unrest and hatred in the world, brought about by two world wars and the great depression of the Thirties, have caused postmillennialists to pause and check their positions. Their doctrines of an earthly utopia are not proclaimed with much zeal today.

5. Amillennialism literally means "no millennium." This is an unfortunate term, however, since the great majority of amillennialists definitely do believe in a millennium based on Revelation 20:1-10. They simply rebel against the hyperliteralism placed on this passage by most of the other schools of millennialism. Amillennialists interpret Revelation 20:1-10 as representing the period of time between the two advents of our Lord, that is, as going on at the present time and ending when our Lord returns. Some believe this reign includes only the souls of those who are already in heaven. Other amillennialists believe that every Christian, living and dead, is reigning with Christ in the present millennium (kingdom). In other words, whereas other millennialists place a literal interpretation upon Revelation 20:1-10, thus gaining an earthly, material kingdom, amillennialists interpret this passage in a spiritual manner, believing it to be figurative language describing the spiritual reign of Christ in the hearts of his people, which is already going on. Amillennialists would be like the postmillennialists in that both believe the millennium precedes the second coming of Christ. They would be like the premillennialist in that both believe good and evil will exist side by side until the end of the world. It is unfair to list amillennialism as an innovation of recent origin, as is often done. This belief can be traced back at least to the time of Origen (A.D.

200). And, contrary to popular opinion, most of the great Protestant reformers would fit into this school of interpretation.

### Kingdom as Millennium

It is my firm belief — and this is the historic Christian belief — that rather than interpret the entire Bible in the light of a literal interpretation of Revelation 20:1-10, one should interpret this one obscure passage in the light of all the rest of the Bible. This necessitates finding a plan, based on the clear teachings of the Bible, in which John's symbolic description will fit. This we shall attempt to do. As the reader should have deduced by now, our approach is definitely not a hyperliteral one. A hyperliteral interpretation of Revelation 20 does violence to a whole host of *clear* passages throughout the Bible.

The kingdom — in its present phase — and the millennium are practically, if not altogether, synoynmous terms. The same people make up both, i.e., those Christians (both Jews and Gentiles) in whose hearts God is presently reigning; both are going on at the present time, both having been inaugurated by the first advent of our Lord. If there be any difference, it is this: the millennium will be *concluded* at the second coming of Christ to earth, whereas the kingdom will be *perfected* at that time and will continue on into the eternal state. Even here one has to split theological hairs in order to distinguish between kingdom and millennium.

A great majority of millennial thinkers agree that the kingdom and millennium are one and the same. This fact is seen in the following definition of premillennialism (J. G. Vos, *Blue Banner Faith and Life*, Oct.-Dec., 1949):

"Premillennialism is that view of the Last Things which holds that the second coming of Christ will be followed by a period of world-wide peace and righteousness, before the end of the world, called '*the millennium*' or '*the Kingdom of God*,' during which Christ will reign as King in person on this earth" (p. 149; italics added).

The above quotation from Prof. Vos shows that premillennialists equate the kingdom with the millennium. This same thing is true of most futurists and dispensationalists, and of course this fits perfectly into the amillennial school of interpretation of Revelation 20. While there is general agreement on the fact that the kingdom is also the millennium, there are great differences of opinion as to the *time* of the kingdom. Most historic Christian theologians have always taught that the kingdom is already in our midst, being the reign of God in the hearts of his people. The premillennialists, however, including the dispensationalists and most futurists, insist that the kingdom of God is not now in the world, and that it will not be instituted until Christ returns.

Clarence Larken (*Dispensational Truth*), who for years has been a leading spokesman for the dispensational school of thought, definitely teaches that the kingdom and millennium are synonymous terms.

"By Pre-Millennial we mean before the Millennium. That is, before the period of a 'Thousand Years' spoken of in Rev. 20:1-6. This period is spoken of in other scriptures as 'The Kingdom,' and is described in glowing terms by the prophets as a time when the earth shall be blessed with a universal rule of righteousness. . ." (p. 10).

If the kingdom proposed by Jesus had been accepted, according to this theory, then the cross would not have been necessary to bring about salvation! People would have been saved by offering the proper animal sacrifices and keeping the law of Moses. This teaching is subscribed to by such leading dispensationalists as S. D. Gordon (*Quiet Talks About Jesus*), who says:

"It can be said at once that His dying was not God's own plan. It was conceived somewhere else and yielded to by God. God has a plan of atonement by which men who were willing could be saved from sin and its effect.

"That plan is given in the Old Hebrew code. To the tabernacle or temple, under prescribed regulations, a man could bring some animal which he owned. The man brought that which was his own. It represented him" (p. 114).

Lewis Sperry Chafer (*The Kingdom in History and Prophecy*) gives the dispensationalists' belief as to what would have happened had the Jews accepted the alleged legal kingdom which they say Jesus offered to them. "It was a bona fide offer, and, had they received him as their King, the nation's hopes would have been realized" (p. 56; italics added).

Here, then, is the gist of much millennial thinking today: Christ offered to Israel a kingdom. This proffered kingdom was to have been an earthly messianic reign, patterned after David's kingdom of the Old Testament. The throne of David was to have been set up in the temple at Jerusalem, where Jesus was to rule with a rod of iron. Israel was to have had a chosen place of authority during this kingdom (millennial) reign. One cannot help but see the great similarity between these teachings and the beliefs of those unbelieving Jews who put Jesus on the cross for not satisfying their material misconceptions of the kingdom. During this millennium, say the dispensationalists, the law and sacrifices were to have been reinstituted, and salvation would have been gained by adherence to these.

If, as most millennialists agree, the kingdom of heaven and the millennium are one and the same, and if, as most historic Christians — including the church fathers, Protestant reformers, and most reputable Bible commentaries — have always believed and taught the kingdom of heaven was established at the first advent of Christ, then simple logic compels the conclusion that Christians are already in the millennium of Revelation 20. This the New Testament clearly teaches.

The millennium — which John, in Revelation 20, describes in symbolic language — is a complete period of time during which God reigns in the hearts of all his people. This period began at the crucifixion (where Christ overcame Satan in fulfillment of Genesis 3:15) and will end at the second advent.

## XIV

## THE FINAL STATE

The second coming of Christ — culminating in the general resurrection and the general judgment — will bring to a close this present age. Then will begin the final state, or, as it is sometimes called, "the eternal state." We prefer the term "final state," because there is a sense in which everything God does is eternal. Actually, the Bible speaks of only two ages — this world (age) and the world (age) to come (Matt. 12:32; Mark 10:30; Luke 18:30; 20:34; John 8:23).

The final state will differ from the present in that the present age is one of preparation, whereas everything in the final state will be in its completed form. The present age is temporary and thus will come to an end, whereas the final age will last throughout eternity. Time, in its terrestrial form, will no longer exist. Man will no longer be bound by space. Heaven will then extend over all space except the area of hell.

Some things existing in the present world will be ushered into the final state, having been made conformable to the new surroundings of that state. Two examples are the people of God and the kingdom of God. Here, again, however, the transformations will be great between the two worlds. Today, God's people are subject to temptations, sin, and suffering. These will not exist among God's people in the final state. In this life, God's people have immortal souls but they are housed in mortal bodies. Before entering the final state, every believer will receive an immortal body. The kingdom, too, is presently in an incomplete form. Not only are members being added to the kingdom of God daily, but all its members are being constantly shaped and refined in order to rid them of the dross of their Adamic nature. Too, the reign of God in the hearts of his people is taking place amid earthly surroundings. In the world to come, the kingdom of God will be in its consummated and perfected form. God the Son will then have turned over the kingdom to God the Father and it will then be marred by no impurities. The full number of the elect — of both Jews and Gentiles — will have come into the kingdom and the number of God's people will be complete. (I believe that, in God's foreknowledge and through his electing, the fullness of the Gentiles will be realized at the exact second the complete number of elected Jews are saved.)

### Immortality

Since immortality reaches perfection only in the final state, perhaps a word of definition is in order here. Immortality really has two definitions: (1) the technical theological meaning listed in the dictionary, and (2) the accepted general meaning with which it usually is associated.

*The Winston (Collegiate) Dictionary* defines immortality as (1) exemption from death; theological: an everlasting existence with God. (2) time which has unending existence.

The following Greek words are from *Strong's Greek Lexicon*: *aphtharsia*, incorruptibility, generally unending existence; *athanasia*, deathlessness, immortality. Here, again, one can see the two definitions of immortality: (1) incorruptibility, and (2) unending existence.

1. Only a genuine believer in Jesus Christ can lay claim to immortality in its theological sense. For only of the believer, one who has been born from above, may it be said that he is exempt from death and will enjoy an everlasting existence with God.

In order fully to appreciate the technical meaning of immortality as distinguished from its general meaning, one must discover a way in which the saint is eternally different from the sinner. Immortality cannot be taken to mean an exemption from physical death since this comes to the saved as well as to the lost. The bodies of both decay in the earth (Ecc. 12:7). Neither is the Christian different from the non-Christian simply because his soul lives forever, for every soul is eternal — the soul of the lost person will spend its eternity in hell, but it will go on existing nonetheless.

In what way, then, is the soul of the Christian uniquely different from that of the person who has never been born again? The physical bodies of both are subject to death, and the souls of both are destined to exist forever. There is one paramount difference between the soul of the twice-born person and that of the unbeliever. That difference is that the former is exempt from the second death which is described in Revelation 20:14; this is a spiritual death of the soul. Herein lies true immortality. Every person who reaches the age of accountability will die a first spiritual death, and every such person will also die a natural death — unless he be living when Christ comes (I Cor. 15:51) — but only the genuine believer is immune to the second death.

What makes a person immortal? John gives the answer to this question in the same twentieth chapter of the Revelation. "Blessed and holy is he that hath part in the first resurrection: over these the second death hath no power. . ." (Rev. 20:6). Our part in the first resurrection was dealt with in an earlier chapter, and was shown to be the new birth or conversion experience (John 5:24,25).

A. Immortality was reflected in the Old Testament. "But now he is dead, wherefore should I fast? Can I bring him back again? I shall go to him, but he will not return to me" (II Sam. 12:23). David was here speaking of his dead infant son, and he had in mind more than going to the grave when he stated that he would be re-united with his son.

Job wrestled with the theological question of immortality when he asked the question: "If a man die, shall he live again?" (Job 14:14). He answered his own question in clear terms in the following statement.

"But as for me I know that my Redeemer liveth and at last he will stand up upon the earth: And after my skin, even this body, is destroyed, Then without my flesh shall I see God; Whom I, even I, shall see, on my side, And mine eyes shall behold, and not as a stranger. . ." (Job 19:25-27).

"And many of them that sleep in the dust of the earth shall awake, some to everlasting life, and some to shame and everlasting contempt" (Dan. 12:2).

Certainly, Daniel's prediction could not come to pass if physical death ended all.

Although the Old Testament does not deal in detail with life after death, we certainly are given glimpses of it through God's inspired prophets. One sees progressive revelation at work as one turns to the fuller light of the New Testament.

B.   Jesus' resurrection proved the doctrine of immortality. Much of Paul's theology is based on the fact of Jesus' bodily resurrection. "If Christ be not risen . . ." says this theologian, then all would be in vain — our faith, our preaching, our hope of a hereafter. But — and here one can almost hear Paul shouting the Hallelujah Chorus — exclaims Paul, Christ *is risen* and has become the firstfruits of those Christians of all ages who sleep the sleep of death. Because of this fact, each believer, in his own order, will be raised and given a glorified body like that of the risen Christ.

Our Lord himself based the future of his followers on the fact that the sepulchre could not hold him. ". . . because I live, ye shall live also" (John 14:19).

C.   Immortality for the individual Christian begins at the new birth. Immortality, like sanctification, is both an act and a process. He who has the Son *has* life, and shall never come into condemnation. To repent of sin and be genuinely converted is to become a recipient of eternal life. It is to pass instantly into spiritual life. "Being therefore justified by faith, we have peace with God through our Lord Jesus Christ: through whom also we have had our access by faith wherein we stand" (Rom. 5:1). "There is therefore *now* no condemnation to them that are in Christ Jesus" (Rom. 8:1).

The preceding, and many similar passages, refer to the *act* of immortality. There is also the *process* through which immortality travels to its completion. There is a definite tension between what the immortal person is and what he is to become. Immortality is like money in the bank — and the check is drawn on a bank which cannot fail — yet, the Christian will not cash the check until the second coming of Christ. The gift of the Holy Spirit, at conversion, is spoken of as a down payment on a much fuller reward which is to come.

"Now he that established us with you in Christ, and anointed us, is God; who also sealed us, and gave us the earnest of the Spirit in our hearts" (II Cor. 1:21,22). "Now he that wrought us for this very thing is God, who gave unto us the earnest of the Spirit" (II Cor. 5:5). ". . . in Christ: in whom ye also, having heard the word of the truth, the gospel of your salvation—in whom having also believed, ye were sealed with the Holy Spirit of promise, which is an earnest of our inheritance, unto the redemption of God's own possession, unto the praise of his glory" (Eph. 1:12-14).

Even though the apostle Paul possessed, and taught, a present-tense salvation (immortality), he also taught that this was merely a shadow or foretaste of the joy of the salvation which is to be the lot of the Christian in the final state. "If we have only hoped in Christ in this life, we are of all men most pitiable" (I Cor. 15:19).

D. Immortality is enhanced at physical death. The intermediate state — although this is not the final state — is, for the Christian, a place of conscious bliss in the presence of the Savior. Jesus said to the believing thief on the cross: ". . . today shalt thou be with me in paradise" (Luke 23:43). Jesus taught that, while life still went on in the earth, Lazarus, the beggar, died and went immediately into paradise (Abraham's bosom) (Luke 16:22).

Paul did not expect to receive his final rewards until the day of the Lord. However, he was inspired to teach that physical death would represent an immediate improvement in his state of immortality: "For me to live is Christ, and to die is gain. . . . But I am in a strait betwixt the two, having the desire to depart and be with Christ; for it is very far better: yet to abide in the flesh is more needful for your sake" (Phil. 1:21-24).

E. Immortality will be consummated at the second coming. Much language of the Bible will be fully realized only in the final state. Nothing this side of eternity completely satisfies the meaning of prophecies concerning the lion lying down with the lamb, perfect peace, perfect laws, every knee bowing at the name of Christ, and the like.

"The Second Advent of Christ will coincide with the final and complete manifestation of the kingdom, when every knee will bow in His name and every tongue confess Him as Lord (Phil. 2:10f), when God's will is to be done on earth as it is in heaven (Matt. 6:10). At Christ's first coming the age to come invaded this present age; at His second coming the age to come will have altogether superseded this present age. Between the two comings the two ages overlap; Christians live temporally in this present age while spiritually they belong to the heavenly kingdom and enjoy the life of the age to come. Biblical eschatology is largely, but not completely 'realized'; there still remains a future element, to become actual at the Second Advent, the *parousia*. . ." (F. F. Bruce, *The Book of Acts, The New International Commentary on The New Testament*, p. 35).

An immortal soul is incomplete without a body. Paul teaches in Romans 8:23 that those who have the firstfruits of the Spirit, i.e., Christians, long for a future redemption of their bodies. Thus the saved soul is in an incomplete state until then. In this life, our souls remain in corruptible bodies; when we depart this life — even though our souls go immediately into the presence of Jesus — they are disembodied souls.

". . . the creation itself shall be delivered from the bondage of corruption into the liberty of the glory of the children of God. For we know that the whole creation groaneth and travaileth in pain together until now. And not only so, but ourselves also, who have the firstfruits of the Spirit, even we ourselves groan within ourselves, waiting for our adoption, to wit, the redemption of our body" (Rom. 8:21-23).

A comparison of other Scripture passages shows that the new body will not be received until the second advent of Jesus. "For our citizenship is in heaven; whence also we wait for a Saviour, the Lord Jesus Christ: who shall fashion anew the body of our humiliation, that it may be conformed to the body of his glory, according to the working whereby he is able even to subject all things unto himself" (Phil. 3:20,21). "When Christ, who is our life, shall be manifested, then shall ye also with him be manifested in glory" (Col. 3:4). "For as in Adam all die, so also in Christ shall all be made alive. But each in his own order: Christ the firstfruits; then they that are Christ's at his coming" (I Cor. 15:22,23).

Only in the final state will the believer enjoy the full benefits of immortality. Only then will he cease to view the things of God through an imperfect mirror (I Cor. 13:12). "For this corruptible *must* put on incorruption, and this mortal *must* put on immortality" (I Cor. 15:53).

2. Although, as stated earlier, the unbeliever does not possess immortality in its strictest theological sense, he does, nonetheless, possess it in its secondary sense, i.e., an unending existence. The soul of the wicked will suffer the second death and will be condemned to spend its eternity separated from God. But it will not cease to exist or to be conscious (Ecc. 12:7). The eternity of the wicked is just as long as that of the saint. If there is an eternal heaven for the saved there is a hell of equal duration for the unsaved. Jesus

spoke of hell as an actual place where their worm dieth not and the fire is not quenched.

a) The wicked are condemned already. Jesus did not come into the world (primarily) for the purpose of judging sinners. His primary mission was to seek and to save the lost. However, those who reject his offer of free salvation thereby seal their own judgment. Unless and until a person comes under the shed blood of Christ, the wrath of God abides on that person.

"He that believeth on him is not judged: he that believeth not hath been judged already, because he hath not believed on the name of the only begotten Son of God. And this is the judgment, that the light is come into the world, and men loved the darkness rather than the light; for their works were evil" (John 3:18,19).

b) Their condition worsens at physical death. The Scriptures make clear the fact that the soul of the wicked, at death, enters into a state of conscious torment. Jesus contrasted for us the intermediate state of the wicked as over against that of the righteous. In Luke 16: ". . . and the rich man also died, and was buried. And in Hades he lifted up his eyes, being in torments, and seeth Abraham afar off, and Lazarus in his bosom. And he cried and said, Father Abraham, have mercy on me, and send Lazarus, that he may dip the tip of his finger in water, and cool my tongue; for I am in anguish in this flame. But Abraham said, Son, remember that thou in thy lifetime receivedst thy good things, and Lazarus in like manner evil things: But now here he is comforted, and thou art in anguish. And besides all this, between us and you there is a great gulf fixed, that they that would pass from hence to you may not be able, and that none may cross over from thence to us" (vss. 22-26).

"The Lord knoweth how to deliver the godly out of temptation and to keep the unrighteous under punishment unto the day of judgment" (II Peter 2:9).

c) The condemnation of the wicked will be finalized at the second coming.

"And to you that are afflicted rest with us, at the revelation of the Lord Jesus from heaven with the angels of his power in flaming fire, rendering vengeance to them that know not God, and to them that obey not the gospel of our Lord Jesus: who shall suffer punishment, even eternal destruction from the face of the Lord and from the glory of his might, when he shall come to be glorified in his saints, and to be marvelled at in all them that believed (because our testimony unto you was believed) in that day" (II Thess. 1:7-10). "He that rejecteth me, and receiveth not my sayings, hath one that judgeth him: the word that I spake, the same shall judge him in the last day" (John 12:48).

Also read Matthew 25:31,32,41,46; and Revelation 20:11-15 in conjunction with these verses.

We noted earlier that the wicked, at death, go immediately into torment (Luke 16:22f). Here we see that their full punishment does not begin until the end of the world. What of their intermediate state? A collation of scriptures would seem to indicate that their punishment, which begins at death, will be compounded at the judgment.

"The Lord knoweth how to deliver the godly out of temptation, and to keep the unrighteous under punishment unto the day of judgment" (II Peter 2:9). "And angels that kept not their own principality, but left their proper habitation, he hath kept in everlasting bonds under darkness unto the judgment of the great day" (Jude 6).

The intermediate state of the wicked is to his final state what the prison death cell is to the gas chamber. The person in the death cell can see the chamber and suffers the mental torment of expectation. But the worst of his punishment is ahead. However, this is merely an earthly analogy and we dare not carry it to extremes. For example, the pain of the gas chamber is short-lived while the pain of hell will continue forever.

### The Final State of the Earth

In the early chapters of Genesis one reads the account of paradise lost. The earth was corrupted by sin; and we believe that the universal flood, which resulted from man's disobedience, changed the very appearance of God's created earth. The closing chapters of the Revelation record paradise regained.

The regeneration of the universe was predicted in the Old Testament. The following passages will serve as examples.

"Of old didst thou lay the foundation of the earth; and the heavens are the work of thy hands. They shall perish, but thou shalt endure; yea, all of them shall wax old like a garment; as a vesture shalt thou change them, and they shall be changed" (Psalm 102:25, 26).

"For, behold, I create new heavens and a new earth; and the former things shall not be remembered, nor come into mind" (Isa. 65:17).

Naturally, these predictions were given in the language of that day. The following quotation, concerning fulfillment, is apropos.

" 'In form,' writes Dr. Albertus Pieters, 'prediction and fulfillment are diverse, in essence they are the same. This principle applies to the New Testament no less than the Old. We are promised eternal life in heaven, and to make us realize it we read of many mansions, of white raiment, of harps of gold, of a river of life, to quench our thirst, of the fruit of the tree of life for food, of medicinal leaves of healing, of golden streets, and a heavenly city that has a wall and twelve gates. Such things are needed to convey to us the purpose of God to supply every need and to cause us to dwell in perfect peace and safety, but in what form the reality will be enjoyed we cannot tell, because we do not know what our situation and needs will be in the disembodied state, or after the soul has been reunited to the body in resurrection. Only we do know that whatever such things would mean to us now, of abundant provision, perfect security and glorious existence, shall be fulfilled, and more than fulfilled' " (quoted from "Prophetic Studies" by Dr. John Wilmot, in the July 25, 1963, issue of *The Gospel Witness*, p. 7).

The following passages are examples of New Testament predictions with reference to the final state of the earth.

"For the creation was subjected to vanity, not of its own will, but by reason of him who subjected it, in hope that the creation itself also shall be delivered from the bondage of corruption into the liberty of the glory of the children of God" (Rom. 8:20,21).

"But the day of the Lord will come as a thief; in the which the heavens shall pass away with a great noise, and the elements shall be dissolved with fervent heat, and the earth and the works that are therein shall be burned up. Seeing that these things are thus all to be dissolved, what manner of persons ought ye to be in all holy living and godliness, looking for and earnestly desiring the coming of the day of God, by reason of which the heavens being on fire shall be dissolved, and the elements shall melt with fervent heat? But, according to his promise, we look for new heavens and a new earth, wherein dwelleth righteousness" (II Peter 3:10-13).

"And I saw a new heaven and a new earth: for the first heaven and the first earth are passed away; and the sea is no more" (Rev. 21:1).

John devotes the last two chapters of the Revelation to an apocalyptic description of the final state. Here we see paradise regained.

In all probability, the scriptural references to the destruction of the present world and the setting up of a new one should be interpreted in the same manner as those which refer to the regeneration of the individual Christians. Although Paul speaks of the believer as a new creation in Christ and says that old things "are passed away," we know that the old self was not annihilated. But the change was so radical that Paul could speak in terms of a destruction of the old and the birth of a completely new person.

So it will be, we suspect, with the universe at the second coming of Christ. We believe that the present earth will be completely renovated, but not annihilated.

"What a mighty, all-comprehensive, and blessed change that will be! We need not proceed on the assumption that the old creation will be entirely annihilated, though the form of it and the conditions prevailing in it will undergo a radical change. The imperfections of the present universe, which resulted from sin, will be removed; heaven and earth will again appear in their pristine beauty. The present world is full of unrighteousness. People are clamoring for righteousness in every domain: in social and civic life, in industry and business, in commercial and international relations, and even in the religious sphere. How different that will be in the new creation! It will be a world characterized by holiness and righteousness. The bitter cries of dissatisfaction and injustice will be replaced by songs of thanksgiving and paeans of victory. It will be a fit dwellingplace for the glorified Christ and his redeemed and glorified Church" (L. Berkhof, *The Second Coming of Christ*, p. 85).

"It should be made clear, however, that annihilation of the earth is not clearly taught in the Scriptures. The word parerchomai which is translated 'pass away' does not mean annihilate. Culver says, 'The meaning is rather to pass from one position in time or space to another. And even granting the most destructive ideas as the meaning of luthestai (be dissolved) and katakaesetai (be burned up, if we adopt the Textus Receptus), the words certainly do not describe annihilation.' Peter speaks of the two world judgments: one by water, the Flood, in which the world 'perished' but was obviously not annihilated; and one by fire, in which the world shall be burned up, but not necessarily annihilated" (Paul Erb, *The Alpha and the Omega*, p. 119).

### Christ's Second Coming Is the Pivotal Point

The present world will come to an end and the final state will begin at the second coming of Christ. In fact, many events will synchronize at the second advent. Both the general resurrection and the general judgment will take place then, the saints will be raptured and rewarded, the wicked will be judged, the earth will be cleansed, Satan will be put down, and the perfected kingdom will be turned over to God the Father by God the Son. Is it any wonder that Paul calls the second coming the Blessed Hope of the Christian?

The present age, which lies between the incarnation and the second coming, might be compared to a woman in pangs of childbirth. The delivery has begun. Each day, each event, sees the birth nearing completion. Paul indeed uses this illustration in Romans 8:23. This could be taken to represent the individual believer, or the church, or the kingdom of God. There is a tension between what we already are and what God has in store for us following the harvest. The Christian has eternal life; he is a member of the kingdom of God; his citizenship already is in heaven. Yet, he has not possessed his possessions.

At the second coming, the tension which now exists between what we are, on the one hand, and fulfilled immortality, on the other, will be removed. In the final state, our bodies will have been made amenable to Spirit rule (Rom. 8:11). The earth will have been cleansed and made suitable for spiritual living. What now is true in heaven will then be true of all creation. God's will then truly will be done on earth as it is in heaven.

This is not to say that everything for the Christian is "pie-in-the-sky-bye-and-bye." Quite the contrary is true. Eternity broke into history at the incarnation. Man has already been initiated into the kingdom of God and has tasted the joys of heaven (Col. 1:13). The kingdom of God is used synonymously with eternal life in the Gospels. However, this is only a foretaste of that which God has in store for his own. The parousia will mark a dividing line between what we are in miniature as compared with the full enjoyment of immortality.

## XV

## OTHERS OF LIKE MIND

Many sincerely believe that premillennialists represent the thinking of a large majority of Bible scholars. This is no doubt because of the wide use of the pen by its adherents, plus the fact that they are more vocal in preaching their beliefs than are either the amillennialist or the postmillennialist. This is not meant as a slur on the premillennialist; on the contrary, it is a compliment to them that they believe their doctrines strongly enough to want to perpetuate them. The present writer found it difficult to break with his former dispensationalist beliefs, mainly because he felt, as a young minister, that to do so was to break away from the historic Christian teachings.

Actually, however, premillennialism (and this is true of both historic premillennialism and present-day dispensational-premillennialism) has always been but a minority belief among Christians. Certainly this fact alone would not hinder it from being the true biblical belief. Our statements are made only to combat the erroneous claims that premillennialism represents the majority opinion. The great majority of the church fathers, Protestant reformers, commentators, and teachers of the Bible have been either amillennial or postmillennial.

This brief chapter is presented somewhat as an appendix. Its purpose is to list, with but few comments, a sampling of the opinions of some outstanding Bible preachers and teachers. These quotations will deal mainly with the millennium, resurrection, and judgment, since one's treatment of these three doctrines determines his views on eschatology.

These quotations are not offered as proof of our position. Our proof and only authority must be the Word of God. Paul said to let God be true, even if it should make every man a liar. However, it is well for us to know how these great minds have interpreted the Scriptures on these points.

John Walvoord, in an article in *Bibliotheca Sacra* (Jan.-Mar., 1951), admits that millennialism was a departure from all the great reformers such as Calvin, Luther, Zwingli, Knox, and so forth. This is a very enlightening statement when one considers that Dr. Walvoord is president of Dallas Theological Seminary, the very headquarters for dispensational thinking and writing today. He is also an avid follower of *The Scofield Reference Bible*. Dr. Walvoord writes: "Reformed eschatology has been predominantly Amillennial. Most if not all the leaders of the Protestant Reformation were Amillennial in their eschatology, following the teachings of Augustine" (p. 111).

Another such admission is made by the late Dr. Scofield. Writing in the introduction of a book by Lewis Sperry Chafer, *The Kingdom in History and Prophecy*, Dr. Scofield said: "Protestant theology has very generally taught that all the kingdom promises, and even the great Davidic covenant itself, are to be fulfilled through the church" (p. 5).

William Masselink (*Why Thousand Years?*) gives Martin Luther's views on millennialism: "A millennial reign of Christ, characterized by a pre-eminent knowledge of the mysteries of God, by a holy life and an earthly prosperity for those involved, is not to be expected by God's children in this world" (p. 279).

### John Calvin

Heinrich Quistorp (*Calvin's Doctrine of the Last Things*) points out that John Calvin counted as heresy the idea of a literal, material millennium. "This kingdom of Christ will be an eternal kingdom because it is the kingdom of God. Calvin emphasizes this with vigor. Hence he decidedly rejects the chiliasm of the fanatics which would make of the kingdom of Christ a purely temporal and transient one. Calvin sees in chiliasm a deceptive fantasy by means of which Satan began to corrupt the Christian hope soon after apostolic times. 'I dismiss the notion that Satan began already in the time of Paul to ruin this hope | of the eternality of the kingdom of God|. But shortly afterwards the Chiliasts |millennialists| arose who fixed and narrowed the conception of Christ's kingdom as being of a thousand years duration' " (p. 158).

It is amusing today to see so many, who pride themselves on being Calvinists, following the millennial teachings (chiliasm) which Calvin so bitterly denounced as being the work of Satan.

### Justin Martyr

"The First Apology of Justin," *The Ante-Nicene Church Fathers*, Justin Martyr: "Justin Martyr, in his *First Apology* (dated between A.D. 147 and 161) speaks of 'two advents . . . the second, when according to prophecy, he shall raise the bodies of all men who have lived, and shall clothe those of the worthy with immortality and shall send those of the wicked, endued with eternal sensibility into everlasting fire with the wicked devils' (p. 180)" (quoted from Ray Summers, *The Life Beyond*, p. 95).

"Dialogue With Trypho The Jew," *The Ante-Nicene Church Fathers*, Justin Martyr: "There was a certain man with us, whose name was John, one of the Apostles of Christ, who prophesied, by a revelation that was made to him, that those who believed in our Christ would dwell a thousand years in Jerusalem; and that thereafter the general, and in short, the eternal resurrection and judgment of all men would take place" (p. 240).

These two statements from Justin Martyr, when taken together, teach that (1) the resurrection and judgment will both take place at the second advent; (2) this will be a general resurrection and judgment *of all the dead*; (3) this will all happen *after* a thousand year reign of the saints.

Many premillennial writers have used Justin Martyr as an example of a well-known church father who embraced premillennialism. Yet, the above two statements by Justin Martyr himself disprove this. In both instances he spoke of a general resurrection and judgment. This alone outlaws a *premillennial* coming of Christ. His statement quoting John as having taught that all believers would dwell in Jerusalem a thousand years could be claimed to make John either a postmillennialist or an amillennialist. However, no stretch of the imagination could make this statement apply to the premillennial school of thought. For Justin Martyr quoted John as having said that the millennium would be followed by a general resurrection and judgment.

Here, the premillennialist cannot have his theological cake and eat it. Whatever interpretation one might put upon the millennium itself, one cannot have Justin Martyr speaking of *a general resurrection and judgment* while at the same time believing one thousand years will intervene between *two separate resurrections and judgments*. The most that could be claimed for Justin Martyr would be to classify him as a very inconsistent premillennialist.

### B. B. Warfield

"The Millennium And The Apocalypse," *Biblical Doctrines* (This first passage from Dr. Warfield will be elaborated on in our next section.):

"John knows no more of two resurrections—of the saints and of the wicked—than does Paul: and the whole theory of an intervening millennium—and indeed of a millennium of any kind on earth—goes up in smoke. We are forced, indeed to add our assent to Kliefoth's conclusion, that 'the doctrine of a thousand year kingdom has no foundation in the prophecies of the New Testament, and is therefore not a dogma but merely a hypothesis lacking all Biblical ground.' The millennium of the Apocalypse is the blessedness of the saints who have gone away from the body to be at home with the Lord" (pp. 661-62).

"The Prophecies Of St. Paul," *Biblical And Theological Studies*, B. B. Warfield (Warfield was dealing with I Corinthians 15, particularly verses 22-24, when he made the following comment):

". . . the context apparently confines the word 'death' in these verses to its simple physical sense, while on the contrary the 'all' of both clauses seems unlimited, and the context appears to furnish nothing to narrow its meaning to a class. They thus assert the resurrection of all men without distinction as dependent on and the result of Adam's sin. 'But,' the Apostle adds, returning to the Christian dead, 'this resurrection though certain, is not immediate; each rises in his own place in the ranks—Christ is the first-fruits, then His own rise at His coming; then is the end' (verses 23,24). The interminable debates that have played around the meaning of this statement are the outgrowth of strange misconceptions. *Because the resurrection of the wicked is not mentioned it does not at all follow that it is excluded*; the whole section has nothing to do with the resurrection of the wicked (which is only incidentally included and not openly stated in the semi-parenthetic explanation of verses 21 and 22), but, like the parallel passage in I Thessalonians, confines itself to the Christian dead. *Nor is it exegetically possible to read the resurrection of the wicked into the passage as a third event to take place at a different time from that of the good, as if the Apostle had said: 'Each shall rise in his own order; Christ the first-fruits,—then Christ's dead at his coming,—then, the end of the resurrection, namely of the wicked'* The term, 'the end,' is a perfectly definite one with a set and distinct meaning, and from Matthew (e.g., xxiv. 6, cf. 14) throughout the New Testament, and in these very epistles (I Cor. 1.8; II Cor. 1.13, 14), is the standing designation of the 'end of the ages,' or 'end of the world.' It is illegitimate to press it into any other groove here. *Relief is not however got by varying the third term, so as to make it say that 'then comes the end, accompanied by the resurrection of the wicked' for this is importing into the passage what there is absolutely nothing in it to suggest.* The word *tagma* does not in the least imply succession; but means 'order' only in the sense of the word in such phrases as 'orders of society.' Neither does the 'they that are Christ's' any more than in Rom. ix. 6, when we hear of 'Israel,' and 'those of Israel,' we expect to hear of 'those not of Israel.' The contrast is entirely absorbed by the 'Christ' of the preceding clause, and only the clumsiness of our English gives a different impression. Not only, however, is there no exegetical basis for this exposition in this passage; *the whole theory of a resurrection of the wicked at a later time than the resurrection of the just is excluded by this passage.* Briefly, this follows from the statement that after the coming of Christ, 'then comes the end' (verse 24). No doubt the mere word 'then' *eita* does not assert immediateness, and for ought necessarily said in it, 'the end' might be only the next event mentioned by the Apostle, although the intervening interval shall be vast and crowded with important events. But the context here necessarily limits this 'then' to immediate subsequence" (pp. 483-84; italics added).

"But we not only learn thus how it happens that Paul dwells so much on the Second Advent when writing to the Thessalonians, but we learn also what is much more important—how he himself thought of the Advent and in what aspect he proclaimed it. Plainly to him it was above all things else the Judgment. It was the Judgment Day that he announced in its proclamation; and this was the lever with which he pricked at Gentile consciences. 'The day in which God will judge the world in righteousness' was what he proclaimed to the Athenians, and that it was just this that was in mind in I Thess. 1:10 is evident from the office assigned to the expected Jesus,—'the Deliverer from the coming wrath.' In harmony with this, every passage in which the Second Advent is adverted to in these Epistles conceives of it pointedly as the Judgment Day . . . he declares that the Day of the Lord will bring sudden destruction upon the wicked (I Thess. v. 3), and will draw a sharp line in justice between the good and bad (II Thess. 1:9). He speaks of the Advent freely as the 'Day of the Lord' (I Thess. v. 2,4; II Thess. 1:10), a term which from Joel down had stood in all prophecy as the synonym of the final judgment" (*ibid.*, p. 465).

### Henry H. Halley

"The Judgment will be complete. Every person from every age and nation will be there. Every deed and motive will have been recorded. It will be the 'Day when God shall Judge the Secrets of men,' spoken of by Paul in Rom. 2:16.

"There will be only two classes: the Saved and the Lost. The 'Books' will have the records of men's lives. The 'Book of Life' will have the roll of the Saved. There are many of such mixed character that we would not know where to place them. But God knows" (*Halley's Bible Handbook*, p. 670).

### Geerhardus Vos

"The idea is in all passages plainly implied, that Jesus' eschatological revelation will bear the features of a strictly momentary, miraculous act. While things preceding and preparing for it do not, of course, lack all gradual and orderly unfolding, yet the event itself is catastrophic in the absolute sense, nay this very idea of suddenness and unexpectedness seems to be intimately associated with the word" (*The Pauline Eschatology*, p. 79).

### G. L. Murray

"It has been the age-old belief of the Christian church that God has, in His own eternal counsels, appointed a day in which He shall bring the members of the human race before His judgment seat to be assigned to their eternal destinies. This belief is amply supported by the Holy Scriptures which speak of the Lord's return, the resurrection of the dead, and the final judgment, as simultaneous events. This is also suggested by the Apostles' Creed which speaks of Christ's return, and the judgment of the quick and the dead, in the same clause. In Scripture, and elsewhere, the time when this series of events shall take place is described as 'the day of the Lord,' or 'the day of Christ' " (*Millennial Studies*, p. 131).

### Adam Clarke

(Commenting on I Cor. 15:26) *"The last enemy]* Death, shall be destroyed: *katargeitai,* shall be *counterworked, subverted,* and finally *overturned.* But death cannot be *destroyed* by there being simply no farther death; death can only be destroyed and annihilated by a *general resurrection;* if there be no general resurrection, it is most evident that death will still retain his empire. Therefore, the fact that *death shall be destroyed* assures the fact that there shall be a *general resurrection*; and this is a proof, also, that after the resurrection there shall be no more death" (*Clarke's Commentary*, Vol. VI, p. 284).

### Loraine Boettner

"The earlier forms of premillennialism as well as the present dispensational doctrines have been held usually, if not always, by a minority of Christian people. The distinctive dispensational doctrines occupy a much less prominent place in European than in American church life" (*The Millennium*, p. 8)

### Confession of the Evangelical Free Church of Geneva, 1848

According to Philip Schaff, *Creeds of Christendom*, Vol. III, p. 785, the following statement "exhibits the Calvinism of the nineteenth century":

"We believe that there will be a resurrection of the unjust as well as of the just; that God has decided a day in which he shall judge the whole world by the man chosen for that purpose; that the unjust will go to everlasting punishment, while the just will rejoice in life everlasting" (Article XIV).

### The Westminster Confession of Faith, 1647:

"God hath appointed a day wherein he will judge the world in righteousness by Jesus Christ, to whom all power and judgment is given of the Father, in which day, not only the apostate angels shall be judged, but likewise all persons, that have lived upon the earth, shall appear before the tribunal of Christ, to give an account of their thoughts, words, and deeds; and to receive according to what they have done in the body, whether good or evil" (chapter 33, "Of the Last Judgment").

### The New Hampshire Baptist Confession of 1833

"We believe that the end of the World is approaching; that at the last day Christ will descend from heaven, and raise the dead from the grave to final retribution; that a solemn separation will then take place; that the wicked will be adjudged to endless punishment and the righteous to endless joy; and that this judgment will fix forever the final state of men in heaven or hell, on principles of righteousness" (Article XVIII, "Of the World to Come").

### Confession of The Free-Will Baptists, 1834

"The General Judgment—There will be a general judgment when time and man's probation will close forever. Then all men will be judged according to their works" (chapter XXI, "The General Judgment and Future Retribution").

### The Augsburg Confession

The Augsburg Confession characterizes all chiliastic (millennial) views as "certain Jewish opinions," and condemns them.

*Edgar Y. Mullins*

"Matthew 16:27 connects the rendering 'to every man according to his deeds,' with the coming of Christ in the glory of his Father. So also in Matthew 25:31-33, Christ comes and sits on the throne of his glory and judges all nations. In John 5:28,29, it is declared that 'the hour cometh' in which all that are in the tomb, both righteous and wicked, shall be raised for judgment. In II Thessalonians 1: 6-10 Christ is represented as coming in flaming fire, and punishing the wicked with 'eternal destruction from the face of the Lord.' In II Peter 3:7,10 again the 'Day of the Lord' is closely connected with the judgment of ungodly men and the destruction of the earth by fire. In Revelation 20:11-15 there is a portrayal of the final judgment, in which all men appear together and eternal awards are declared" (*The Christian Religion In Its Doctrinal Expression*, pp. 467-68).

*Augustus H. Strong*

"The Subjects of the Final Judgment: All men—each possessed of body as well as soul,— the dead having been raised, and the living having been changed" (*Outlines of Systematic Theology*, p. 268).

"While the Scriptures describe the impartation of the new life to the soul in regeneration as a spiritual resurrection, they also declare that, at the second coming of Christ, there shall be a resurrection of the body and a reunion of the body to the soul from which, during the intermediate state, it has been separated. Both the just and unjust shall have part in the resurrection. To the just, it shall be a resurrection unto life; and the body shall be a body like Christ's—a body fitted for the uses of the sanctified spirit. To the unjust, it shall be a resurrection unto condemnation; an analogy would seem to indicate that, here also, the outward form will fitly represent the inward state of the soul—being corrupt and deformed as is the soul which inhabits it. Those who are living at Christ's coming shall receive spiritual bodies without passing through death. As the body after corruption and dissolution, so the outward world after destruction by fire, shall be rehabilitated and fitted for the abode of the saints" (*ibid.*, pp. 264-65).

"The perfect joy of the saints, and the utter misery of the wicked, begin only with the resurrection and general judgment" (*ibid.*, p. 262).

"While the Scriptures represent great events in the history of the individual Christian, like death, and great events in the history of the church, like the outpouring of the Spirit at Pentecost and the destruction of Jerusalem, as comings of Christ for deliverance or judgment, they also declare that these partial and typical comings shall be concluded by a final, triumphant return of Christ, to punish the wicked and to complete the salvation of his people" (*ibid.*, p. 262).

". . . we discern a striking parallel between the predictions of Christ's first, and the predictions of his second, advent. In both cases the event was more distant and more grand than those imagined to whom the prophecies first came. Under both dispensations, patient waiting for Christ was intended to discipline the faith, and to enlarge the conceptions, of God's true servants. The fact that every age since Christ ascended has had its Chiliasts and Second Adventists should turn our thoughts away from curious and fruitless prying into the time of Christ's coming, and set us at immediate and constant endeavor to be ready, at whatsoever hour he may appear" (*ibid.*, p. 263).

"The Scripture foretells a period, called in the language of prophecy 'a thousand years,' when Satan shall be restrained and the saints shall reign with Christ on the earth. A comparison of the passages bearing on this subject leads us to the conclusion that this millennial blessedness and dominion is prior to the second advent. One passage only seems at first sight to teach the contrary, *viz.*: Rev. 20:4-10. But this supports the theory of a premillennial advent only when the passage is interpreted with the barest literalness. A better view of its meaning will be gained by considering:

"(a) That it constitutes a part, and confessedly an obscure part, of one of the most figurative books of Scripture, and therefore ought to be interpreted by the plainer statement of other Scriptures.

"(b) That the other Scriptures contain nothing with regard to a resurrection of the righteous which is widely separated in time from that of the wicked, but rather declare distinctly that the second coming of Christ is immediately connected both with the resurrection of the just and the unjust and with the general judgment.

"(c) That the literal interpretation of the passage—holding, as it does, to a resurrection of bodies of flesh and blood, and to a reign of the risen saints in the flesh, and in the world as at present constituted—is inconsistent with other Scripture declarations with regard to the spiritual nature of the resurrection-body and of the coming reign of Christ" (*ibid.*, pp. 263-64).

### Herschel H. Hobbs

(Hobbs is a former president of the Southern Baptist Convention.)

"In all probability the Scriptures speak of only one coming, open, dramatic, and with great noise (I Cor. 15:51, 52; I Thess. 4:16; II Thess. 1:6-10; 2:1-8) (*Fundamentals of Our Faith*, p. 153).

"However, Paul's word about a first resurrection simply means that 'the dead in Christ shall rise first' (I Thess. 4:16), before living Christians are 'caught up together with them in the clouds, to meet the Lord in the air' (I Thess. 4:17). Elsewhere Paul referred only to the resurrection of the saints without reference to the wicked (I Cor. 15:50ff). Here he was thinking only of saved people. In Acts 24:15, however, he spoke of the resurrection both of the just and the unjust. Jesus spoke of the resurrection of the just (Luke 14:14) but also of the just and the unjust (John 5:29). It would appear that both Jesus and Paul thought of only one resurrection.

"The New Testament seems to speak of one coming of Christ with one resurrection both of the just and the unjust. The 'first resurrection' idea in Revelation 20:5 poses many questions, but in view of the souls of them that were beheaded for the witness of Jesus (Rev. 20:4), of martyrs, and the 'rest of the dead' (Rev. 20:5), plus the fact that there is no specific mention of a second resurrection of the wicked, plus uses of Jesus and Paul of 'the just and the unjust,' the evidence shows that one resurrection is taught in the New Testament. This is where our case lies" (*ibid.*, p. 157).

### B. H. Carroll

"All commentators, radicals, and conservatives, pre-and post-millennialists agree that Daniel here refers to a real and final resurrection of the bodies of the just and the unjust.

"The interpretation of Daniel 12:2 by Tregelles, the premillennialist, separating by a long interval the resurrection of the just from that of the unjust, finds no support in any text or version, and so far as I know in any great commentary" ("Daniel And The Interbiblical Period," *An Interpretation of the English Bible*, pp. 143-44).

"After Jesus comes in his final advent, the soul-saving time is ended forever. Whoever is not ready will then never be ready. The idea of Christ coming and thousands of years passing on after he comes and men living and dying, and the gospel being preached or men being saved by some other means, is wholly foreign to the teaching of our Lord. No one can get ready then. His coming is a windup" ("The Four Gospels," *ibid.*, p. 272).

### Edward A. McDowell

"THE RESURRECTION, THE JUDGMENT, AND THE END OF DEATH—Revelation 20:11-15 . . . Here, then, pictorially conceived, are the great realities of the final judgment, of the general resurrection, of the ultimate separating of good and evil, of the condemnation of the wicked, of the final reward of the righteous" (*The Meaning and Message of the Book of Revelation*, p. 205).

### Ray Summers

"When the entire New Testament is studied, it teaches one general resurrection (of both good and evil) and one general judgment (of both good and evil), both of which are directly related to the second coming of Christ which brings to an end this world order and ushers in the eternal heavenly order" (*Worthy Is the Lamb*, p. 206).

"This statement from Jesus [John 5:28,29] is one of the foundation statements for the view of one general resurrection at the last day. The best of the expositors affirm this interpretation and hold that there is no basis whatever for the idea of two separate resurrections at two different periods of time. The contrast here is not between two different times when men are to be raised but between the different kinds of men who are to be raised, those who have practiced good and those who have practiced evil" (*The Life Beyond*, p. 55).

### H. I. Hester and J. W. Pearse

"JUDGING THE NATIONS (Matthew 25:31-46). The Son of man sits on his throne with the nations of the earth before him. All of the nations are present, Gentiles and Jews, Christians and non-Christians. The purpose of the assembly is for judgment. This is in keeping with the pictures of the judgment given in the New Testament. A judgment for individuals and nations is a necessity. The fact [sic] of right and wrong, good and bad, righteousness and unrighteousnesss, require a reckoning. Right doing must be rewarded; wrong doing must be punished. We must give an answer for the deeds of the body. Moral law makes this a necessity.

"The Son of man is the Judge, for this is his right. He has completed his work as revealer of God and the Saviour of men, and now exercises his authority as Judge" (*Broadman Comments, 1961*, p. 372).

### Summary

Interestingly enough, no major denomination teaches, or has ever taught, that there is to be more than one resurrection and judgment. Yet, the chiliast belief of two or more of each, separated by one thousand or more years, has infiltrated just about every denomination, bringing with it confusion, strife, and misunderstanding.

## XVI

## OTHERS OF LIKE MIND *(Continued)*

Futurism, like premillennialism, is presented by some of its advocates as being a majority opinion in biblical interpretation. And it has grown to a commanding position since its founding in 1830. It has, in fact, infiltrated practically every denomination. However, futurists are still in the minority among Christians of the world.

This fact was brought forcibly to the writer's attention during seminary days. Having been reared in surroundings where it seemed that the only school of thought was the futuristic one, I was disturbed as a deeper study of God's Word brought out the inconsistencies of what had been memorized from the footnotes of *The Scofield Reference Bible.* Doubts concerning futurism had begun shortly after my call to preach and were simply sharpened during college and seminary.

Finally, I went to the dean of the seminary and told him of my consternation. He smiled, then made a statement which I since have verified through much research. He stated that while the school of thought with which I had broken was by far the most vocal, thus giving the appearance of representing the majority opinion, actually it has always represented only a small minority of Christian thinkers. So that, rather than making a great discovery, I had merely gotten into step with the apostles, many of the church fathers, most, if not all, of the Protestant reformers, most recognized Bible commentaries, as well as most present-day teachers and writers.

Although, as stated above, futurism has gained a wide following among many denominations, it would seem that this influence has been waning during recent decades. *Christian Life* magazine (March 1956, pp. 17,18, "Is Evangelical Theology Changing?") included this statement: "The trend today is away from dispensationalism — away from the Scofield notes. . . ."[1]

---

[1] Most writers do not distinguish between dispensationalism and futurism, but use the terms as synonyms. This will be evident from the contemporary

In the first chapter of this book a futurist was defined as one who centers his theological beliefs around national Israel, and believes that most prophecies concerning Israel are to have a literal fulfillment in the future, after the Christian church has been taken out of the world. In view of this definition the quoted matter in this chapter by those opposed to futurism will be limited, for the most part, to statements concerning Israel and the church and the alleged future millennial reign. Many quotations already have been used throughout the book, and others could be heaped one upon another. These will suffice to show that futurism by no means has a corner on theological thought.

Dr. G. Campbell Morgan in 1943, two years before he died, wrote to a correspondent concerning the union of Israel and the church: "I am convinced that all the promises made to Israel have found, are finding, and will find their perfect fulfillment in the Church. It is true that in the past, in my expositions, I gave a definite place to Israel in the purposes of God. I have now come to the conviction, as I have just said, that it is the new and spiritual Israel that is intended" (Letter to Rev. H. F. Wright, Baptist pastor, Brunswick, Victoria, quoted from *A New Heaven and a New Earth*, Archibald Hughes, p. 123).

Hughes, in discussing Revelation 20, says: "Who, without great assumption, can read into this passage a golden age on earth with Jewish national supremacy for a millennium?" (*ibid.*, p. 61).

F. F. Bruce states, commenting on Acts 2:40, ASV of 1901 ("And with many other words he testified, and exhorted them, saying, Save yourselves from this crooked generation.") :

"Peter bore his reasoned witness to the gospel facts and to the promise of salvation. The generation to which his hearers belonged had been upbraided by Jesus Himself as a 'faithless and perverse generation' (Luke 9:41), as an 'evil generation' because of its repudiation of Him whom God sent as Israel's anointed Saviour (Luke 11:29; 17:25). But there was a way of deliverance from the judgment which such faithlessness inevitably incurred. The salvation of which Joel had spoken was to be enjoyed by a 'remnant' of the

---

comments quoted throughout this chapter. In *An Examination of Dispensationalism*, by the present writer, the lines between five different millennial interpretations are clearly drawn, after which dispensationalism is dealt with in detail.

whole people; so now Peter urged his hearers to make sure by repentant calling upon the Lord that they would belong to this remnant and so save themselves from that 'crooked generation.' *The new believing community was, in fact, the faithful remnant of the Old Israel and at the same time the nucleus of the new Israel, the Christian Church'* (*The Book of Acts*, pp. 78,79).

Nygren points up well the teaching of Scripture, Old and New Testaments, concerning two Israels. Nor does Nygren allow that Romans 9-11 is parenthetic, as most futurists do, to the rest of Romans. He proves that Paul is still very much on the subject in these chapters. "Our task is to show that there is no distinction between the righteousness of faith and the promises of God. That is true, too, of Christ's relation to Israel. According to the flesh, He belongs to Israel; but 'according to the Spirit,' He is 'God who is over all, blessed forever'" (*Commentary on Romans*, p. 357).

Nygren points out that, according to Paul, the promises were not given to the entire nation of Israel, but only to the remnant, i.e., those who would believe.

"But, Paul holds, 'Not all who descended from Israel belong to Israel.' We must distinguish between 'Israel according to the flesh' and 'Israel according to the Spirit.' Only to the latter, only to the spiritual Israel were the promises given" (*ibid.*, pp. 361-62).

"God has made righteousness and salvation depend on faith. Only they who believe are the 'children of promise.' Therefore, he who does not believe must be rejected. Israel does not believe, therefore, rejection is inescapable" (*ibid.*, p. 388).

H. Wheeler Robinson remarks: "Judaism and Christianity are the work of a single Sculptor, just as much as the twin statues of them in the porch of Strasbourg Cathedral" (*The History of Israel*, p. 144).

In commenting on Romans, especially the third chapter, William Sanday had this to say: "The Jew looked at the Old Testament and he saw there Law, Obedience to the Law or Works, circumcision, descent from Abraham. Saint Paul said, Look again and look deeper, and you will see . . . not Law but promise, not works but Faith . . . of which circumcision is only the seal, not the literal descent from Abraham but spiritual descent. All these things are realized in Christianity" (*International Commentary on Romans*, p. 96).

"And then further, whereas Law (all Law and any kind of Law) was only an elaborate machinery for producing right action, there too Christianity accomplished, as if with the stroke of a wand, all that the law strove to do without success" (*ibid.*, p. 97).

Dr. Ray Summers and Dr. B. H. Carroll — both of whom are recognized authorities in both the Greek language and the New Testament — give the generally accepted opinion among Baptists on this subject.

". . . the futurist method is associated with a materialistic philosophy of the kingdom of God and a basis of triumph for the cause of righteousness which appears to be unscriptural throughout. Any system which turns from the purposes of grace and the cross of Christ to methods of victory of any other description becomes repulsive to the sincere Christian mind. Futurism does this very thing, whether it will admit it or not. This dispensationalism is Jewish theology, largely of the apocryphal literature, and not New Testament theology" (Ray Summers, *Worthy Is the Lamb*, p. 34).

"After Jesus comes in his final advent, the soul-saving time is ended forever. Whoever is not ready then will never be ready. The idea of Christ coming and thousands of years passing on after he comes and men living and dying, and the gospel being preached or men being saved by some other means, is wholly foreign to the teaching of our Lord. No one can get ready then. His coming is a windup" (B. H. Carroll, *An Interpretation of the English Bible*, Vol. XI, p. 272).

Dr. Allis speaks on this subject out of years of study and research. He gives the following resume of Christian thought with reference to the subject: "The history of Dispensationalism has not been marked by inner conflict to the same extent as has that of Brethrenism. But it is a significant fact that some of the most vigorous opponents of the movement have come out of its own ranks. More than fifty years ago Robert Cameron and Nathanael West took issue with their colleagues of the Niagara Bible Conference over the question of Pretribulationism. They were followed by others, notably by W. J. Erdman and Henry W. Frost. The cause of Posttribulationism is vigorously advocated today by the Sovereign Grace Advent Testimony (London), which represents the views of B. W. Newton, who broke with Darby about a century ago over this and related issues. One of the most active opponents of Dispensationalism in recent years, Philip Mauro, is also to be numbered among those who at one time ardently advocated its teachings. Another is A. W. Pink" (Oswald T. Allis, *Prophecy and the Church*, pp. 14,15).

Dr. B. B. Warfield has been classed as one of the great theologians of all time. Boettner ranks him, along with Augustine, Calvin, and Charles Hodge, as one of the four outstanding theologians in the entire history of the church. The following quotation gives Dr. Warfield's opinion on the subject at hand.

"What, then, is the eschatological outline we have gained from a study of [Revelation 20]? Briefly stated it is as follows. Our **Lord Jesus Christ** came to conquer the world to Himself, and this He does with a thoroughness and completeness which seems to go beyond even the intimations of Romans 11 and 1 Corinthians 15. Meanwhile as the conquest of the world is going on below, the saints who die in the Lord are gathered in Paradise to reign with their Lord, Who is Lord of all, and Who is from His throne directing the conquest of the world. When the victory is completely won there intervenes the last judgment and the final destruction of the wicked. At once there is a new heaven and a new earth and the consummation of the glory of the church. And this church abides forever (22:5) in perfection of holiness and blessedness. In bare outline that is what our section teaches. It will be noted at once that it is precisely the teaching of the didactic Epistles of Paul and of the whole of the New Testament with him. No attempts to harmonize the several types of teaching are necessary, therefore, for their entire harmony lies on the surface. John knows no more of two resurrections — of the saints and of the wicked — than does Paul: and the whole theory of an intervening millennium — and indeed of a millennium of any kind on earth — goes up in smoke. We are forced, indeed, to add our assent to Kliefoth's conclusion, that 'the doctrine of a thousand year kingdom has no foundation in the prophecies of the New Testament, and is therefore not a dogma but merely a hypothesis lacking all Biblical ground.' The millennium of the Apocalypse is the blessedness of the saints who have gone away from the body to be at home with the Lord" (B. B. Warfield, *Biblical Doctrines*, pp. 661-62).

Scofield himself realized that he was listening to another drummer in advocating Darby's theory concerning Israel and the church.

He made the following admission: "Especially is it necessary to exclude the notion — a legacy in Protestant thought from post-apostolic and Roman Catholic theology — that the Church is the true Israel, and that the Old Testament foreview of the kingdom is fulfilled in the Church" (*Scofield Reference Bible*, p. 989).

Hughes quotes the above statement by Scofield, then makes the following comment: "The authority Dr. Scofield rejects is not only 'post-apostolic and Roman Catholic' as he calls it; it is apostolic as well. Dr. Scofield's Futuristic Theory was derived principally from Mr. J. N. Darby, one of the founders of the 'Brethren' movement, in the nineteenth century; and the originators of the theory were R. Bellarmine and F. Ribera, Jesuit priests who promulgated it during 1576-1589 (*The Impelling Force of Prophetic Truth*, L. R. Conradi, pp. 346-48). It was certainly entirely unknown to the writers of the New Testament! When the theory was first preached it was vigorously rejected by all Protestant Churches and by some Roman Catholic theologians. It lay dormant until 'awakened' by J. N. Darby, and now flourishes principally through the *Scofield Reference Bible*" (Archibald Hughes, *A New Heaven and a New Earth*, p. 148).

Murray makes a plea for more systematic Bible study on the part of the futurists. His point is well taken. "We pass on to our readers at this point a rather amusing incident reported by the late Dr. Rowland Bingham, at one time editor of the *Evangelical Christian*, and General Director of the Sudan Interior Mission, in his book, *Matthew the Publican and His Gospel*: 'My wife set the investigating machinery going one day by saying, "Rowland, where do you get the Secret Rapture idea in the Bible? I have to teach the Second Coming to my class of young women on Sunday and I have been hunting for some proof of the Secret Rapture." I quite glibly replied, "First Thessalonians four." "But," she said, "I have been reading that and it is about the noisiest thing in my Bible. The Lord shall descend from heaven with a shout, with the voice of the archangel and the trump of God. . . ." I tried a second thrust by suggesting that there was the type of Enoch being secretly translated while Noah went through the judgment, to which there came the counter blow that knocked me out of the ring as she said, "You know, Rowland, that you cannot build a doctrine on a type." Later I said to my unsatisfied wife, "My teachers all affirmed that the Greek very clearly differentiates between the Secret Rapture of the church and the public manifestation to the world. The word parousia always indicates the rapture, while epiphaneia always has to do with the appearing of Christ with His Church. . . ." But that help-meet of mine wanted to do what I had never done, check up on those two Greek words. And so there was nothing for it but to get out my Young's Concordance and turn to every text in which the word parousia appeared. It smashed the theory of the Secret Rapture so hopelessly that I marvelled at the credulity with which I had swallowed my "Authorities." ' It is a pity that there are not more Bible students with this discernment, for then many baseless theories would not find such ready acceptance" (G. L. Murray, *Millennial Studies*, pp. 137-38).

These are but a few of the available contemporary comments by men well versed in theology who look on futurism as being far to the left of apostolic teachings as handed down to us through the inspired words of the New Testament.

### Summary

The theory of futurism concerning Israel is only a comparatively recent teaching, having originated about 1830. It takes this long for a dogma to get itself clearly before the people and to "prove its mettle." It would seem that this teaching has failed to stand the test of close scrutiny in the light of the Scriptures, and that consequently it is on its way out. The *Scofield Reference Bible* even now is in the hands of revisers; more and more Bible schools are relaxing their grip (although grudgingly) on hyperdispensationalism; and books are being written by fundamental men criticizing the positions held by their own schools of thought (e.g., George Ladd's book on *Crucial Questions About the Kingdom of God*).

If some readers should still hold to the futurist view, it is suggested that they owe it to themselves to attempt to find New Testament scriptures to warrant their acceptance of the *assumptions* listed herein. These after all form the framework for this school of thought. If these assumptions cannot be supported by the Word of God, then it would seem logical to drop this theory.

Perhaps another definition ought to be made at this time—a definition of thought. This section is not meant to teach—nor has the author ever taught — that "God is through with the Jew" or that "there is no future for the Jew." What the author does teach is that God's plan for the Jew — since Calvary tore down the middle wall of partition — is now essentially the same as God's plan for the Gentile. That is to say that a remnant of Jews is marked out for final salvation, and that this salvation will come about in the present age (which the author looks on as being the final *historical* age). The author does not believe that every Jew living at the return of Christ will be given a second chance and that every living Jew then will be saved (this the futurist teaches).

The author's sincere acceptance of Scripture passages such as "Today is the day of salvation," rules out there being *another* day of salvation. This belief causes the author to want to go to "the Jew first, and also to the Gentile" and preach to them that if they fail to accept Christ, before the trumpet sounds the signal that time shall be no more, they will be hopelessly lost and will "cry for the rocks to fall on them" in the day of Christ's coming in judgment (compare II Cor. 6:2; Matt. 24:27-29; Rev. 1:7).

To drop Darby's theory is not to leave the Scriptures, nor to lose their beauty. On the contrary, it opens up new vistas. Instead of one's interest being a small spot on the map, called Palestine, that interest becomes "all the world." Instead of the Christian being a member of a church that is "parenthetic" (for that is what Darby makes it), he becomes a member of the bride and body of Christ. And instead of being interested in a desolate Jerusalem (see Matt. 23:38), the child of God, Jew and Gentile, will have his hope fixed upon the "New Jerusalem" (Rev. 21:2), which will some day come down out of heaven and encompass every believer in our precious Lord Jesus Christ.

# XVII

## SUMMARY AND CONCLUSION

There is a constantly growing interest in final things (eschatology). People sincerely want to know what the Bible has to say on this important subject. Although theories are legion, the contest in our day, with reference to final things, is between amillennialism and dispensationalism.

There are comparatively few conservative postmillennial writers in America today. Among premillenarians in this country, dispensationalists serve as spokesmen for the majority. Futurists and historic premillenarians have defaulted to the more vocal dispensational writers and speakers.

Amillennialism is the majority opinion among conservative Christian scholars. It is, in the opinion of this writer, representative of the faith once delivered to the saints. Amillennial doctrines are spelled out in the New Testament. A vast majority of the church fathers, and practically all of the Protestant reformers were amillenarians—following, in the main, the teachings of Augustine.

Dispensationalism, which is militantly opposed to amillennialism, is a new dogma which was crystallized by John Nelson Darby around 1830. Darby was a Plymouth Brethren. C. I. Scofield was so much impressed by Darby's teachings that he compiled *The Scofield Reference Bible* for the purpose of propagating Darby's teachings. Though Darby's teachings were called "rediscovered truths," most of them were unheard of until the nineteenth century. Historic premillennialism may be traced to the early centuries A.D. However—and this needs to be stressed—there is very little resemblance between historic premillennial doctrines and those doctrines put forth by dispensational premillenarians.

Although dispensationalism is a relatively young dogma, and although this dogma forms a definite minority opinion among Christians—this dogma is made a test of fellowship by most of its adherents. They castigate as liberals those who hold any other interpretation of Scripture. A quotation or two will suffice to show the haughty attitude of dispensationalists toward other Christians, as well as their utter disdain for those who hold to the historic Christian faith.

"I know of very few of the old commentaries that are trustworthy when it comes to prophecy. Nearly all of them spiritualize the predictions of the Old Testament prophets and confuse the kingdom with the Church. Hence their interpretations are worthless" (Oswald J. Smith, *When The King Comes Back*, pp. 13,14).

"None of [Isaiah 11:1-13; 12:1-6] was fulfilled at the first advent, and none of it can be spiritualized, for it has no fulfillment in the Church, in spite of what the great commentators say. God did not see fit to enlighten them" (*ibid.*, p. 63).

"In fact, until brought to the fore, through the writings and preaching of a distinguished ex-clergyman, Mr. J. N. Darby, in the early part of the last century, [the dispensationalist teaching that the church is not prophesied in the Old Testament] is scarcely to be found in a single book or sermon throughout a period of 1600 years! . . ." (Harry A. Ironside, *Mysteries of God*, p. 50).

"Protestant theology has very generally taught that all the kingdom promises, and even the great Davidic covenant itself, are to be fulfilled in and through the Church. The confusion thus created has been still further darkened. . ." (Lewis Sperry Chafer, *The Kingdom in History and Prophecy*, p. 5).

"Most if not all the leaders of the Protestant Reformation were Amillennial in their eschatology, following the teachings of Augustine" (John Walvoord, *Bibliotheca Sacra*, Jan.-Mar., 1951, p. 11).

This is why the present writer felt it necessary to contrast the teachings of this book with dispensationalist beliefs. The two schools stand poles apart on just about every doctrine dealt with herein.

The stated purpose of this book is twofold: (1) to present from the Scriptures a clear arrangement of God's plans and program for the future, and (2) to help eradicate from our minds some things not taught in the Bible. The best way to unlearn unscriptural teachings is to get a running account of "what saith the scripture" on such matters. It is impossible to understand "final things" apart from a knowledge of "former things."

The first eleven chapters of our Bible record God's dealings with the entire human race. Beginning with chapter 12 of Genesis, however, the record narrows. From there to the end of Malachi the record is almost entirely an account of God's dealing with a race of people, Israel. So-called rediscovered truths concerning national Israel have done more than any other single thing to bring confusion into the field of eschatology.

God made two sets of promises to Abraham, the father of all the righteous. One set of promises had to do with national Israel; the other set related to Abraham's spiritual descendants, the Israel of God which is made up of all believers—Jew and Gentile. Israel's national promises were conditional. All of these promises have been either fulfilled or invalidated through disobedience. The Scriptures state clearly that God made of Israel a great nation, made her people more numerous than the stars, gave her *all* the land which he promised through Abraham, caused her to build the temple, drove her out of the land, caused her to return and rebuild the temple, and sent the Messiah through her.

Israel lived under the old covenant. However, Jeremiah predicted a new covenant. Jesus established this new covenant at his first advent. Each communion service reminds the Christian of the new covenant: "This is my blood of the new covenant. . . ," said Jesus as he instituted the Lord's Supper. Jesus was, and is, the only hope of Israel. He came as the king of Israel. To as many of his own as received him gave he power to become the sons of the living God. We need to be reminded that all of these things took place at the *first* advent. His second coming will be a consummation, not a beginning.

The incarnation set eschatology in motion. Jesus established the new covenant with the church, the Israel of God. The covenant promises were given to Israel as a nation. They were fulfilled—rather, they are being fulfilled—through Israel as a church. The Christian church is Israel, full grown. The church, in its infancy, was a Jewish group. All of the apostles, all of the writers of the New Testament, were Jews. The Christian church is built upon the foundation of the Jewish prophets and Jewish apostles, Jesus Christ being the chief cornerstone. Jewish historians have estimated there were nearly two million Jewish converts to Christianity during the first century A.D. The church succeeded Israel as God's chosen people.

The church does not constitute a second body of God. God has but one body (John 10:16; Eph. 2:14-16). Gentile believers were grafted into the same olive tree, i.e., into the root and stock of Hebrew Abraham (Rom. 11:16-18).

Nor is this a minor point among theologians. Many curious ramifications have grown out of the minority belief that God has two separate bodies, Israel and the church, and that these two peoples have separate destinies. Historic Christian theologians have always held that God has but one people and one plan of salvation.

Even as God has but one chosen people and one plan of salvation, so he has but one kingdom. The kingdom is primarily a reign rather than a realm. It is the reign of God in the hearts of his people. God's kingdom is eternal (Psalms 145:13). Therefore, it is highly unscriptural to limit it to one thousand years duration. The "new" kingdom ushered in by our Lord at the first advent was actually a new manifestation (a new phase) of the one eternal kingdom of God.

Millenarians agree that the kingdom and the millennium are one and the same. To prove, therefore, that one is present is to prove *ipso facto* that the other has arrived. The millennium is that phase of the eternal kingdom which began at the incarnation and will be consummated at the second advent.

An earthly millennium lasting only one thousand years may be arrived at only through a hyperliteral interpretation of isolated passages of Scripture. Six verses in the book of Revelation dare not be allowed to contradict clear passages of Scripture. And the Old Testament predictions of a golden age, so often used to "prove" an alleged materialistic millennium have at least two other possible meanings. Either they refer to the present age—for certainly they were spoken in poetic language, governed by the usage in the prophet's day—or else they will be fulfilled in the final state, wherein the saints will reign on the renewed earth throughout eternity. The present writer feels that the answer lies in a combination of both of these possibilities. That is to say, the poetic language of the Old Testament, referring to a golden age, is finding partial fulfillment in the present age; but it will not find complete fulfillment until the arrival of the final state following the second advent of Christ.

The New Testament speaks of two kinds of resurrections. The first of these is the new birth, whereas the second resurrection will be a literal, physical resurrection of the body. It is this first resurrection, or new birth, which causes the Christian to reign with Christ in the present ongoing millennial kingdom. His part in this first resurrection also assures him that the second death will have no power over him (Rev. 20:6,14).

Without the new birth, every person is spiritually dead (II Cor. 5:13-15; Eph. 2:1). To accept Christ is to be made spiritually alive (John 5:25; Eph. 2:1,5). The rest of the dead, i.e., they who do not accept Christ, live not (spiritually) during this thousand year millennial kingdom reign (Rev. 20:5). They remain dead in trespasses and sin. Nor do they live (spiritually) after the thousand years are finished (Rev. 1:7).

The second resurrection will take place at the harvest, which Jesus said is the end of this present age. This will be a general resurrection (Matt. 25:31; John 5:28,29). All who are in the graves will come forth.

The general resurrection will precipitate a separation of the righteous from the unrighteous. When all who are in the graves come forth, the saints will be caught up (raptured) in the air to escort their King to the earth. The unsaved will see the joy of the resurrected saints, but will have no part in it. Rather, because they see their doom approaching, they will cry for the rocks to fall on them. They will seek death (annihilation), but find it not.

The general resurrection will be immediately followed by a general judgment. Again, all will be there. The saints will be there to give an account of their stewardship and to receive their rewards. The wicked will be there to hear those terrifying words, "Depart from me. . . ." Another grave error on the part of those who accept Darby's alleged rediscovered truths is their teaching that the righteous will not be present at the judgment scene. What saith the scripture? ". . . for we shall all stand before the judgment-seat of God. . . . So then each one of us shall give account of himself to God" (Rom. 14:10-12). Need the reader be reminded that Paul was a Christian theologian writing to Christians?

Satan, whose power to hinder people from hearing the gospel was bound at the first advent, will be loosed for a little season just preceding the second coming of Christ. He, in the person of antichrist, will be leading his forces in a final attack against the church when Christ appears. The brightness of Jesus' coming will put down Satan for the final time, and he will be cast into hell ahead of his followers.

The whole earth will be judged, cleansed, and incorporated as an integral part of heaven. Then righteousness will literally cover the earth as the waters cover the sea. And Jesus will literally reign on the earth with his church. This reign, however, will not be of a limited duration. It will last throughout eternity.

"Blessed and holy is he that hath part in the first resurrection: over these the second death hath no power . . . but they shall reign with him. . . ."

# BIBLIOGRAPHY

ALLIS, O. T. *Prophecy and the Church.* Philadelphia: Presbyterian and Reformed Publishing Company, 1945.

BARROW, E. R. *Companion to the Bible.* New York: The American Tract Society, 1867.

BERKHOF, L. *The Second Coming of Christ.* Grand Rapids: Wm. B. Eerdmans Publishing Company, 1953.

————. *Systematic Theology.* Grand Rapids: Wm. B. Eerdmans Publishing Company, 1953.

BIRD, T. C. *Drama of the Apocalypse.* Boston: Roxburgh Publishing Company, 1912.

BLACKSTONE, W. E. *Jesus Is Coming.* Chicago: Moody Bible Institute, n.d.

BOETTNER, LORAINE. *The Millennium.* Philadelphia: Presbyterian and Reformed Publishing Company, 1957.

BRIGHT, JOHN. *The Kingdom of God.* New York: Abingdon Press, 1953.

BUIS, HARRY. *A Simplified Commentary on the Book of Revelation.* Philadelphia: Presbyterian and Reformed Publishing Company, 1960.

BULLINGER, E. W., *The Foundation of Dispensational Truth.* London: Eyre & Spottiswodde, 1931.

CALVIN, JOHN. *Institutes of the Christian Religion.* (Vol. II). Grand Rapids: Wm. B. Eerdmans Publishing Company, 1957.

CAMPBELL, RODERICK. *Israel and the New Covenant.* Philadelphia: Presbyterian and Reformed Publishing Company, 1954.

CARTLEDGE, SAMUEL A. *A Conservative Introduction to the Old Testament.* Athens: University of Georgia Press, 1944.

CHAFER, L. S. *Dispensationalism.* Dallas: Dallas Seminary Press, 1951.

————. *The Kingdom in History and Prophecy.* Chicago: Fleming H. Revell, 1915.

————. *Systematic Theology.* Dallas: Dallas Seminary Press, 1948.

CHAMBERLAIN, W. D. *The Church Faces the Isms.* (Edited by Arnold Black Rhodes.) New York: Abingdon Press, 1958.

COX, W. E. *Amillennialism Today.* Philadelphia: Presbyterian and Reformed Publishing Company, 1966.

————. *An Examination of Dispensationalism.* Philadelphia: Presbyterian and Reformed Publishing Company, 1963.

————. *In These Last Days.* Philadelphia: Presbyterian and Reformed Publishing Company, 1964.

————. *The Millennium.* Philadelphia: Presbyterian and Reformed Publishing Company, 1964.

————. *The New-Covenant Israel.* Philadelphia: Presbyterian and Reformed Publishing Company, 1963.

DODD, C. H. *The Parables of the Kingdom.* New York: Charles Scribner's Sons, 1961.

Douty, Norman F. *Has Christ's Return Two Stages?* New York: Pageant Press, Inc., 1956.

Erb, Paul. *The Alpha and the Omega.* Scottdale, Pa.: Herald Press, 1955.

Evans, William. *Outline Studies of the Bible.* Chicago: Moody Press, 1913.

Gaebelein, A. C. *The Prophet Daniel.* Grand Rapids: Kregel Publications, n.d.

Gordon, S. D. *Quiet Talks About Jesus.* Chicago: Fleming H. Revell, 1906.

Halley, H. H. *Halley's Bible Handbook.* Grand Rapids: Zondervan Publishing Company, 1962.

Hamilton, F. E. *The Basis of Millennial Faith.* Grand Rapids: Wm. B. Eerdmans Publishing Company, 1955.

Hendricksen, William. *More Than Conquerors.* Grand Rapids: Baker Book House, 1949.

————. *Three Lectures on the Book of Revelation.* Grand Rapids: Zondervan Publishing Company, 1949.

Henry, Carl F. H. *The Uneasy Conscience of Modern Fundamentalism.* Grand Rapids: Wm. B. Eerdmans Publishing Company, 1947.

Hester, H. I., and Pearce, J. W. *Broadman Comments, 1961.* Nashville: Broadman Press, 1961.

Hobbs, H. H., *Fundamentals of Our Faith.* Nashville: Broadman Press, 1960.

Hodges, Jesse Wilson. *Christ's Kingdom and Coming.* Grand Rapids: Wm. B. Eerdmans Publishing Company, 1957.

Hughes, Archibald. *New Heaven and New Earth.* Philadelphia: Presbyterian and Reformed Publishing Company, 1957.

Ironside, H. A. *Lectures on Daniel the Prophet.* New York: Loizeaux Brothers, 1953.

————. *The Mysteries of God.* New York: Loizeaux Brothers, 1908.

Johnston, George. *The Doctrine of the Church in the New Testament.* New York: Cambridge University Press, 1943.

Josephus, Flavius. *"Wars of the Jews," The Works of Josephus.* (Translated by William Whiston.)

Kik, J. M. *Matthew XXIV.* Philadelphia: Presbyterian and Reformed Publishing Company, 1948.

————. *Revelation XX.* Philadelphia: Presbyterian and Reformed Publishing Company, 1955.

Ladd, G. E. *The Blessed Hope.* Grand Rapids: Wm. B. Eerdmans Publishing Company, 1956.

————. *Crucial Questions About the Kingdom of God.* Grand Rapids: Wm. B. Eerdmans Publishing Company, 1952.

Larkin, Clarence. *Dispensational Truth.* Philadelphia: Rev. Clarence Larkin, Est. 1920.

————. *Rightly Dividing the Word.* Fox Chase, Philadelphia: C. Larkin, 1921.

Martyr, Justin, *"Dialogue With Trypho the Jew," The Ante-Nicene Church Fathers.* New York: The Christian Literature Company, 1890.

————. *"The First Apology of Justin," The Ante-Nicene Fathers.* (Edited by Alexander Roberts and James Donaldson.) Grand Rapids: Wm. B. Eerdmans Publishing Company, 1956.

Masselink, William. *Why Thousand Years?* Grand Rapids: Wm. B. Eerdmans Publishing Company, 1930.

Mauro, Philip. *The Gospel of the Kingdom.* Boston: Hamilton Bros., 1928.